TRANSFIGURATIONS

TRANSFIGURATIONS
Theology and the French Feminists

Edited by

C. W. Maggie Kim
Susan M. St. Ville
Susan M. Simonaitis

FORTRESS PRESS *Minneapolis*

To B. T. Stull

TRANSFIGURATIONS
Theology and the French Feminists

Photo of volume editors by Rebekah Miles

Chapter 7, "Sporting Power," by Sharon D. Welch draws in part on her earlier published works: "Ideology and Social Change," in *Weaving the Visions: New Patterns in Feminist Spirituality*, edited by Judith Plaskow and Carol P. Christ (San Francisco: HarperCollins, 1989), 337, 341–42; *A Feminist Ethic of Risk* (Minneapolis: Fortress Press, 1990), 18, 160, 170–71; "An Ethic of Solidarity," in *Postmodernism, Feminism, and Cultural Politics: Redrawing Educational Boundaries*, edited by Henry A. Giroux (Albany: State University of New York Press, 1991), 84–86.

Chapter 8, "Irigaray and the Divine," by Elizabeth Grosz appears by permission of SUNY Press, Albany, New York, and is reprinted from *Transitions in Continental Philosophy*, edited by Stephen Watson, Arleen Dallery, and Marya Bower (State University of New York Press, 1994).

Library of Congress Cataloging-in-Publication Data

Transfigurations : theology and the French feminists / edited by C. W. Maggie Kim, Susan M. St. Ville, and Susan M. Simonaitis.
p. cm.
Includes bibliographical references.
ISBN 0-8006-2697-4
1. Feminist theology. 2. Feminist theory—France. 3. Kristeva, Julia, 1941– —Religion. 4. Irigaray, Luce—Religion. 5. Cixous, Helene, 1937– —Religion. I. Kim, C. W. Maggie, 1961– II. St. Ville, Susan M., 1963– . III. Simonaitis, Susan M., 1963–
BT83.55.T73 1993
230′.082—dc20 93-26608
CIP

The paper used in this publication meets the minimum requirements of American National Standard for Information Services—Permanence of Paper for Printed Library Materials, ANSI Z329.48-1984. ∞™

Manufactured in the U.S.A. AF 1–2697

97 96 95 94 93 1 2 3 4 5 6 7 8 9 10

Contents

Acknowledgments

Speaking in one voice and in three, our first thanks are to each other. This project has allowed us to experience firsthand the process of cooperative scholarship, strengthening our respect for each other as colleagues and as friends. The majority of the papers in this volume were presented at a conference we organized on "Feminist Theologies and French Feminisms: Possibilities and Problems," which took place at the Divinity School, the University of Chicago, on April 26–28, 1991. We would like to thank Anne Carr, who served as faculty advisor for the conference, as well as Dean Clark Gilpin, who encouraged our efforts and provided generous financial support. We recognize also the intellectual community at the Divinity School, which continues to shape and to challenge our feminist concerns. Finally, we give special thanks to Bradford T. Stull, our friend and reading companion, who initially suggested the idea of a conference and who enthusiastically helped to make it (and this book) a reality.

—*C. W. Maggie Kim*
Susan M. St. Ville
Susan M. Simonaitis

Contributors

Ellen T. Armour is Assistant Professor of Religious Studies at Rhodes College, Memphis, Tennessee. She is working on a book that builds an alliance between feminist theology and the work of Derrida and Irigaray on issues of race and gender.

Rebecca S. Chopp is Associate Professor of Systematic Theology, Candler School of Theology, Emory University, Atlanta, Georgia, and author of *The Power to Speak: Feminism, Language, God* (1989) and *The Praxis of Suffering: An Interpretation of Liberation and Political Theologies* (1986).

Elizabeth Grosz is Associate Professor in Critical Theory at Monash University, Clayton, Victoria, Australia. She is author of *Sexual Subversions: Three French Feminists* (1989), *Jacques Lacan: A Feminist Introduction* (1990) and *Volatile Bodies: Toward a Corporeal Feminism* (1994).

Amy Hollywood is Assistant Professor of Religion at Dartmouth College, Hanover, New Hampshire. At present, she is working on a book about body, will, and work in Mechthild of Magdeburg, Marguerite Porete, and Meister Eckhart.

Serene Jones is Assistant Professor of Systematic Theology at Yale Divinity School, New Haven, Connecticut. She is currently working on a book on rhetoric and doctrine in Calvin's *Institutes*, and one on feminist theory and Christian theology.

Cleo McNelly Kearns is Associate Professor of Humanities, New Jersey Institute of Technology, Newark, New Jersey, and is author of *T. S. Eliot and Indic Religions: A Study in Poetry and Belief* (1987).

Françoise Meltzer is Professor of Romance Languages and Literatures and in the Committee on Comparative Studies in Literature at the University of Chicago, Chicago, Illinois. She is author of *Salome and the Dance of Writing: Portraits of Mimesis in Literature* (1987) and editor of *The Trials of Psychoanalysis* (1988).

Sharon D. Welch is Associate Professor and Director of the Women's Studies Program at the University of Missouri, Columbia, Missouri, and author of *Communities of Resistance and Solidarity* (1987) and *A Feminist Ethic of Risk* (1990).

Introduction

Since the late 1980s, a growing number of feminist theologians have discovered provocative and challenging insights in the writings of the "French feminists."[1] Until recently, however, only a few scholars have produced texts that reflect a sustained conversation between these two spheres. This volume, then, presents the leading efforts of an emerging area of scholarship within feminist theology. Yet, as will become evident, this new area of scholarship encompasses conflicting perspectives, and deliberately so. The following essays harbor real differences in both approaches taken and positions argued. We welcome this diversity because we think it reveals not only multiple opportunities for innovative thought but also important disagreements among those feminist theologians drawn to the work of the French. These disagreements are about both the nature and task of feminist theology itself and the extent to which the theories of the French can be resources for religious reflection. While this volume offers no simple response to these concerns, the essays, taken collectively, highlight central issues of debate and point toward fruitful lines of further conversation with the French.

1. The work of the French feminists is mentioned in such books as Marilyn Chapin Massey's *Feminine Soul: The Fate of an Ideal* (Boston: Beacon Press, 1985), Margaret R. Miles' *Carnal Knowing: Female Nakedness and Religious Meaning in the Christian West* (Boston: Beacon Press, 1989), Naomi Goldenberg's *Returning Words to Flesh: Feminism, Psychoanalysis, and the Resurrection of the Body* (Boston: Beacon Press, 1990), and Sharon Welch's *A Feminist Ethic of Risk* (Minneapolis: Fortress Press, 1990). Perhaps the theological work most influenced by the French theorists is *The Power to Speak: Feminism, Language, God*, by Rebecca Chopp (New York: Crossroad Publishing Company, 1989).

Our own "turn to the French" emerged as a response to the challenges raised by women of color, on the one hand, and postmodern theorists, on the other. Although radically different from each other in many respects, they pose similar questions for feminist theology. Just as feminists have criticized prevailing patriarchal theologies for their male bias, so women of color have begun to criticize earlier feminist theologies for race and class biases. Writers such as Katie G. Cannon, Jacquelyn Grant, and Ada María Isasi-Díaz have argued that the alternative theological constructions offered in the name of women by prominent feminist theologians reflect only the experience of women who are white and upper class.[2] When feminist theologians fail to acknowledge the differences that exist between groups of women, we have little to say to women who are on the margins, women who are victims not only of sexism but of racism, classism, and other forms of oppression as well. The consequences of such oversights are sinister. Just as the neglect of women's experience in patriarchal theology allows it to function as an active force in the oppression of women, so too feminist theology's failure to acknowledge the diversity of women results in complicity with discrimination by race and class.

At the same time, feminist theology has been challenged by postmodern views that reject modernity's claims to universal truth and, in so doing, put into question the theological enterprise in general as well as inquiries (theological or not) based on gender analysis. The works of such diverse thinkers as Michel Foucault, Jacques Derrida, Jean-François Lyotard, and Jacques Lacan reveal the inescapable effects of power, language, and the unconscious on all claims to knowledge.[3] According to postmodernists, theories

2. For example, see Katie G. Cannon's *Black Womanist Ethics* (Atlanta: Scholar's Press, 1988), Jacquelyn Grant's *White Women's Christ and Black Women's Jesus* (Atlanta: Scholar's Press, 1989), and essays in *Inheriting Our Mothers' Gardens*, Letty Russell, Kwok Pui-lan, Ada María Isasi-Díaz, Katie Geneva Cannon, eds. (Philadelphia: Westminster Press, 1988).

3. Michel Foucault, *The History of Sexuality*, trans. Robert Hurley (New York: Pantheon Books, 1978), *Discipline and Punish: The Birth of the Prison*, trans. Alan Sheridan (New York: Pantheon Books, 1978), *The Order of Things: An Archaeology of the Human Sciences* (New York: Random House, 1970), and *The Archaeology of Knowledge and the Discourse of Language*, trans. A. M.

claiming universality, be they theological or feminist, deny the inevitable conditionedness and partiality of any theory and must, therefore, be rejected. Taken seriously, postmodernism, which challenges the possibility of any theory that purports to be relevant across space and through time, requires feminist theologians to reconsider both how we speak about God and in what sense we speak for women.

Connections between the challenges posed by women of color and by theorists of postmodernity are evident. In trying to understand why feminist theology has tended to repeat the errors of patriarchy, some theorists argue that the criticisms made by women of color point to more than a simple gap in the content of feminist theology. Instead, they assert that the problem lies at the level of methodological assumptions. Two related essays by Sheila Greeve Davaney exemplify such an argument and demonstrate well the connection between the two sets of challenges.[4] Her essay "The Limits of the Appeal to Women's Experience" focuses on criticisms of feminist theology by women of color, while "Problems with

---

Sheridan Smith (New York: Pantheon Books, 1972). Jacques Derrida, *Of Grammatology,* trans. Gayatri Chakravorty Spivak (Baltimore: Johns Hopkins University Press, 1976), *Dissemination,* trans. Barbara Johnson (Chicago: University of Chicago Press, 1981), *Margins of Philosophy,* trans. Alan Bass (Chicago: University of Chicago Press, 1982), and *Writing and Difference,* trans. Alan Bass (Chicago: University of Chicago Press, 1978). Jean-François Lyotard, *The Postmodern Condition: A Report on Knowledge,* trans. Geoff Bennington and Brian Massumi (Minneapolis: University of Minnesota Press, 1984), and *The Differend: Phrases in Dispute,* trans. Georges Van Den Abbeele (Minneapolis: University of Minnesota Press, 1988). Jacques Lacan, *Ecrits: A Selection,* trans. Alan Sheridan (New York: Norton, 1977), and *Feminine Sexuality: Jacques Lacan and the école freudienne,* ed. Juliet Mitchell and Jacqueline Rose, trans. J. Rose (New York: W. W. Norton, 1982).

4. Sheila Greeve Davaney, "The Limits of the Appeal to Women's Experience," in *Shaping New Vision: Gender and Values in American Culture,* Clarissa W. Atkinson, Constance H. Buchanan, and Margaret R. Miles, eds. (Ann Arbor: U.M.I. Research Press, 1987) 31–50, and "Problems with Feminist Theory: Historicity and the Search for Sure Foundations" in *Embodied Love: Sensuality and Relationship as Feminist Values,* Paula M. Cooey, Sharon A. Farmer, and Mary Ellen Ross, eds. (San Francisco: Harper & Row, 1987) 79–95.

Feminist Theory: Historicity and the Search for Sure Foundations" draws on the work of Michel Foucault to outline the problems faced by contemporary feminist thinkers. In both essays, Davaney argues that feminist theologians have inherited the methodological assumptions of our Enlightenment-era forebears and, along with those assumptions, a serious dilemma. Like other modern theories in our contemporary situation, the writings of feminist theologians are caught in a struggle between foundationalism and relativism. Davaney agrees with the common characterization of modern scholarship as driven by the "Enlightenment-inspired" desire to uncover an ontological truth that serves as the standard by which the validity of all claims can be assessed. Yet this quest for certainty has been met by the counter-modern recognition that, when scrutinized, all claims to universal truth contain the biases of the specific historical and social situations from which they emerge. Relying on the work of Foucault, Davaney argues that to recognize that truth is determined by historical forces is to recognize that truth is a matter of power. The standard by which the validity of perspectives is judged is inevitably the perspective of those who are politically privileged in a society.

According to Davaney, even though contemporary scholars and thinkers acknowledge the political and historical character of thought, we are reticent to abandon the modern desire to establish unquestioned standards of truth and knowledge, thus creating a methodological tension. In feminist theology, this dilemma can be seen in the dual role given to the category of "women's experience." In our critical practice, feminists have appealed to women's experience to challenge the supposedly universal norms claimed by earlier male theologians. In constructing alternative theological formulations, however, feminists have tended to make "women's experience" the ontological standard of theological sources and interpretations. Davaney contends that when we claim ontological validity for our views, feminist theologians implicitly assume that all perspectives on the divine that differ from our own are invalid. Feminist theology seems here to undercut its liberating potential. For, as the writings of women of color and poor women reveal, the group of discredited viewpoints may include the perspectives of women whose social location is radically different from the privileged position held by the most prominent feminist theologians.

Not all scholars accept Davaney's reading of the central texts in feminist theology.[5] Nor do all agree with her conclusion that feminist theologians must embrace a radical relativism. Still, when combined with the criticisms from women of color, Davaney's methodological critique helps to frame some key issues debated in contemporary feminist theological circles. Increasingly, we are challenged to rethink our understanding of the task and practice of feminist theology so that it allows women to articulate interpretations of the divine that attend to the particular perspectives of women who are different from each other. This challenge demands reflection on two related issues. First, feminists must attempt to uncover any hidden metaphysical assumptions underlying the methodologies we use in our theological practice. Second, given the centrality of the category of "women's experience," feminists must rethink the anthropological assumptions that inform our work. How do we understand the subject "woman" whose perception of the divine is of such importance? More tellingly, how do we understand and account for the diversity of subjects who are indicated by the name "woman"?

With these questions, it becomes clear why feminist theologians have turned to the texts of the French feminists. Questions about the methodological presuppositions that shape our thought and the implications these hold for our understanding of human persons have been central to their inquiries. The French writers most often called upon by American feminists—Julia Kristeva, Luce Irigaray, and Hélène Cixous—stand with the postmodern intellectuals who seek to reveal the assumptions of universality and subjectivity undergirding Western thought. But, it is not only the deconstructive projects of the French that appeal to American feminist theologians. Sensitivity to the particularity of different persons and perspectives has led the French feminists to undertake constructive

5. For example, see "Embodied Thinking: Reflections in Feminist Theological Method," by Carol P. Christ, *Journal of Feminist Studies in Religion,* 5 (Spr. 1989): 7–15.

projects as well. In many of their writings they attempt to articulate new ways of thinking and speaking that empower rather than silence the variety of voices that exist in any culture. Thus the possibilities for conversation between French feminists and American theologians are numerous.

Turning to the essays, we begin this volume with a cautionary note. In "Transfeminisms," Françoise Meltzer, a literary theorist and an "outsider" to religious studies, points to the difficulties involved in any discussion of French feminisms, beginning with the term itself. In the United States, "French feminisms" has become a widely used label for a fairly large and diverse group of women writers in France. But, Meltzer warns us, just as there are multiple meanings for the word *feminism,* so too for *French*. We must not fall back into the trap of binary oppositions, whether male vs. female or French vs. American. There are significant differences among the three "French feminists" most frequently referred to in this text: Cixous, Irigaray, and Kristeva. In addition, Meltzer points us to the work of several other women writing in France who have yet to be recognized by feminist theologians in the States, an oversight which can be explained only partially by the slow translation of French texts. In any case, what Meltzer makes exceedingly clear is that feminist theologians, as latecomers to the scene, have just scratched the surface of what might fall under the problematic but pragmatically useful label "French feminisms."

Meltzer also sketches the figures and movements that have shaped the French feminists themselves and the reception of their work in the United States. The work of the French feminists is critical of but also highly indebted to the "fathers of contemporary critical discourse in France"—from Plato, Sigmund Freud, Karl Marx, G. W. F. Hegel, and Claude Lévi-Strauss to Jacques Derrida, Michel Foucault, and Jacques Lacan. In light of this inheritance, Meltzer offers two caveats when we look to the writings of the French feminists. First, female-centered terms can be substituted for male-centered terms without challenging the latter's underlying assumptions and, second, the very vocabulary inherited from the "father texts" (for example, the vocabulary of psychoanalysis) is "loaded with often unquestioned misogynist premises."

The problem of inheritance, of course, is not unique to the French. In "From Patriarchy into Freedom: A Conversation between American Feminist Theology and French Feminism," Rebecca Chopp argues that it is important for American feminist theologians to understand what we have inherited from American intellectual traditions as well as how we are called to transform these traditions. It is in undertaking this task of transformation that Chopp believes the work of Julia Kristeva can be helpful. In Chopp's view, feminist theology is best understood within the context of the American scholarly traditions of pragmatism and public theology because it shares with both the political end of transforming the public order and the insistence that human persons cannot be understood apart from the social community in which they live and act. Viewing feminist theology in this context, Chopp argues that women's experience should be understood as a pragmatic rather than an ontological norm. According to Chopp, the experience of any subject is understood by feminist theologians to be particular, intimately bound up with the social community, and marked by qualities of plurality and ambiguity. While the appeal to "women's experience" is important, it remains simply a moment in the larger task of feminist theology, which is "best described as productive strategies of critique and transformation . . . [that] offer persuasive discourses of personal and social flourishing."

In contrast to its inherited context of pragmatism and public theology, American feminist theology carries its diagnosis of social ills to the level of the fundamental norms and terms that order society. Thus, as feminist theologians, we face the "double task" of deconstructing the terms that allow for meaning in patriarchy and of discovering new terms that would give rise to a more just society. For Chopp, Kristeva's analysis of the "monotheistic logic" of patriarchy makes clear the need for a theological critique of cultural systems of meaning. At the same time, her notion of the "semiotic modality of language" provides a place from which we can both resist and transform patriarchy. Finally, her concern with the process of meaning coming to be rather than with particular meanings already given offers us a new way to think about the practice of theology.

In "Kristeva and Feminist Theology," Cleo Kearns, too, asserts that Kristeva's reflections on theological discourse and religious practice reveal much to theologians about our enterprise. For Kristeva, most theological discourse is that of "credal religion": the language of theology generally bears an overabundance of the symbolic aspect of the signifying practice. That is, it relies on and reinforces those sets of linguistic meanings that have been socially sanctioned under the "law of the Father." As such, theological discourse in its most repressive mode can and does "batten our persuasion that some authority can support our denial of mortality or suspend its operations on our behalf." Kearns agrees with Kristeva's rejection of this type of theological discourse because its only possible effect can be to stall the formation of innovative ideas and to limit the possibilities for the renewal of religious subjects.

Yet Kearns points out that Kristeva does not herself entirely relinquish theological language, in part because "even in psychoanalysis proper there is a persistent experience both in therapy and beyond it, which insists on using the apparently dated language of Judeo-Christian passion and ethics." Within a context created by *analytic listening* and *aesthetic practice*, religious language renders forth *un autre sens* (another sense or meaning). Theological discourse and religious practices can encourage the subject to accept itself as a *sujet en procès*, a provisional and flexible self, constantly negotiating between the "law of the Father" (the symbolic realm) and the corporeal, material rhythms and patterns of the semiotic realm. Kearns elaborates on Kristeva's understanding of the problems and possibilities of theological discourse by conducting an extensive exegesis of two Kristevan aphorisms, "I am mortal and speaking" and "Taboo forestalls sacrifice." With this understanding of theological language before her, Kearns briefly examines two sacramental expressions, the Thomist understanding of the eucharist as needing a signifying word and a material substance, and Emily Dickinson's poem on the eucharist, to show how Kristeva's work can be used to open "a new world of significations and possibilities, of affirmations as well as denials" within feminist theology.

Kristeva's understanding of language and theories of textual interpretation also inform the essay by Amy Hollywood, albeit in a very different way. In "Violence and Subjectivity: *Wuthering Heights*, Julia Kristeva, and Feminist Theology," Hollywood conducts a reading of Emily Brontë's novel to show its relevance for current theological reflection. For Hollywood, novels such as *Wuthering Heights* are an unconventional but important resource for feminist theologians, provided we can uncover the meanings offered by a discourse that is at once literary and religious. Here, Kristeva's nuanced theory of poetic language offers an interpretive tool. At the same time, *Wuthering Heights* acts as a corrective to Kristeva's narrow understanding of religion because the novel makes "explicit the religious implications of its poetic language and the proximity of the poetic to the mystical and the sacred."

In her reading of *Wuthering Heights*, Hollywood concentrates on what the novel can add to the feminist view of human subjects and the violence they experience in their lives. Feminist theologians, Hollywood notes, tend to direct attention toward the violence inflicted on women by the hierarchical structures of patriarchal society. Hollywood argues, however, that this understanding of violence, and the feminist demand for its eradication, is one-dimensional and cannot account for the types of violence present in texts like *Wuthering Heights* or for the fascination such violence holds for readers. In this instance, Kristeva's account of subjectivity and the violence inherent in its formation offers a more adequate framework for explaining these examples of disruption. Hollywood argues that the abuses commonly highlighted by most feminist theologians are "only the most visible manifestations of a much more variegated and prevalent phenomenon." Beyond the obvious forms of physical and destructive violence, we must acknowledge the violence "of and in subjectivity." Such a recognition influences our feminist response to violence. Hollywood contends that since no person and no society can avoid the violent drives and forces that are its underpinnings, "it is how we negotiate and control violent drives . . . that must be subject for discussion, rather than how to do away with violence entirely, an impossible task that can lead to the worst kinds of oppression."

In "This God Which Is Not One: Irigaray and Barth on the Divine," Serene Jones draws together French feminism and theology through a comparative analysis of the writings of Luce Irigaray and Karl Barth. Although Irigaray and Barth seem an odd pair, Jones argues that within their different intellectual contexts, their work is guided by a shared concern. Of chief interest to both is the status granted the "other" in the traditions of Western thought, where the other for Irigaray is woman and for Barth, God. Through her critique of the "logic of the Same," Irigaray shows that Western phallocentric systems of meaning are blind to the real differences that separate women from men and so are incapable of granting women an identity of our own. In a similar manner, Barth argues that liberal theology, which finds its starting point in the religious experience of the human subject, inevitably fails to acknowledge the radical otherness of the Christian God.

In addition, both thinkers formulate strategies to open their respective thought worlds to the excluded other. Irigaray's practice of mimicry exposes the inadequacy of the role granted women within Western discourse. Barth, on the other hand, destabilizes religious language through both his insistence that all God-talk has the form of an "analogy of faith" and his refusal to privilege any one philosophical tradition in his theological writing. In a more constructive vein, Irigaray imagines the shape of a new rationality, patterned after the female body, which would be better able to welcome the differences within and between its various terms. Likewise, Barth's paradoxical description of God as a trinity marked by internal difference and radical relationality allows him to construct a theology that values the otherness at the center of any relation, including the relation between God and humanity.

There are, of course, points at which Irigaray and Barth call each other into question. According to Jones, Irigaray would challenge, among other things, the "lingering phallocentrism" in Barth's tendency to place God in a hierarchical relationship to humanity. Barth, on the other hand, would charge that Irigaray's understanding of a divine that reflects the differentiated image of the female body refuses to recognize God's radical otherness. Jones suggests that Irigaray's failure to recognize difference in the normative relationship betweeen God and humanity undermines her attempt to construct an ethic that celebrates difference between individuals. Not surprisingly, Jones' comparison does not end with a neatly packaged conclusion but rather with questions to prompt further inquiry. Is it possible to speak of the difference between God and humanity without reinstating a hierarchy? If so, will this conception of the God-human relationship engender an openness to otherness in the arenas of human thought and action?

Ellen Armour's essay draws on the work of Irigaray for a very different type of project, namely, to gain insight into what is at stake in critiques by women of color. In "Questioning Woman in Feminist/Womanist Theology: Irigaray, Ruether, and Daly," Armour follows the discussions of race and class in the writings of Mary Daly and Rosemary Radford Ruether. Armour notes that both women have heard and attempted to respond sensitively to the voices of poor women and women of color, but she maintains that a close study of their writings shows the inadequacy of their responses. Despite Daly's and Ruether's intentions, Armour argues, the presuppositions which structure their thinking and give shape to their writings at the level of discursive practice do not allow them to acknowledge the real distinctions between women.

Drawing upon Irigaray's critique of the "discourse of the Same" that marks Western thinking, Armour reveals that Daly and Ruether have not broken free from discursive practices which produce a "latent essentialism" in their texts. According to Armour, an underlying discursive structure "inscribes/prescribes/proscribes" in their writings a liberal view of "woman-as-such," which precludes full recognition of the "play of difference" between women. Further, Armour suggests that Irigaray's attempt "to write and think otherwise" might be a constructive resource for feminist theologians. The discursive oppression manifested by the "discourse of the Same" sets a "hegemonic trajectory" that limits the way we write and think. It also limits our attempts to embody solidarity with women who represent difference to us. By contrast, thinking and writing the feminine imaginary (again, a notion drawn from Irigaray) may indeed help feminist theologians avoid "false exits" from patriarchal oppression.

In an interesting contrast to Armour's essay, Sharon Welch's "Sporting Power: French Feminisms, American Feminism, and an Ethic of Conflict" advocates a more cautious use of French feminist theories by American feminist theologians. Welch directly engages the methodological challenge (used in Armour's essay, initiated by a number of French feminists, and articulated in the Davaney articles) to the category of women's experience. In response to charges that an oppressive essentialism operates in the works of Elisabeth Schüssler Fiorenza, Daly, and Ruether, Welch offers "another narrative account of the fate of the appeal to women's experience." She argues that, while *logically* it may seem that the political impact of the discourse of classical feminist theology would be a continuation of racism and classism, the *actual* impact of this discourse has been quite different. Women of color often claim that it is precisely the appeal to women's experience that prompted them to articulate their own experiences in all their particularity. Thus, "far from silencing women who are different, the appeal to women's experience" has allowed for the "freeing up of voices." This panoply of voices has resulted in an important process of discussion and reflection in feminist theology.

Welch suggests that feminist theologians would be wrong to seek a theory "free of conflict." The challenge before us is rather to formulate an "ethic of conflict" that provides procedures for evaluating the clashes that occur in feminist discussions between different communities of women. While Welch is troubled by a too hasty appropriation of the French feminist theories, which, for her, seem to be concerned more with the constitution of individual subjects than with the relations between subjects, she does suggest that the insights of the French feminists can be useful in formulating an ethic of conflict. Hélène Cixous and Luce Irigaray, in particular, help describe the "logic of naming, the logic of identity formation" that marks the process of assent and dissent inherent in our current feminist theological discussions. Irigaray's description of the love between two women which cannot be captured by patriarchal logic or Cixous' notion of an economy of gift may help feminist theologians envision the shape of our own interaction.

In the final essay of this volume, "Irigaray and the Divine," Elizabeth Grosz, herself not a theologian, offers a different critical context in which to understand Irigaray's interest in the divine. Grosz notes that Irigaray, like many American feminists, clearly does not advocate "a return to piety, and to a mode of devotion represented by that well-worn emblem of female devotion, St. Theresa." Yet, in a move that differs from that taken by most feminist theologians, Grosz points out that Irigaray's concern with God needs to be seen in the context of her projects to create an ideal *for women*. In other words, Irigaray's project attempts to "tie together" concepts of God with feminist concepts and practices. As such, Irigaray's discursive use of the "divine" and the familiar referent of theologians cannot be simply equated, an important cautionary note for theologians such as Jones who consider Irigaray's references to God exclusively within a theological framework. According to Grosz, Irigaray's God is a "sensible transcendental," that is, "a term designating a material process of completion and integration, a movement always tending towards, becoming its own ideal."

Grosz reminds us that Irigaray is fully aware that appeals to "God" have been the source and justification of patriarchal philosophical and theological "knowledges"; she shares with Lacan and other contemporary French thinkers the rejection of an ontological "certainty" ensured by "Good old God." Yet she does not abandon the category of the "divine." Because of this, we can understand why her work is appealing to American feminist theologians. But Grosz notes that Irigaray's understanding of the status of the divine becomes more clear in her more recent work, only now being translated. Though different from the other essays in this anthology, Grosz's exegesis of the category of the divine in Irigaray's more recent work may serve as a corrective to constructive feminist theologies that refer to (more often than not, translations of) Irigaray.

We hope that Grosz's essay, along with the other essays in this volume, will spark conversations and debates within feminist theology. As Grosz, Meltzer, and Chopp explicitly say, and as the other authors suggest, all writing, to various degrees, is writing within, whether for or against, inherited theories and discourses. Consequently, it is important to note that it is not only the "fathers" who have left us an inheritance. Along with the heritage of Lacan or Derrida or the patriarchs of pragmatism, we have that of the "mothers" of feminist theology. Thus today feminist theologians must not only criticize and transform the work of the "fathers," we must also critically assess our own growing tradition. As both Welch and Armour insist, we undermine our most valued goals if we fail to listen and respond to the insights and criticisms of women whose experiences are different from our own.

The theological authors in this volume have turned to the French feminists to add new dimensions to their conversations with and against the theological traditions in which they work. Chopp, Jones, and Kearns, in spite of their differences, clearly share the goal of transforming and renewing Christian theology and practice. Chopp explores the insights of Kristeva's work to examine how we can move the traditions of pragmatism and public theology, and the feminist theologies they inform, "from patriarchy into freedom." Juxtaposing Irigaray's work with that of a theological "father," Karl Barth, Jones argues that both reveal to theologians the importance of attending to otherness. However, she faults Barth for his misogynism and Irigaray for what Jones finds to be an inadequate understanding of God. Relying on the work of Kristeva, Kearns examines what she believes to be "improper" theological discourse and practice and suggests that a more adequate understanding of theology can lead to a renewal of the sacraments in Christianity.

In contrast, Hollywood seeks to broaden the theological discipline by exploring a text not generally recognized as part of that tradition. Kristeva's theory of subjectivity provides a place from which Hollywood can suggest to feminist theologians that we need to consider a different sort of anthropology as well as a different sort of theological text. Finally, Armour and Welch both begin with an explicit commitment to the emerging voices of women of color in theological discourse. Armour, relying on the work of Irigaray, proceeds from this commitment to criticize the oppression embedded in the methodologies of two prominent feminist theologians, despite their best intentions. Welch proceeds from the same commitment to defend the methods of the feminist theological tradition, based on its *actual* effects as opposed to its theoretical implications. For Welch, the French feminists are helpful not for criticizing feminist theological method but for imaging an "ethic of risk" that seeks solidarity in the midst of genuine conflict.

Taken together, the essays will leave the reader with a sense of the conflicts present in American feminist theology today as well as with ideas for the ways in which the American feminist conversation might be forwarded by looking to the French feminists. As editors of this anthology, we not only recognize the tensions between the essays, we welcome them. Our own experiences of organizing the conference that gave rise to most of these essays and of editing the essays to create this volume have taught us that it requires less work to call for collaborative efforts than to accomplish them. What is so obvious and yet so understated about the notion of collaboration is that the intention to work cooperatively usually takes place in the midst of, and often in spite of, genuine but conflicting commitments.

—1

Transfeminisms

FRANÇOISE MELTZER

If one is going to undertake, as I am about to do, a discussion of "French feminisms," one is naturally going to encounter several irrevocable and (more importantly) necessary difficulties. The first is that there is in fact no single French (or, I would maintain, any other) "feminism" (at least one of the essays in this collection states this quite clearly). Nevertheless, as soon as "French" gets put next to "American," or "theology" in contradistinction to "literary theory," the reductive binaries, not to mention essentialisms, begin to proliferate.

Such binaries can be pushed, of course, to a *reductio ad absurdum*: what is intended to be a multicultural concern can quickly turn into ethnocentristic assumptions and defensiveness. What, for example, does *French* mean here? Does it mean Francophone writings? Work by women of color in France? Poor women? Women living in the French provinces? Does it include men in France? The answer to all these questions, needless to say, is a firm no. *French* here means white, first-world women of the latter part of the twentieth century, who have received an elite education in Paris and who work out of the "*métropole*" as their intellectual and institutional base.

And then there is the problem of what *feminism* means. The label *French feminisms* itself was certainly not generated by this volume. There is, for example, the important book published by Elaine Marks and Isabelle de Courtivron, *New French Feminisms: An Anthology,* published in 1981;[1] or the *Yale French Studies* special issue of the same year, entitled *Feminist Readings: French Texts/American Contexts,*[2] which undertakes a similar sort of juxtaposing; and *French Feminist Thought: A Reader,* edited by Toril Moi.[3] During the eighties, many articles also appeared containing the terms "French feminisms," "Feminisms in France," and so on, in their titles.

In the texts of the essays collected here, however, "French feminisms" seems to mean, quite precisely, a specific trilogy: Hélène Cixous, Luce Irigaray, and Julia Kristeva. No doubt this is in part because all three of these writers have addressed themselves specifically to the issue of the divine. Nevertheless, such a trinitarian economy seems, from the point of view of an outsider, curiously resonant in a theological context. But if this is what "French feminisms" shakes down to here, then I would suggest that we[4] stop saying "French" and "feminisms" and the combination thereof and just say Kristeva when that is what we mean, and Irigaray if we

1. Elaine Marks and Isabelle de Courtivron, eds., *New French Feminisms: An Anthology* (Amherst: Unversity of Massachusetts Press, 1980).

2. *Feminist Readings: French Texts/American Contexts,* special issue of *Yale French Studies* 61–62 (1981).

3. Toril Moi, ed., *French Feminist Thought: A Reader* (Oxford and New York: Basil Blackwell, 1987).

4. Throughout this introduction, I use "we" in a fairly ambivalent and ambiguous sense, which is not merely (although it certainly is partially) the result of confusion. At times I use "we" simply to mean the readers of this volume. At others, I want it to mean the community of women in the United States that reads about feminisms and cares about the stakes of such a discourse; at yet other times, my "we" can mean the same from the French perspective. Such a criss-crossing "we" not only figures my own, biographical transatlanticism; it is also (somewhat more pretentiously) intended to destabilize any contained notion of nationalism and/or of a single feminist sensibility. Thus my "we" serves, I hope, to undercut the essentialism it claims to espouse. The same holds true for the instances in which I use "I." In other words, pronoun politics have become so difficult and burdensome, that I am basically taking the easy way out by using irony to undercut any firm pronoun position.

are referring to her texts, and *mutatis mutandis*, Cixous. It would be easier, and would avoid some unnecessary complications from, for example, a "French" literary theorist's point of view, which is the one I have been asked to represent (an equally dangerous term) here.[5] There are, of course, scores of women writing in Paris today who have their own agendas for everybody they imagine to be lined up under the sign of (as Lacan put it) "Women." Almost none of these writers is mentioned in these essays, a point which needs to be kept in mind when the phrase "French feminisms" appears.[6]

One of the most pressing problems in all of this is language, and at many levels. First at the obvious level: "We translate what the American women write," notes Cixous at the opening of *New French Feminisms*, "they never translate our texts."[7] In the more than ten years since this sentence was uttered, things have changed. Irigaray, Cixous, and Kristeva have all been dutifully put into English.[8] The fact remains, however, that not everybody reads French,

5. Similarly, for example, saying "Baudelaire" or "Mallarmé" or "Rimbaud" is finally easier than using the term "the Symbolists," given that great energy must be wasted explaining how each of these poets is utterly different from the other two. Labels, of course, have great pragmatic value; but I have come to believe that the distortions they create (univocity, e.g., or the reinforcement of nationalist sentiments) are not worth the convenience they profess to ensure.

6. For a sampling of many of these unmentioned writers, see Marks's and de Courtivron's introduction to their *New French Feminisms*.

7. Ibid., ix.

8. Among English translations of Cixous, Irigaray, and Kristeva are the following: Hélène Cixous, *Writing Difference: Readings from the Seminar of Hélène Cixous*, ed. Susan Sellers (New York: St. Martin's Press, 1988), *Reading with Clarice Lispector*, trans. Verena Andermatt Conley (Minneapolis: University of Minnesota Press, 1990), *"Coming to Writing" and Other Essays*, ed. Deborah Jenson, trans. Sarah Cornell *et. al.* (Cambridge, Mass: Harvard University Press, 1991), *Readings: The Poetics of Blanchot, Joyce, Kafka, Kleist, Lispector, and Tsvetayeva*, ed. and trans. Verena Andermatt Conley (Minneapolis: University of Minnesota Press, 1991), *The Book of Promethea*, trans. Betsy Wing (Lincoln: University of Nebraska Press, 1991), and Hélène Cixous and Catherine Clément, *The Newly Born Woman*, trans. Betsy Wing (Minneapolis: University of Minnesota Press, 1986); Luce Irigaray, *Speculum of the Other Woman*, trans. Gillian C. Gill (Ithaca, New York: Cornell University Press, 1985), *This Sex Which Is Not One*, trans. Catherine Porter with

and that a good many of the Parisian women absent from theological speculations on feminism (or vice versa, I imagine) have simply not been translated yet. Maybe they never will be. Some, however, have. Sarah Kofman's brilliant *The Enigma of Woman: Woman in Freud's Writings,* for example, was published in translation in 1985.[9] Catherine Clément, Michele Montrelay, and Monique Wittig have all been translated.[10] Language is a barrier so obvious that it is frequently forgotten as such, but it is also the case, as I will discuss later, that who gets translated and who gets read are not entirely serendipitous.

Language is a problem at a second level as well because some terms cannot be translated, and so a lot of time is spent explaining them. *Jouissance,* for example, became the *Aufhebung* word of the eighties—the term, in other words, that is both untranslatable and

---

Carolyn Burke (Ithaca, New York: Cornell University Press, 1985), *Marine Lover of Friedrich Nietzsche,* trans. Gillian C. Gill (New York: Columbia University Press, 1991); and these titles by Julia Kristeva: *Desire in Language: A Semiotic Approach to Literature and Art,* trans. Thomas Gora, Alice Jardine, and Leon S. Roudiez (New York: Columbia University Press: 1980), *Powers of Horror: An Essay on Abjection,* trans. Leon S. Roudiez (New York: Columbia University Press, 1982), *Revolution in Poetic Language,* trans. Margaret Waller (New York: Columbia University Press, 1984), *About Chinese Women,* trans. Anita Barrows (London; New York: M. Boyars dist. in U.S. by Scribner, 1986), *The Kristeva Reader,* ed. Toril Moi (New York: Columbia University Press, 1986), *In the Beginning Was Love: Psychoanalysis and Faith,* trans. Arthur Goldhammer (New York: Columbia University Press, 1987), *Tales of Love,* trans. Leon S. Roudiez (New York: Columbia University Press, 1987), *Black Sun: Depression and Melancholia,* trans. Leon S. Roudiez (New York: Columbia University Press, 1989), *Language—The Unknown: An Initiation into Linguistics,* trans. Anne M. Manke (New York: Columbia University Press, 1989), and *Strangers to Ourselves,* trans. Leon S. Roudiez (New York: Columbia University Press, 1991).

9. Sarah Kofman, *The Enigma of Woman: Woman in Freud's Writings,* trans. Catherine Porter (Ithaca: Cornell University Press, 1985).

10. For example, see Catherine Clément's essay "Enslaved Enclave" in *New French Feminisms,* 130–36, and *The Newly Born Woman,* trans. Betsy Wing (Minneapolis: University of Minnesota Press, 1986), co-authored with Hélène Cixous; Michèle Montrelay's essay "Inquiry into Femininity," trans. Parveen Adames, first published in *m/f* 1 (1978): 83–101, and reprinted in *French Feminist Thought;* and Monique Wittig's *Les Guérillères,* trans. David LaVay (London: Owen, 1971).

vitally important. Endless footnotes have been dedicated to this difficulty. As Jane Gallop notes, "*jouissance* may, in fact, now function as a synecdoche for the broader problems of assimilation of what the French women write. And, because it has frequently appeared untranslated in the English-speaking context, *jouissance* may have taken on a new connotation; it has come to serve as an emblem of French feminine theory."[11] *Jouissance,* then, standing in bald French on the English page, reminds us of otherness, of the resistance to assimilation, of the danger of dreaming of transcendental signifiers, of the insidiousness of essentialism (ever rearing its Aristotelian head)—of everything that we all have agreed for the time being to be bad.

There is also another term, as long as we are about it: *écriture féminine* usually gets put into French, ostensibly because "female writing," "woman's writing," "feminine writing," to name a few attempts, sound clumsy ("gynography," a relatively recent term, seems to me a more successful variant). But the other reason is simply that such foreign terms are often purposely exclusionary, warning the reader as to the erudition of the author in question. *Ecriture féminine* signals that I have read Cixous or Irigaray, at the very least. It also signals that if I am reading these Parisian intellectual white women, I too am erudite and need not be intimidated. I am what Alice Jardine calls a "Transatlantic feminist."[12]

But by sprinkling my text with such high-culture Frenchifications, I would have company. Sigmund Freud, for example, in his German text, uses the following phrase to demonstrate that he (unlike others, presumably), calls things by their real names: "J'appelle un chat un chat" (I call a cat a cat), he writes in perfect French. An odd choice for an Austrian who writes in German and wants to claim that he doesn't beat around the bush when it comes to language. The point in all this, however, is that language is a problem not only in terms of available translations, but also because some words either resist being translated, have a history of being

11. Jane Gallop, *Thinking through the Body* (New York: Columbia University Press, 1988), 120.

12. Alice Jardine, "Pretexts for the Transatlantic Feminist," *Yale French Studies* 62 (1981): 220–36.

imagined as untranslatable, or serve as phatic moments for lining up political and intellectual ducks.

Third, language is a problem for metaphysical reasons. "Woman" is inscribed in a gridwork of signifiers that are masculine and by which she is written as enigma (and not only by Freud); she is a metaphor standing for incomprehensibility, lack, and an eternally synecdochical economy. It is here that the story of woman as Adam's rib becomes not only funny but also a narrative of origin that reflects the scandal of woman and how she is to be inscribed in the masculinist (read: metaphysical) text, and that propagates that scandal with increasing conviction and stridency even into the present. Theology in this context becomes collaborator, and I mean this in the least charitable sense, in the face of the patriarchal forces occupying female subjectivity.

Language is never innocent; but this is a fact that directly affects any attempt to rearticulate the place of woman in the metaphysical text. To this dilemma Monique Wittig proposes a cognitive subject, one that exists before language and that is therefore free to use language as a tool rather than to be structured by it. Irigaray and Cixous imagine a feminine language (*écriture féminine*) that will counter the pervasive masculinist one; Kristeva refuses the whole notion of woman as metaphor and proposes what she calls "semanalysis," a new way of thinking the concept of text. She (like many others, I should add) sees the development of the subject within the political and social climate that surrounds it.

It is in part because of the literary theory of deconstruction that we think with (or in) certain terms now; that we locate the sites of logo-, phallo-, euro-, and ethnocentrisms—all of which are issues at the heart of any notion of feminism. It is deconstruction that speaks of "the Tradition," arguing that the text of Western metaphysics is in place by the time and dialogues of Plato, and that whether we put Mallarmé, Céline, Levinas, or Rousseau up against the words of Socrates, we will always (already) bump up against the same notion of *mimesis,* of truth as word, of writing as secondary, of woman as the (unknowing) site of truth and as lack and/or supplement. Deconstruction is "French" for the American context. That is, it "means" the writings of Jacques Derrida and Paul De Man (I note almost in passing that Derrida is from Algeria and De Man was Belgian, so that here "French" means writing in French). In some ways, then, deconstruction reinforced the belief in what Frederic Jameson once called the prisonhouse of language (for different reasons).[13]

It is from the writings of Michel Foucault and his analysis of the relations between the subject and power that we now critique the sovereignty of the subject. But any notion of the subject is churned out by that same machine (to use Derrida's word) of Western metaphysics, and so it problematizes the ground upon which "woman" is to question her own status as subject. This is especially the case when those institutions that Foucault studies, and whose mechanisms he dismantles with respect to power, are products of a system that never gave (in this case) French women legal status as subjects until about fifty years ago. Men can contemplate, for example, the death of the subject—only to return to a firm footing in their daily lives. Women, on the other hand, have not had much sovereignty as subjects on the level of everyday life; abstractions such as "the death of the subject" can be seen as mental games for the leisured. For the dispossessed, in other words, as Gayatri Spivak notes, essentialism and the empowered subject it frequently implies can become a powerful weapon.

It is from the writings of Freud that we begin to separate biological sex and gender, and from the difficult work of Jacques Lacan that we talk of the phallus as signifier without signified, as transgendered, and so on. On the other hand, psychoanalysis sees woman as enigma, a "shadowy and incomplete" object of scientific study, and problematizes her entry into the Symbolic (Lacan's term for the realm of language, taboo, Oedipal conflict) by inscribing her within an Oedipal model that, simply put, does not fit her.

By putting the phallus in the Symbolic register, Lacan frees the notion from a biological fact confirmed by ocular discovery. Freud's notion of penis envy was articulated as a visual scene: the little girl "sees that the little boy has it, that she doesn't have it, and that she wants it." Lacan transmutes such a moment into a

13. Frederic Jameson, *The Prisonhouse of Language: A Critical Account of Stucturalism and Russian Formalism* (Princeton: Princeton University Press, 1972).

linguistic appropriation of power and desire, one which at least in theory insists upon a nongendered account of lack. This plus Lacan's interest in the development of a split subject from an existential (in the Sartrean sense) rather than biological place is how Lacan's work can be used in a feminist agenda, and how he can himself be said to have produced feminist (albeit problematic, of course) texts. In this sense, Lacan must be taken into account by any narrative or tallying of "French feminism." Just as Kofman's book *The Enigma of Woman* is an allusion to Freud, so Irigaray's title, *This Sex Which Is Not One* is a direct allusion and response to Lacan's discussion of the "woman question."

Derrida, Foucault, Lacan—but also Plato, Freud, Marx, Hegel, Lévi-Strauss, Saussure—these are the fathers of contemporary critical discourse in France; they are also the textual fathers of Cixous, Irigaray, and Kristeva. And therein lies, of course, the problem. It would be impossible for texts that address themselves to the place of "woman" (or, for that matter, to any other theoretical issue) not to take the works of these (male) progenitors into question. But there is a danger that, it seems to me, is twofold for feminist concerns: first, the father texts can elicit alternative models from within the same economy. Irigaray's substitution of "two lips" in the place of the single male economy of one, for example, might be read in this light. As Donna Haraway notes, "substitutes do not destabilize; they replicate." She continues, "Substitutes are tied to identifications. Male-centered and masculinist accounts cannot or may not be replaced by female-centered and feminist accounts provided by women writing from the point of view of themselves being females or women."[14]

So too, I would argue, the notion of *écriture féminine* can (I do not say does) run the risk of being such a substitute: female writing as against male. It is not just that we are back to binaries; by substituting instead of destabilizing (to keep Haraway's language) the terms of the patriarchal text, we do not, finally, question its assumptions.

Related to the problem of identification through substitution is the fact that the father texts provide a vocabulary loaded with

14. Donna Haraway, *Primate Visions: Gender, Race, and Nature in the World of Modern Science* (New York: Routledge, 1989), 310.

often-unquestioned misogynist premises and, ultimately, with what I would call an ideological architecture. I use the metaphor of architecture because it often seems that, once inside a given system (whether it be Marxism, psychoanalysis, or Derridian deconstruction, to name a few), the door slams behind you and you are left inside a building that structures your moves for you. Thus, if you work within a psychoanalytic framework, for example, you are stuck with notions such as penis envy, castration complex, the Oedipal struggle, and a male libido. All these notions are thoroughly misogynist; but they are imposed by a classical (which means Freudian) psychoanalytic approach, so that you are forced to enter into debate concerning these issues, whether you intended to or not. More importantly perhaps, you are forced to answer questions that are not necessarily your own (for example: Why is woman an enigma?).

Psychoanalysis is not a random example here. Two of the three writers who, as we have noted, are most present in feminist theological writings (if this volume is any indication) are, in fact, psychoanalysts who have practiced in the past or who are practicing now, and the third writer (Cixous) has been highly influenced by psychoanalysis. This means, among other things, that an understanding of Kristeva, Cixous, or Irigaray necessarily means a thorough grasp of Freud's and Lacan's writings. The problem is double: does one teach these feminist texts, for example, by beginning with what I am calling the fathers? How much of the writings of these three theorists is trapped (we are back in the building) by the architecture that psychoanalysis insists upon? For theologians who call themselves feminist, it seems to me that there is another difficulty: to what extent is the Freudian unconscious a convenient metaphor for the divine and, if it is such, how conscious are these theologians of the ideological (that is, specifically misogynist) baggage that such a metaphor already entails? What will theology do with God-the-father, the figure Lacan calls "this good old God"? Proposing a mother god is once again substitution, a mere replacement of terms within an equation that is not necessarily ours.

The feminist trinity here is not merely the result of who get translated, although that is certainly part of it. These writers appeared in American texts largely as a consequence of the feminist interpreters of Lacan and Derrida in this country. Jane Gallop and Shoshana Felman were among the first to study Lacan; Barbara Johnson and Gayatri Spivak translated Derrida.[15] These women critics have shaped the present critical discourse in America; it was they who began, some twenty years ago, writing about psychoanalysis and literature, philosophy and history, and, finally, theories of the feminine. Kristeva first, then Irigaray and Cixous, began to appear in footnotes. Thus the trio is partly inspired by the fact that the American critical theorists of the seventies concentrated on the texts of Derridean deconstruction and Lacanian psychoanalysis, which are both discourses that have been elucidated and critiqued by Kristeva, Irigaray, and Cixous. But the same can be said of Kofman, Wittig, Montrelay, and Clément, to name a few.

The textual kinships grow fast and furious in this landscape; it is nearly impossible to avoid reading the theorists who are reading each other. Moreover, in a peculiar circular logic, it becomes difficult not to *want* to read French after a while, so that the untranslated texts can be readable and the puns accessible. It should be remembered, in this context, that deconstruction, Lacan, and the texts of the "French feminists" in question here came into the American discourse largely through university French departments. Barbara Johnson, Shoshana Felman, Gayatri Spivak, Naomi Schor, Jane Gallop, Elaine Marks, to name just a few of these "interpreters," were trained in French literature and at one point or another were members of either French or comparative literature departments or both.

Kristeva, of course, is of particular prominence. Her work is emphasized by such feminists as Alice Jardine, Judith Butler, Toril Moi (whose *Kristeva Reader* attests to Kristeva's impact), and Teresa de Lauretis, who are well-known by feminists in this country (again,

15. Shoshana Felman, *Jacques Lacan and the Adventure of Insight: Psychoanalysis in Contemporary Culture* (Cambridge, Mass.: Harvard University Press, 1987). Jane Gallop, *The Daughter's Seduction: Feminism and Psychoanalysis* (Ithaca: Cornell University Press, 1985). Jacques Derrida, *Of Grammatology,* trans. Gayatri Chakravorty Spivak (Baltimore: Johns Hopkins University Press, 1976), and *Dissemination,* trans. Barbara Johnson (Chicago: University of Chicago Press, 1981).

to name a very few).[16] British feminists, on the other hand, have "recuperated" Lacan for their projects: Juliet Mitchell, Jacqueline Rose, and the film critic Laura Mulvey, for example, all rely on Lacan's theory of the phallus, and on his notions of the constitution of the subject, for their specifically feminist inquiries.[17]

It seems odd from my perspective of "outsider" that none of the essays in the collection here mentions or uses the work of one of our few "mothers": Simone de Beauvoir. At a time when her life is very much in vogue—the less than attractive aspects of it seem to inspire particular interest—when biographies about her, or her and Jean-Paul Sartre, proliferate, her monumental work, *The Second Sex,* seems as if too obvious even to mention.[18] As Toril Moi remarks,

> many feminists have been made uneasy by Beauvoir's seemingly effortless escape from the female condition. Is she not embracing patriarchal values? Should she not have made a greater effort to praise the traditional domain of women? Does her exceptional life (no husband, no children, no permanent home until she was almost fifty) somehow disqualify her from speaking "as a woman"?[19]

16. Alice Jardine, "Opaque Texts and Transparent Contexts: The Political Difference of Julia Kristeva," *Poetics of Gender,* ed. Nancy Miller (New York: Columbia University Press, 1986), and "Theories of the Feminine: Kristeva," *enclitic* 4 no. 2 (Fall 1980), 5–15. Judith Butler, "The Body Politics of Julia Kristeva," *Hypatia* 3 no. 3 (Winter 1989) and *Gender Trouble: Feminism and the Subversion of Identity* (New York: Routledge, 1990). Toril Moi, ed., *The Kristeva Reader* (New York: Columbia University Press, 1986); *Sexual/Textual Politics: Feminist Literary Theory* (London and New York: Methuen, 1985). Teresa de Lauretis, *Alice Doesn't: Feminism, Semiotics, Cinema* (Bloomington: Indiana University Press, 1984).

17. Juliet Mitchell and Jacqueline Rose, eds., *Feminine Sexuality: Jacques Lacan and the Ecole Freudienne,* trans. Jacqueline Rose (New York: W. W. Norton, 1982). Jacqueline Rose, *Sexuality in the Field of Vision* (London: Verso, 1986). Laura Mulvey, *Visual and Other Pleasures* (Bloomington: Indiana University Press, 1989).

18. Simone de Beauvoir, *The Second Sex,* trans. and ed. H. M. Parshley (New York: Vintage Books, 1974).

19. Toril Moi, "An Intellectual Woman in Postwar France," *A New History of French Literature,* ed. Denis Hollier with R. Howard Bloch (Cambridge, Mass.: Harvard University Press, 1989), 987.

Or (as Moi also notes) was she unexceptional, spending too much time and ink on Jean-Paul Sartre?

Perhaps one can put these questions into perspective by suggesting that they are gendered. If we trivialize Beauvoir's importance by dismissing her life as not feminist [*sic*] enough, we lose the intelligence and wealth of information (the sheer research of the book is breathtaking) that *The Second Sex* provides. It was Beauvoir, by the way, who first said that a woman is made, not born. It is she who said that the answer to a man's comment, "You only think this because you are a woman," is, "I think it because it is true." It was Beauvoir who articulated the scandal of misogyny from an international perspective and who incurred the wrath of enraged men in reviews as soon as *The Second Sex* emerged (in excerpts) in 1948.

Beauvoir did not, of course, declare herself to be a feminist until very late, in 1971. But it should be remembered here that, apart from the fact that such labels are not of the utmost importance (how many self-proclaimed "feminists" do we know who, for example, hate women?), the term *féministe* in France has far more negative connotations than does that of "feminist" in the States. A *féministe* in France is still largely regarded (including by intellectual women such as Kristeva and Cixous) as an angry, unpleasant woman who hates men. The women in France who do what feminists do here, who believe in a feminist agenda, do not necessarily label themselves in any particular fashion. While I am perfectly aware that many (young) women in the States today shy away from the term as well, in France such avoidance is neither generational nor necessarily ideological: *le féminisme* seems overly aggressive to many women writing in France or in French, women whom Americans have no difficulty in placing in the feminist camp. It is a difference of style, in part; but it is also a difference of understanding where the female subject is articulated. For Kristeva, it is in philosophy, as it is for Kofman. For Cixous, it is in the act of writing itself. Feminism is seen as "aggressive" not merely for obvious (and unfortunate) reasons. It is "aggressive" because it assumes a stridency and a limited agenda that risks seeing the inscription of the female subject in the Western metaphysical text as something more specific than that, something more parochial. Thus "feminism" can be viewed as reinforcing the very essentialism and marginalization it professes to critique. It is in this sense that I mean "aggressive."

So we are back to language as the focal point of difficulty. Lately in this country, gender studies are beginning to replace (and rethink) women's studies, feminism, and so on. But the gender issue has itself been compared to language: "The sexes," writes Barbara Johnson, "stand in relation to each other not as two distinct entities but as two foreign languages." If reading is gendered, she adds, "the reading process is less a love story than a story of failed translation."[20] What is important, at the very least, is to keep such a failure from proliferating—whether it be transatlantic, transgender, transdiscipline, or any other *trans*.

As Simone de Beauvoir reminds us, it is because women have always been kept separate from each other—separate either by class, or language, or sexual competition, or physical attributes and the male judgments thereof, or education (to name a few on a very long list)—that they have so rarely mobilized to make demands of (indeed to take power from) the patriarchy and its political and epistemological hegemony. Both "French" and "feminism" can, in fact, fuel such separation; just as, conversely, the elision of difference can sponsor a dangerous, indeed deadly, brand of essentialism. The debate between difference and essentialism is a no-win struggle, because both are absolutely necessary and, alone, absolutely wrong. There is no answer here except, as Haraway puts it, to change the stories.

I no longer believe that criticizing or revising the fathers is an option, because it will not, in my opinion, destabilize the narratives on women. Irigaray, Cixous, Kristeva, Montrelay, Clément—all struggle with Freud and Lacan. The late advent of Freud into France (during the sixties) explains, to a large degree, why these differing "feminists" choose psychoanalytic models from which to extract their own versions of the feminine (whatever that may mean). Psychoanalysis was a field of far greater excitement in the France of 1968—where it was quite new and was reshaped by Lacan and where it was identified with the student revolt, with the left, with

20. Barbara Johnson, *A World of Difference* (Baltimore: Johns Hopkins University Press, 1987), 37.

the new intellectuals, with the texts of Hegel, Saussure, Lévi-Strauss—than it was in the States, where the reassurances of ego psychologists homogenized it into mainstream, self-help business.

But that was, in fact, some time ago. What is called "French feminism" in these pages has moved on (and out). If the excitement in France was in the late sixties and seventies; the excitement here was in the eighties, when the writers mentioned were beginning to be read by Americans. So theological "feminists" are themselves coming quite late to all of this. But good things, I repeat, come of delay. Delays destabilize texts and their narratives by virtue of looking at them with different assumptions. The Freudian unconscious, for example, was radically destabilized when read through linguistics by Lacan. The texts of Lacan were in turn destabilized by the vision of a Cixous, or Irigaray, or Kristeva. We look to the late advent of "feminist" theologians for a similar enrichment.

2

From Patriarchy into Freedom

A CONVERSATION BETWEEN AMERICAN FEMINIST THEOLOGY AND FRENCH FEMINISM

REBECCA S. CHOPP

I begin my conversation between American feminist theology and French feminism by stating two convictions: first, the need to situate oneself as well as the other in a conversation and, second, the need to establish the framework of the conversation.

By the first conviction, I mean that in any dialogue one needs to be as clear as possible about one's own context, categories, perspectives. Thus I am going to concentrate on American feminist theology and theory. I want to try to understand the historical precedents for feminist theory and feminist theology as forms of cultural politics located within the changes in the lives of American women in this century.[1] These changes, bridging the political and

1. Ethel Klein, *Gender Politics: From Consciousness to Mass Politics* (Cambridge, Mass.: Harvard University Press, 1984). Ethel Klein has identified three of these: changes in marriage and divorce practices; the advent of birth control; and the movement of women, across race and class lines, into the work force. Though Klein concentrates on white middle- and working-class women, these and other changes affect all women in the United States. The shift in the dominant ideology of what it is to be a woman has dramatically changed in the United States, with popular women's magazines now promoting the hegemonic idea of the superwoman instead of that of the suburban housewife.

the personal, are the locus for American feminism. American feminist theology needs to be understood in the context of the women's movement, which I define as a broad-based social movement of women who address problems in the cultural and political arenas relating to the needs of women and children.

Second, given my contextualization of American feminist theology, I want to establish a framework for the conversation between American feminist theology and French feminist theory. I will begin by suggesting that feminist theology, placed as it is in the history of pragmatism and American public theology, works for the transformation of political and personal life away from patriarchy into freedom. Given this turn to radical transformation, I want to explore a conversation with French feminism, for I think that French feminism offers us some useful guides for pursuing strategies of diagnosis and transformation. My attempt at a conversation between American feminist theologies and French feminism is going to follow my understanding of American feminist pragmatism, the attempt to use all there is to be used in terms of addressing the problems of the day. I will argue that French feminism is helpful as we address a particular set of problems having to do with the radical transformation of our narratives, our language, and our practices by giving us particular strategies of self-reflexive critique and transformation.

I do not mean that French feminism offers us all the answers or all the strategies that we need, but simply that there is a certain self-reflexivity in French feminism that pragmatically is helpful when we struggle with the terms of our own transformation. For instance, it is now commonly assumed in feminist theory that there is no universal "woman," for the differences among women are many and great. Yet the gender critique of feminism—the basic ordering of practices, values, institutions as marked by man and woman—is central to an analysis of patriarchy, understood as oppressive practices and structures that affect all women, despite, through, and in the midst of their differences. French feminism can help theologians think through the necessity of emancipation from a binary ordering of gender and think toward transformation of a cultural politics of difference.

FEMINISM, PRAGMATISM, AND PUBLIC THEOLOGY

In recent years American feminist theorists and American feminist theologians have responded to French theory with cries about the death of the subject. Perhaps most frequently quoted is Nancy Hartsock's provocative question, "Why is it that just at the moment when so many of us who have been silenced begin to demand the right to name ourselves, to act as subjects rather than objects of history, that just then the concept of subjecthood becomes problematic?"[2] Feminist theologians such as Elisabeth Schüssler Fiorenza, Susan Brooks Thistlethwaite, and Mary McClintock Fulkerson have all voiced similar concerns in relation to French poststructuralist thought.[3] As important and necessary as the concern for our subjecthood is, and I take it to be almost nonrefutable, it is well worth reflecting on the nature of the American response. What is at stake in this particular response to the French critique of the subject?

It is especially curious since French feminism, in the context of poststructuralism, shares with American feminism the resistance to the universal, autonomous subject of Cartesianism. Whereas American feminism has tended to focus on the critique of foundationalism, French feminism has focused on the critique of humanism, that is, the notion that there is a real or true self buried in the unconscious or secured in an ontology or phenomenology of the subject. And whereas American feminism focuses on the representative functions of language, French feminism concentrates on the performative functions of language. To state the difference perhaps too vividly, American feminism tends to epitomize the phrase "the personal is the political"; French feminism tends to represent another phrase, "the political is the personal." American

2. Nancy Hartsock, "Foucault on Power: A Theory for Women?" in *Feminism/Postmodernism*, ed. with intro. by Linda J. Nicholson (New York: Routledge, 1990), 163.

3. American feminist theologians are just in the initial states of responding to French feminism. See Elisabeth Schüssler Fiorenza, "The Politics of Otherness: Biblical Interpretation as a Critical Praxis for Liberation," in *Expanding the View: Gustavo Gutiérrez and the Future of Liberation Theology*, eds. Marc H. Ellis and Otto Maduro (Maryknoll, N.Y.: Orbis, 1990), 140–156.

feminism has focused on economic distribution, social equality, violence against women, and women's rights. French feminism has focused on sexuality, desire, music and aesthetics, and philosophical texts. But if, as I have suggested, American feminist theology is placed within the vast changes in the lives of American women and in the context of the women's movement, we may at least begin to identify the particularity of the American response of privileging the political.

American feminism addresses itself to a variety of questions of American democracy, including the proper utilization of laws, economic practices, and distribution of goods and services for the equal and fair treatment of women as citizens. At the same time, American feminism questions the ongoing interpretation of democratic culture. For democracy is never just a set of laws about equal and fair treatment. Rather it is an ongoing interpretation of itself, an ongoing production of new practices and narratives, of new values and forms of social and personal life that constitute a democracy. If the narrative of the citizen in most democratic theory is tied to male roles in society, what happens when women begin to fill these roles? Or when the rhetoric of democracy is stretched to include not only the rights of the many but responsibilities for the many, and the many now include the vast numbers of children of working mothers?

This is the reason why so many American feminist theorists insist on labelling their work as a form of politics. At one level, the claim is rather incredible—feminist theory includes no sound bites, pleas for office, suggestions for quick political solutions to current national and international problems. But at another level, especially given the history of the role of the pragmatic intellectual in American culture, it makes perfect sense. For as a form of politics, American feminism, at home in the pragmatic tradition, attempts to provide the theoretical analysis, the poetical provocation, and the utopian realism necessary for change in democratic culture. The philosophical tradition of American pragmatism opposed epistemologically-centered philosophy with its spectator view of the human subject; pragmatism understood philosophy as critical reflection on problems of the age. Cornel West in *The American Evasion of Philosophy* maps out this territory, identifying pragmatism as a rich and diverse tradition, characterized by future-oriented thinking and defined as "a cultural commentary or set of interpretations that attempt to explain America to itself at a particular historical moment."[4] West describes philosophy as a wisdom, focused on truth as that which "enhances the flourishing of human progress."[5] Pragmatist philosophy arises out of problems and dysfunctions of a particular situation, and the desire that things can and must be different. Philosophy is the effort to make the future different out of the sufferings, problems, facts of the present. As West says, "These efforts take the forms of critique and praxis, forms that attempt to change what is into a better what can be."[6]

The identification of feminist theology in the U.S. must, first, be placed within this pragmatic tradition of American feminism. As such, feminist theology is a form of politics, addressing problems of the social and personal good, including problems not only of specific legal and economic practices but also cultural and personal practices. American feminist theology is a part of American feminism in general in its pragmatic scope of addressing the needs of the times and anticipating personal and social transformation.

There is another context for American feminist theology, one privileged by its location in the history of American theology. I want to contend that feminist theology takes as its own and remakes the long history of American public theology.[7] The task of demonstrating how feminist theology is a reconstruction of American

4. Cornel West, *The American Evasion of Philosophy: A Genealogy of Pragmatism* (Madison, Wis.: University of Wisconsin Press, 1989), 5.

5. Ibid., 230.

6. Ibid.

7. There are some movements toward reconstructing a public theology that need to be noted. First the theologies of both Gordon Kaufman and Francis Schüssler Fiorenza, drawing on pragmatism, can be construed as types of public theology. Second, William Dean's *History Making History: The New Historicism in American Religious Thought* (New York: State University of New York Press, 1988) provides excellent resources for public theology as Dean retrieves the radical empiricism of William James, John Dewey, and the Chicago School in relation to contemporary neopragmatists. Third, Ronald F. Thiemann has recently called for the development of a public theology, *Constructing a Public Theology: The Church in a Pluralistic Culture* (Louisville, Ky: Westminster/John Knox Press, 1991).

public theology exceeds the limits of this essay. Nonetheless to identify this history is necessary, for not only does it provide a certain theological context, it also aids in clarifying the tasks of feminist theologies.

What is necessary, then, is to construct a model for understanding the theological counterpart to pragmatism, which I will call public theology. Now I can by no means offer an extended argument about the diverse tradition of American theology, so allow me to paint broadly a picture drawn from Sidney Mead.[8] This will not be the only picture, but one, like West's view of pragmatism, that allows us to name a heterogeneous way of doing theology in the American situation. Sidney Mead's reading of American religious history suggests that the particular theological assumptions behind the Constitution, the role of free churches, and the persuasive power of religious morality combined to associate the church with the role of forming, through religious beliefs, the kind of persons and associations necessary for life together in the republic. Mead states, in *The Lively Experiment*:

> The free churches accepted, or had forced upon them the duty and responsibility to define, articulate, disseminate, and inculcate the basic religious beliefs essential for the existence and well-being of society—and of doing this without any coercive power over the citizens at all, that is, armed only with persuasive power.[9]

Public theology fulfilled its duty and responsibility by producing images of, definitions of, and judgments on America, by

8. Like the dilemma I faced in a quick survey of pragmatism, it is difficult in a short essay to cite all the sources necessary to make the argument historically for a model of public theology. Again, for the sake of brevity, I will stick primarily to the work of Mead. Sidney Mead, *The Lively Experiment: The Shaping of Christianity in America* (New York: Harper & Row, 1963); *The Nation with the Soul of a Church* (New York: Harper & Row, 1975); and *The Old Religion in the Brave New World: Reflections on the Relation between Christendom and the Republic* (Berkeley and Los Angeles: University of California Press, 1977). I am also drawing upon two anthologies: *The Lively Experiment Continued*, ed. Jerald C. Brauer (Macon, Ga.: Mercer, 1987), and William R. Hutchison, ed., *Between the Times: The Travail of the Protestant Establishment in America, 1900–1960*).(Cambridge and New York: Cambridge University Press, 1989).

9. Mead, The Lively Experiment, 65.

training citizens in the space of churches (as the place in American society where public and private met), and by forming discourses of morality (we might now say discourses of subjectivity) necessary for life together as well as for individual flourishing.

American public theology begins not in distinguishing Christian tradition from common human experience, but in the movement of Christian practice speaking to the problems, doubts, and desires within the American situation. American public theology has functioned, at times, covertly and overtly to affirm oppressive practices.[10] The ambiguities and distortions of American public theology cannot be ignored. In the midst of claims about freedom, liberty, and justice, American public theology has often become a discourse of oppression. Yet its prophetic spirit, its relation to morality and public judgment, its employment of religious metaphors to criticize the public also allowed for debates within American public theology about its own oppressive practices. Such ambiguities of American public theology must be continually criticized in order to discover ways in which theological discourse can criticize, form, and transform American society. In this theological model, theology functions to criticize the present situation and to anticipate new possibilities, to create communities for public and personal good, and to offer discourses of subjectivity.[11] When feminist theologians attempt to provide new images of being human, to offer new discourses to the public, to criticize the gender division of public and private, they are working out of this rich model of American public theology.

FEMINIST THEOLOGY AS CULTURAL CRITIQUE

Related as it is to feminism as a form of pragmatism and to American theology as a form of American public theology, feminist theology

10. For one discussion of the ambiguities of such discourse, see Ronald C. White, Jr., *Liberty and Justice for All: Radical Reform and the Social Gospel*, foreword by James M. McPherson (San Francisco: Harper & Row, 1990).

11. Emerson is a good example of a thinker who argued for a view of individuality that was socially and naturally grounded.

constitutes itself as a form of cultural politics around the critique of patriarchy. But precisely as such, it is forced to move beyond the limits of traditional understandings of both pragmatism and public theology. For pragmatism and public theology have been discourses of the dominant culture that attempt to include others into the center of that culture, trying to develop or correct or improve those "others" to ensure successful inclusion. If feminist theology sought only to achieve women's full participation in the public sphere, the confines of pragmatism and public theology would remain secure. But as feminist theology begins to question the very structure, narratives, and ordering of the political, a position of radical transformation occurs. That is, as feminism questions the very nature of the political, pragmatism and public theology become transformed through the critical theory of patriarchy. This critical theory operates through gender analysis, which, according to Joan Scott, arose in feminist theory as a way of getting at "the fundamentally social quality of distinctions based on sex."[12] Gender studies have been helpfully applied in textual studies, in history, in culture, and of course in economics. Indeed, gender studies have become not simply an analysis of how society sees/makes men and women as different, but also how different categories and structures are marked and constituted through a patriarchal ordering of gender division. As Scott maintains, gender is both a "constitutive element in social relations based on perceived differences between the sexes and a primary way of signifying relationships of power."[13] A critical theory of gender construction analyzes not only the division of male and female, but diagnoses the very terms of division itself.

It is the diagnosis of this particular ordering, the seemingly incessant drive to impose an ordering through assigning masculine and feminine categories, where the masculine term is always higher and more valued and the feminine is other and lesser in value, that brings feminism to a position advocating radical transformation in

12. Joan W. Scott, "Gender: A Useful Category of Historical Analysis," in *Coming to Terms: Feminism, Theory, Politics*, ed. Elizabeth Weed (New York: Routledge, 1989), 82.

13. Ibid., 94.

its forms of cultural politics. Feminist theology seeks to critique the binary opposition of values, terms, and practices through gender. Thus it questions the relations of gender terms as descriptive and prescriptive, as interlocking relations of value and power controls. Further, feminist theology seeks to emancipate us from these binary terms and the incessant valuing of one term through the expulsion and devaluation of the other. Feminist theology desires a transformation in which new ways of flourishing, new practices of being human, new discourses of subjectivity are created.

This is, of course, an enormous task. Feminist theologies, and feminist theory in general, must simultaneously address the sufferings of the present age with as much aid as possible and undergo the work of radical transformation. Such a transformation—with the dismantling of the old values, the dominant ways of ordering, the destructive psychic and political constructs of patriarchy, and with the creation of new values, orders, psychic and political constructs of difference—involves a great deal of practical, theoretical work. It is in this dismantling and creating of spaces for transformation that American feminist theology may find French feminism helpful in providing strategies of diagnosis and transformation.

JULIA KRISTEVA AND TRANSFORMATIVE DISCOURSE

I want to use, in an exemplary way, the work of Julia Kristeva to explore some ways in which French feminism may be helpful to American feminist theology. I choose Kristeva because of her interest in transforming discourses and the transformation of discourses. I understand Kristeva to be centrally concerned not with adaptation or restitution, but with transformation of subjectivity, language, and politics, and with envisioning the possibility of transformation outside the gendered ordering of patriarchy. I think Kristeva provides a space for us, minimally, to ask about the ways in which theology must operate to promote not only the correction of the abuses of patriarchy but also the radical transformation from patriarchy into freedom. In speaking about women in Europe in her essay "Women's Time," Kristeva asks the same type of question that we must struggle with:

> *What can be our place in the symbolic contract?* If the social contract, far from being that of equal men, is based on an essentially

> sacrificial relationship of separation and articulation of differences which in this way produces communicable meaning, what is our place in this order of sacrifice and/or of language? No longer wishing to be excluded or no longer content with the function which has always been demanded of us (to maintain, arrange and perpetuate this socio-symbolic contract as mothers, wives, nurses, doctors, teachers . . .), how can we reveal our place, first as it is bequeathed to us by tradition, and then as we want to transform it?[14]

This often-quoted and frequently reprinted essay suggests, especially in Kristeva's notion of the third generation of feminism, the immensity of the task before us: the need to question and resist the very ordering of man/woman and thus the formation of not only politics, culture, and language, but even personal identity based on gender division.

Let me use Kristeva's work then as a space to pursue the difficulty and complexity of the transformation from patriarchy into freedom within the context of American feminist theology.[15] At its

14. Julia Kristeva, "Women's Time" in *The Kristeva Reader*, ed. Toril Moi (New York: Columbia University Press, 1986), 199. [Editors' note: Kelly Oliver helpfully summarizes Kristeva's first two generations of feminism: "The first (pre-'68) feminism is the feminism of suffragettes and existentialists. It is a struggle over the identity of woman as rational citizen, deserving of the 'rights of man.' The ideal 'woman' contains the same characteristics of the ideal 'man' and the struggle is to insert her in man's linear history. The second (post-'68) feminism is the feminism of psychoanalysts and artists. It is a struggle against reducing the identity of woman to the identity of man by inserting her into his linear time. These feminists assert a unique essence of woman or the feminine that falls outside of phallic time and phallic discourse." (*Reading Kristeva: Unraveling the Double-Bind* [Bloomington: Indiana University Press, 1993], 157) The third feminism, which Kristeva advocates, is a mixture of the first two generations. It seeks insertion into history, but, in the name of difference, it refuses to be limited by linear history's time. This generation recognizes that there is no such thing as Woman or Man and rejects the "very dichotomy man/woman . . . as belonging to *metaphysics*." See "Woman's Time," 209.]

15. For important criticisms of Kristeva see Alice Jardine, "Opaque Texts and Transparent Contexts: The Political Difference of Julia Kristeva," and Domna C. Stanton, "Difference on Trial: A Critique of the Maternal Metaphor in Cixous, Irigarary, and Kristeva," in *The Poetics of Gender*, ed. Nancy K. Miller (New York: Columbia University Press, 1986); Judith But-

center, I think this type of transformation is deeply theological, that is I understand this notion of the transformation from sin (equating patriarchy with sin, of course) into freedom to be the movement of the Christian promise. American feminist theology, in my understanding, has as its overarching task the construal of this transformation, and I will address that task in three ways: (1) a critique of the depth texture of patriarchy, (2) the theological possibility of transformation from patriarchy, and (3) theological practices of envisioning personal and social flourishing.

1. A critique of the depth texture of patriarchy

Kristeva, like many of the French thinkers drawing on structuralism and psychoanalysis, suggests that the symbolic order—the ordering of language that gives symbolic meaning—is both the ordering of the subject and the social contract.[16] For Kristeva, the present symbolic order constitutes and is constituted through a binary opposition of gender relations. These relations, according to Kristeva, operate through cultural, linguistic, political, and psychic constructs of power and abjection, meaning and nonmeaning, order and chaos.[17] In the West, these gender relations function through what she calls monotheism, the ordering principle of a symbolic, paternal community that requires men and women to have different relationships to the symbolic. This difference is the condition of relations between men and women.[18]

---

ler, *Gender Trouble: Feminism and the Subversion of Identity* (New York: Routledge, 1990); and Elizabeth Grosz, *Sexual Subversions: Three French Feminists* (Sydney: Allen & Unwin, 1989).

16. Julia Kristeva, *Revolution in Poetic Language*, intro. by Leon S. Roudiez, trans. Margaret Waller (New York: Columbia University Press, 1984).

17. One of Kristeva's most interesting notions is that of abjection. See Julia Kristeva, *Powers of Horror: An Essay on Abjection*, trans. Leon S. Roudiez (New York: Columbia University Press, 1982). For the use of this notion in the context of American feminist theory, see Iris Marion Young, *Justice and the Politics of Difference* (Princeton: Princeton University Press, 1990).

18. For her most explicit development of this notion, see Julia Kristeva, "About Chinese Women" in *The Kristeva Reader*, ed. Toril Moi (New York: Columbia University Press, 1986), 138–59.

What Kristeva suggests in her analysis of the symbolic order as "monotheistic" is that there is a certain ordering to the functioning of society, subjectivity, and language that continually constitutes patriarchal relations. Now if this analysis takes the ordering to be ontological, as structured into the very nature of being, then certainly it is neither helpful for change nor useful for interpretation. But if instead this analysis presents the ordering as a heuristic device, a portraiture of the general structures of the situation, it serves as a way to draw relationships between needed changes in subjectivity, politics, and language. I want to suggest that something like a notion of the symbolic order or dominant culture is extremely important as a way of rendering explicit how patriarchy is not just isolated acts of injustice but a systematic fault within the present situation, invading our practices of personal narratives, childrearing, linguistic practices, and institutional structures. One of the most important tasks of feminist theology as a continuation and transformation of American public theology is to render judgment upon structures and systems of patriarchy. To do this, theology must be able to portray, at least heuristically, how patriarchy operates through institutions, linguistic practices, forms of subjectivity, and so forth.

Of course, theologians will stumble on the term Kristeva uses to label her depth texture of patriarchy, the term *monotheism*. Though the term has had varied uses in the history of Christian theology, it is generally taken as a critical principle that relativizes all ordering in relation to God.[19] It is tempting to rename Kristeva's concern as "monologism" and to argue that she is using a theological term incorrectly. But it may also be helpful for theologians to pursue monotheism itself as a problematic term in feminism for at least two reasons. First, the monotheism of the Christian God has been tied to the patriarchy of the West, and the critique of it must be traced and analyzed through our historical records and present practices. In what way has patriarchal ordering affected Christian notions of God and vice versa? Second, the logic of monotheism, in Kristeva's understanding, secures the identity of the

19. For a different reading of monotheisms, see *Monotheism*, ed. Claude Geffre and Jean-Pierre Jossua, trans. Marcus Lefebure, Concilium series (Edinburgh: T&T Clark, 1985).

one through the devaluing and marginalizing of the other. Now monotheism as it has functioned as a religious doctrine has many other uses. But this problematic ordering that is associated with monotheism—the securing of identity through absolutizing of one and the casting out of all others—bears careful scrutiny.

One implication of a depth texture of monotheism in patriarchy for feminist theology is the need for a careful examination of the role of religion and gender in the U.S. In part, feminist theologians need to insist that theorists pay more attention to the distinctiveness of American history, especially the role played by religion. American feminist theorists have constructed their arguments about private/public in relation to the theories of Jean-Jacques Rousseau, Thomas Hobbes, and John Locke.[20] As influential as these models of liberalism might be, there is another side of the story. To understand fully the models of the American public, it is necessary to understand not only liberalism but also civic republicanism, and to understand particularly the role of churches in American public life, roles both in training of citizens, and also as place of intersection between public and private. Feminist theologians need to call into question American feminist theories that consistently privilege European models of the division of private and public without attention to the particularities of American history, especially since both public and private have been formed in relation to the role of the church as a voluntary association in the United States.

If feminist theology, and feminism in general, needs to pursue a critique of the history of the depth texture of patriarchy—the relation between subjectivity, language, and politics—and the ways in which Christianity has contributed to or resisted this, a great deal of analysis of the present situation must also be done. Why,

20. See, for instance, Jean Bethke Elshtain, *Public Man, Private Woman: Women in Social and Political Thought* (Princeton: Princeton University Press, 1981), and Zillah R. Eisenstein, *The Radical Future of Liberal Feminism* (Boston: Northeastern University Press, 1986). These books make invaluable contributions, but we also need work that looks not only at liberal theories and North American feminism but also at North American feminism in the context of North American traditions of liberalism and civic republicanism.

in this land of democracy and freedom, has half the population consistently been denied self-determination and freedom? What is it about this so called secular nation that as late as 1982 the Equal Rights Amendment to the Constitution can fail to be ratified? What Kristeva helps us to reflect on is a theological critique of patriarchal ordering, an ordering of the whole and the parts, the ultimate and the penultimate, that consistently and thoroughly places women as less than and other.

2. The theological possibility of transformation from patriarchy into freedom

Is there a way for us to create a space other than patriarchy from which to render this judgment and to work for transformation into freedom? How do we speak of something more and something other than patriarchy without losing the radicality of critique?

Kristeva points us toward thinking of new possibilities for strategies of transformation in her notion of the semiotic modality of language and its function of enlarging the arena of meaning and representing the currently unrepresentable. Kristeva's point of departure from Lacan is her refusal to privilege the symbolic order as the only point of analysis. Kristeva posits that the symbolic order works in relation to the semiotic, the dimension of drives and motility, attesting to "the process that exceeds the subject and his communicative process."[21] Thus Kristeva focuses on language as discourse enunciated by a speaking subject as well as the "conditions of the production of meaning as on the (static) meaning produced."[22] Drawing upon resources in psychoanalysis and linguistics, Kristeva produces a subjectivity that is always heterogeneous and decentered, a subject-in-process. For Kristeva, the subject in process is a blend of both the symbolic and the semiotic, with the symbolic being constituted through the social contract of meaning, and the semiotic being the transgressive, that which ruptures, irrupts into, and enlarges the symbolic. The signifying practices of art, and increasingly psychoanalysis, open up and transform the signifying subject. For critique, not only as analysis but also as

21. Kristeva, *Revolution in Poetic Language*, 16.
22. John Lechte, *Julia Kristeva* (New York: Routledge, 1990), 100.

transformation, it is necessary to be able both to enlarge the domain of meaning and to open up the rules of meaning-making. Kristeva does this by refusing to look simply at meaning in a static sense, focusing instead on the process or production of meaning and subjectivity.

I have already explored this point in relation to theological discourse in *The Power to Speak*, in which I use Kristeva's notion of the semiotic to open up theological discourse about God.[23] Feminist theological discourse must resist assertions of eternal division between Word and experience, the ordering of the socio-symbolic contract with its static split of subject and object, and must explore the relation of Word within experience, and experience as always conveying Word, in a manner somewhat parallel to Kristeva's exploration of the semiotic. Word, rather than the paternal law that rules experience, explodes in the semiotic modality to open and transform experience. What Kristeva directs us toward is the recognition that we cannot simply change metaphors or add new experiences to our dominant theological stew and stir, but that we must transform the very terms, patterns, and ordering of how language, culture, politics, and subjectivity work. We can criticize gender opposition and affirm theological practices of difference by opening up the realm of meaning and the rules of meaning-making.

3. Theological practices of envisioning personal and social flourishing

Again, I think Kristeva's work is very suggestive in terms of the procedures of her own work. What Kristeva interrogates is not the symbolic order, the realm of the subject and meaning, but, as she insists, the speaking subject—the subject in process who is always surpassing herself, who speaks in ambiguities, expressing desires and wants she may not consciously recognize.[24] Kristeva

23. Rebecca S. Chopp, *The Power to Speak: Feminism, Language, God* (New York: Crossroad, 1986), 10–39.

24. Julia Kristeva, "The System and the Speaking Subject," *The Kristeva Reader*, 24–33. See also Julia Kristeva, *Tales of Love*, trans. Leon S. Roudiez (New York: Columbia University Press, 1987), and *In the Beginning Was Love: Psychoanalysis and Faith*, trans. Arthur Goldhammer, intro. by Otto F. Kernberg, M.D. (New York: Columbia University Press, 1987).

continually seeks to uncover the process of the ongoing production of subjectivity. In her early work on the semiotic, she explores the openness of signs and introduces the concept of *negativity* as the process of semiotic generativity that destabilizes the posited unity of the symbolic. In her writings on aesthetics, she is concerned not so much with particular meaning, but with the process of meaning coming to be. As John Lechte has observed, Kristeva views art "less as an object, and more as a process or practice that 'creates' the subject."[25] And with her work on psychoanalysis, she turns to the journey of the soul, to use an Augustinian phrase, to explore how contemporary persons might learn to love. Kristeva argues that it is necessary, at present, to enlarge the imaginary in culture, and that both aesthetics and psychoanalysis must be seen as practices that create new forms of subjectivity, language, and perhaps by extension politics.

Feminist theology can use Kristeva's focus on meaning coming to be to think of itself as practices, not of interpreting meaning already given, but of envisioning personal and social flourishing through new forms of subjectivity, language, and politics. In a sense, this is where French feminism's critique of humanism is very necessary for American feminism as it envisions new forms of freedom utterly without patriarchy.

We might helpfully call this process rhetorical hermeneutics, for feminist theology is best described as productive strategies of critique and transformation seeking, in the tradition of American public theology, to offer persuasive discourses of personal and social flourishing. The concern for hermeneutics in feminist theology rests not in tradition or experience, though these can both be important moments, but in transforming the culture.[26] Feminist theology turns to hermeneutics as a practice, a practice of cultural politics. In much contemporary hermeneutical theory, the real of hermeneutics is the

25. John Lechte, "Art, Love and Melancholia," in *Abjection, Melancholia and Love: The Work of Julia Kristeva*, ed. John Fletcher and Andrew Benjamin (New York: Routledge, 1990), 24.

26. If hermeneutics is employed in explaining, say, the work of systematic theology in interpreting religious classics, a focus on the tradition will dominate. See David Tracy, *The Analogical Imagination: Christian Theology and the Culture of Pluralism* (New York: Crossroad, 1981).

subjective experience of the textual object. When coupled with an assumed position of tradition or with simply the notion of text as encompassing experience, what is being sought is a type of revelation or overwhelming experience from the object side of the subject/object split. In this process, which is referred to as the play of the text and interpreter,[27] the text incorporates our experience or discloses to our experience some originary meaning in the text. Yet, within a feminist rhetorical hermeneutics, the play of text and interpreter cannot be isolated as an autonomous act between a subject and an object. For the play—the play of text, subjectivity, and discourse in interpretation—always already occurs within the practices of cultural politics. Play, from the perspective of a critical theory of gender deconstruction, always involves some form of the politics of culture. For example, when girls play with dolls they are formed in a morality, a subjectivity of relationships; and when boys are given guns and footballs they are formed in a morality of aggression and competition. If we use the metaphor of play we must recall that play is always embodied in social history and, at least in part, is always a form of cultural politics. The practice of hermeneutics in feminist theology brings to the surface the awareness that play is not just letting go, but being formed to a particular form of subjectivity that takes in and assumes as natural, important, or delightful a certain set of norms and values.

But if feminist theology diagnoses the practice of reading through the play of cultural politics, it also functions to open up the process, that is to engage in play as fantasy, utopia, reconstruction. Feminist theologians need to transform the process of hermeneutics itself through what Kristeva calls poetics, stressing, for instance, not what metaphor conveys, but what metaphor opens up and creates. In this sense, theology, especially a theology in the context of the transformation of public theology, is a constitutive practice forming the process of becoming subjects, individually and collectively. Indeed, several recent works by theologians such as

27. The metaphor of play is an important one for current hermeneutical theories, and one that I think needs a great deal of deconstruction especially in terms of how the deconstructionists use it. See John Caputo, *Radical Hermeneutics: Repetition, Deconstruction and the Hermeneutic Project* (Bloomington: Indiana University Press, 1987).

Sharon Welch and Elisabeth Schüssler Fiorenza might be read as moving in the direction of offering new nonpatriarchal discourses of personal and social flourishing for the American culture.[28]

Thus French feminism, at least as represented in the work of Julia Kristeva, offers to American feminist theology some productive strategies of transformation in terms of a critique of the depth texture of patriarchy, some modes of possibility for transformation from patriarchy into freedom, and some new ways of understanding the nature and tasks of theology as practices that envision personal and social flourishing. This is not to suggest there are not other points of contact between French feminism and American feminist theology, including points of conflict and even contradiction. Indeed, this essay should be read as one starting point for the conversation of American feminist theology with French feminism, a starting point that will encourage the serious consideration of the distinctiveness of each feminist project and the differences between American and French feminisms. Yet I hope this essay also makes a point that we who work in feminism dare not forget: patriarchy is a systematic fault that runs through the small capillaries and the large vessels of power, wreaking its havoc and destruction through institutions, metaphysics, popular narratives, laws, economic practices, and even the representative and performative functions of language. The task we have as feminists in a large sense is the critique of all the specific acts of patriarchy as well as the critique of patriarchy as the dominant form of life, a form which I have suggested we can only speak of in heuristic fashion. To meet the task of moving from patriarchy into freedom, feminism may well need to understand itself as many different approaches working together to create a reality in which difference itself is a way of life that is celebrated.

28. Sharon D. Welch, *A Feminist Ethic of Risk* (Minneapolis: Fortress Press, 1990), and Elisabeth Schüssler Fiorenza, "The Politics of Otherness."

3

Kristeva and Feminist Theology

CLEO McNELLY KEARNS

A Word that breathes distinctly
Has not the power to die
Cohesive as the Spirit
It may expire if He—
"Made flesh and dwelt among us"
Could condescension be
Like this consent of Language
This loved Philology.
—Emily Dickinson

Dans le thème de notre discussion se dissimulent peut-être la souffrance du discours religieux comme celle due rationalisme, ainsi que tel ou tel malaise, ou inquiétude, plus strictement personnels. Essayons simplement de les acqueillir et éventuellement d'ouvrir nos oreilles à un autre sens.

—Julia Kristeva

French feminism and feminist theology, if I can use two such monolithic terms, have recently undergone an unexpected *rapprochement*. For not only have Anglo-American feminist theologians begun to recognize the importance of figures such as Julia Kristeva, Hélène Cixous, and Luce Irigaray, but French feminists themselves,

Kristeva and Irigaray among them, have begun to make explicit the way in which the Judeo-Christian tradition continues to inform their work, even where they seek to challenge it.[1] This essay is an attempt to further this *rapprochement*, though not, I hope, without a certain resistance on both sides. For there is a difference—an alterity or alterities—to use the current terms, between French feminism and American feminist theology that should not be erased, lest the critical perspective each can offer the other be lost.

For my particular contribution to this complex intersection, I have chosen to focus primarily on the work of Julia Kristeva, for several reasons. First, Kristeva gives serious attention to the problem of suffering and to the reality of death, and she does so in the context of a broad grasp of the historical and cultural factors that condition human experience. At the same time, she demonstrates a certain openness to religious discourse unusual for her circle and milieu, although from a different position than those traditionally assumed from within faith communities. Then, too, her emphasis on the wavering lines between psychological, somatic, and spiritual experiences and on the different ways of drawing these lines in different religious traditions poses new problems for feminist the-

1. See the interview between Hanhoko Nishikawa and Julia Kristeva in *Iichiko Intercultural* 2 (1990): 18, where, apropos of the Japanese writer Mishima, Kristeva says "*C'est une voie tres loin de celle qui est la mienne et qui suit le christianisme aussi bien que le freudisme surtout, et de ma sexualite de femme*." Translation: "It's a path very far from my own, which follows from Christianity and above all from Freudianism and from my sexuality as a woman." See also *Les Cahiers du GRIF*, 32 cited in Toril Moi, ed., *The Kristeva Reader* (New York: Columbia University Press, 1986), 20. Here Kristeva is quoted as saying "For me, in a very Christian fashion, ethics merges with love, which is why ethics also merges with the psychoanalytic relationship." For Luce Irigaray, see her *Marine Lover* (New York: Columbia University Press, 1991), 164–90.

A general introduction to French feminism in its diverse manifestations is Toril Moi, ed., *French Feminist Thought: A Reader* (London: Basil Blackwell, 1987). On the intersection of Kristeva's thought and theology, see *Body/Text in Julia Kristeva: Religion, Women, and Psychoanalysis*, ed. David Crownfield (Albany: State University of New York Press, 1992)]. For a discussion of the ambivalence toward religion in Kristeva's work, see Jean Graybeal, "Joying in the Truth of Self-Division: Kristeva on Religion" in the Crownfield anthology.

ology and offers new ways of articulating its perspectives and visions.

I am also drawn to Kristeva for her insistence on the importance and specificity of literary language in understanding religious history and discourse. Literary language, especially as it has evolved in the West, not only offers a royal road to the particular sensibilities of women. It also points the way toward new, subversive, and sometimes prophetic religious and theological insights. Kristeva takes seriously the works of Western literature that explore the nature and fate of the soul, and she looks for a postmodern critical, psychological, and religious discourse adequate to their range and depth. Finally, her work has a striking and at times uncanny power to wrench into language certain almost unspeakable states of minds, to articulate moments of prophetic vision, and to register a profound pathos, as she tries to invoke and encourage a way of being that lies on the most distant, perhaps most unattainable horizon of human possiblity.[2]

We must acknowledge, however, that when it comes to Kristeva's extensive and by no means monolithic body of work, there is much potential for confusion and misunderstanding. Some of this is due to the very different cultural matrices from which American and French feminism and theology spring, and some is due to substantive differences of style, principle, and approach that are not always kept in view. For although there are many important feminist critiques and appropriations of Kristeva,[3] and even a num-

2. John Lechte describes Kristeva's work as having "analytic effects." See his *Julia Kristeva* (New York: Routledge, 1990), 124. For other introductions to Kristeva's work, see Toril Moi, ed., *The Kristeva Reader* (New York: Columbia University Press, 1986), 1–22, and John Fletcher and Andrew Benjamin, *Abjection, Melancholia and Love: The Work of Julia Kristeva* (New York: Routledge, 1990).

3. For me, the sharpest expressions of this critique are those of Spivak, Butler, Kuykendall, and Wyschogrod. See Gayatri Spivak, *In Other Worlds: Essays in Cultural Politics* (New York: Routledge, Kegan, Paul, 1988), 134–53; Judith Butler, "The Body Politics of Julia Kristeva," *Hypatia* 3 (Winter 1989): 104–117; Eleanor H. Kuykendall, "Questions for Julia Kristeva's Ethics of Linguistics," *The Thinking Muse: Feminism and Modern French Philosophy*, ed. Allen Leffner Allen and Iris Young (Bloomington: Indiana University Press, 1989); and, above all, Edith Wyschogrod in *Saints and*

ber of interesting attempts to apply specific Kristevan insights in religious and theological studies,[4] there is only a very tentative consensus about the implications of Kristeva's work for either feminism or theology. Certainly, too, her views have been as often caricatured as they have been summarized.

Among the many factors that make Kristeva's work resistant to easy theological appropriation is her participation in a long tradition of skepticism and anti-clericalism in French letters. When she came to France from Bulgaria in 1966, Kristeva came with the full resources of an Eastern European perspective well in hand, but she also carried with her the seeds of a profound rebellion against Catholic and Marxist pieties alike. She had been given what she calls a "francophone and francophile" education, steeped not only in Hegel and Marx, but also in Voltaire, Anatole France, and Victor Hugo. Her education had included a reading knowledge of Russian, an awareness of the work of the important dissident Russian critic Mikhail Bahktin, but also on another level a strong interest in French avant garde modernist writers, including Maurice Blanchot and Ferdinand Céline.

Making her debut in Paris as the protégé of the literary critics Lucien Goldmann, Tzvetan Todorov, and Roland Barthes, Kristeva began to attend as well, perhaps even more profoundly, to a slightly older generation of French intellectuals, among them the linguist

---

Postmodernism (Chicago: University of Chicago Press, 1990). There are also, however, a number of cogent defenses of Kristeva's position, among them those of Toril Moi in her *Sexual/Textual Politics* (London: Methuen, 1985); Jacqueline Rose in *Sexuality in the Field of Vision* (London: Verso, 1986); Susan Suleiman in Garmenr, Kahane, and Sprengnether, *The (M)other Tongue: Essays in Feminist Psychoanalytic Interpretation* (Ithaca: Cornell University Press, 1984); Fletcher and Benjamin, eds., *Abjection, Melancholia and Love: The Work of Julia Kristeva* (New York: Routledge, 1990); Theresa Brennan, ed., *Between Feminism and Psychoanalysis* (New York: Routledge, 1989); and, largely by implication, Diana Fuss, *Essentially Speaking: Feminism, Nature and Difference* (New York: Routledge, 1990).

4. Most notably in Martha J. Reineke, " 'This is My Body': Reflections on Abjection, Anorexia, and Medieval Women Mystics," in *Journal of the American Academy of Religion* 58 (1990): 245–67 and in *Body Text,* which contains articles by Diane Jonte-Pace, Marilyn Edelstein, David Crownfield, Martha Reineke, David Fisher, Cleo McNelly Kearns, and Jean Graybeal.

Emile Benveniste, the dark theorist of religion and eros George Bataille, and the panoptic structural anthropologist Claude Lévi-Strauss. At the same time, she took for comrades-in-arms the circle of intellectuals and writers around the literary journal *Tel Quel*, which included Philippe Sollers and, somewhat more distantly, Jacques Derrida. As her own work developed, Kristeva came to participate in the new prestige of psychoanalysis in France, training in the school of the neo-Freudian revisionist Jacques Lacan. Last but not least, she participated in sometimes acerbic but always intense dialogue, public and no doubt private as well, not only with women and intellectuals in these countries, but with such French feminists as the magisterial Simone de Beauvoir, the corrosive and visionary Luce Irigaray, the fantastic, not to say fantasmatic Hélène Cixous, the acute Sarah Kofman, and the politically committed Catherine Clément. She also engaged throughout this period in extensive travel, which brought her into contact with (largely secular) women's movements in places as diverse as the United States and Maoist China.[5]

Although part of Kristeva's interest for us lies in the way she qualifies and shapes the assumptions and perspectives of her milieu, she shares in its sense of the sheer and not always benevolent *weight* of Western culture—including, perhaps especially, its religious culture. For her, the Judeo-Christian tradition has a hegemony, a totality, and a power that seem to exceed certainly that of the individual and at times even that of the modern state. Religion and literature often appear from this point of view more complicit with the powers-that-be than resistant to their totalizing force. The result, especially for those who wish to contest or open up this

5. Kristeva supplies her own gloss to biographical accounts of her life in her "Memoire," *L'Infini* 1 (1983): 39–54, and in "My Memory's Hyperbole," most accessible in Domna Stanton, ed., *The Female Autograph* (Chicago: University of Chicago Press, 1984), 219–37 though first published by Jeanine Pairiser Plottel in the *New York Literary Forum*, 12-23. "My Memory's Hyperbole" provides not only a sense of Kristeva's intellectual tradition but of the political and social milieu of her early years. Scattered remarks in her *In the Beginning Was Love*, trans. Arthur Goldhammer (New York: Columbia University Press, 1987) speak of her convent schooling and its struggles.

monolithic cultural hegemony to other voices and perspectives, is a major investment in skeptical critique, often of a highly technical nature, combined with a deep pessimism about the possibilities for articulating and inaugurating real social change. Again, Kristeva is a partial exception here, but it is important to remember what she is an exception *to*.[6]

Americans tend by contrast neither to grant culture and religion such totalitarian powers nor to take the work of their critique quite so seriously. Of course, the task of dissecting and dissolving human bondage to dogma, clericalism, and obscurantism is not alien to us, nor are we unaware of the complexity and difficulty of the styles and modes of exposition it demands. But our society has been shaped almost from the first by open frontiers, by internal alterities of religion, ethnicity, race, and gender, by the ferment of Latin American and Pacific Rim societies on our borders. We presume a kind of natural frontier to every discourse, art and religion included, a frontier that may be opened up—so that we can "light out for the territories"—whenever and wherever the closures of cultural hegemony threaten to come down too hard. As Kristeva herself says of this extraordinary American insouciance, to view it merely as a surface phenomenon would be "to ignore the individualist and universalist, desperate and jubilant aloofness, with its solitary atomism and its neutralized polyglotism, which substitutes for community in this country of immigrants."[7]

Needless to say, this characterization of the differences between French and American attitudes toward culture and religion is to some extent reductive, caught up in the very binary oppositions we would most like to avoid. Perhaps it is also out of date, for, as our society rigidifies, our borders close, and our arts and religions become more and more paralyzed, complicit, decadent and/or marginal to the central culture (a center which is itself in the process

6. An excellent introduction to the background of French postmodernism is Eve Tavor Bannet, *Structuralism and the Logic of Dissent: Barthes, Derrida, Foucault, Lacan* (Urbana: University of Illinois Press, 1989).

7. "My Memory's Hyperbole," 235. Kristeva's valorization of the United States as the society of the future brought her into conflict with much of the American and French intelligentsia. See her "Why the United States?" in *The Kristeva Reader,* 272–91.

of disintegration), these oppositions themselves may soon be erased or superceded. Then we too, no doubt, will develop darker and more skeptical critiques of culture and more intense, highly wrought styles for debating their terms. In the meantime, however, I think it wise to bear in mind these opposing perspectives, and to try as much as possible to allow for them by developing a sort of third ear for their resonances. For texts like Kristeva's are, at first look, at once fascinating and disconcerting to our sensibilities, and we need to attend both to their difference and to their familiarity to understand the disturbing intimacy with which they can sometimes speak to us.

KRISTEVA AND RELIGION

There are three aspects of Kristeva's approach to religion and theology that might solicit the attention of feminist theologians: (1) her reading of religious history, which seeks to integrate the structural and psychoanalytic perspectives of Freud and Claude Lévi-Strauss with a basic Hegelian-Marxist model; (2) her attitude toward theology, a critical but interested attitude, informed by but not limited to the perspectives of postmodern theory; and (3) her indication of the direction of a new and liberating future through the development, especially among and on behalf of women, of what she calls *analytic listening* and *aesthetic practice*. Across all of these areas Kristeva deploys her analytic concern for the development of what she calls the speaking subject, or *sujet en procès*, the subject "in progress" and/or "on trial." This subject or self or identity is at once a psychological and a cultural construct. In coining this phrase, Kristeva seeks to articulate a view of the self or community less as an entity, a given either of history or of nature, than as a provisional but necessary fiction. "You do not take place as such," she reminds us, but, in a phrase usefully highlighted by Jean Graybeal, "as a stance essential to a practice."[8] The stance in question is not an

8. Kristeva develops her concept of the speaking subject in *Desire in Language: A Semiotic Approach to Literature and Art*, ed. Leon S. Roudiez (New York: Columbia University Press, 1980), 23–35. See also *The Kristeva Reader*, 24–33.

easy one to strike; it necessitates the negotiation and renegotiation of contradictions of body and mind, self and other, inside and out, continuity and discontinuity, which entail great risk as well as great opportunity and which are never reconciled with impunity, even in our most intense moments of orgasmic joy or *jouissance*.

Kristeva's analysis of religious history and psychology is focused on the different ways in which this *sujet en procès* is articulated and supported in different religious and cultural formations. This analysis is most fully developed in her *Powers of Horror* (1980), though there are foreshadowings and elaborations of her views in her early work in literary linguistics, scattered remarks in her later essays on psychoanalytic theory, and some considerations with respect to the early Christian attitude toward otherness in her *Strangers to Ourselves* (1987). *Powers of Horror* is one of Kristeva's major attempts at synthetic thought, and among her most important books for the study of religion and theology. In it she seeks to explain the deep structure and psychocultural functions of various religious formations ranging from ancient Judaism through Greek humanism and Christianity to the postmodern secular ethos of our own day.

Kristeva's treatment of these formations is organized around two laws or maxims, which she attempts to draw together. These are: *I am mortal and speaking* and *Taboo forestalls sacrifice*. Even in themselves, these formulations are evocative. The *I* of *I am mortal and speaking*, for instance, indicates the necessity of constructing an always provisional sense of self or subject, and the *mortal*, of the inevitable change and death, even minute by minute, that makes this task a constant test of our strengths and limitations. *Taboo forestalls sacrifice* sums up, in a succinct phrase, the structuralist and anthropological matrix of Kristeva's work and her attempt to understand the function of religion in history and culture as well as in psychology. It points to her view that religious ritual draws out and defers through language and signification the murderous as well as loving impulses that help to found our identities, both collective and individual. Both of these formulations or maxims point to Kristeva's clear-sighted recognition of the realities of human limitation and pain, recognition which is for her the necessary ground of reconstruction and healing, both at the individual and the collective levels.

To understand the import of these formulations, however, we must grasp the full extent of Kristeva's ambition in developing them. For her purpose here—a purpose her impassioned, psychically charged and impressionistic style sometimes masks—is not just to make pithy statements or aphorisms, but to adumbrate structural principles. She is attempting, in effect, nothing less than the revision of Freud's *Totem and Taboo* in terms of the insights afforded by Melanie Klein, D.W. Winnicott, René Girard, and Mary Douglas, but above all by Jacques Lacan and Claude Lévi-Strauss.[9] In doing so, she hopes to explain the forces that generate not only religion, but also patriarchy, psychosis, language and culture, and generate them all at one and the same time.

Sigmund Freud, she argues, saw part of the pattern of these forces when he understood the importance of the incest taboo. Lacan saw another when he stressed the coincidence of that taboo with language formation. And Lévi-Strauss detected yet another when he perceived, in a notorious formulation or aphorism of his own, that men exchange "women, language and money." Girard and Douglas understood the social functions of these reciprocities, especially the function of scapegoat and sacrifice in "purifying" the body proper and the politic of taboo elements. As far as Kristeva is concerned, it remains only to combine these insights and to add to them a deeper understanding of the nature and function of religious discourse to have a new and very powerful explanation not only of the history of religion but of religious psychology as well.

Kristeva begins to work toward that explanation by indulging at the very start of her book *Powers of Horror* in an impressionistic and quasi-phenomenological account of the psychic state of abjection, a state of potentially psychopathological horror and disgust

9. The influence of Lévi-Strauss on Kristeva has, I think, been much underestimated, even by Lechte and Moi. Martha Reineke has treated the role of René Girard in her "The Mother in Mimesis: Kristeva and Girard on Violence and the Sacred," in Crownfield, *Body Text*. Lévi-Strauss appears, thinly disguised, as Professor Strich-Meyer in Kristeva's novel, *The Samurai* (New York: Columbia University Press, 1992).

which in her view haunts and destablizes the relationship between mother and child, and later between father and child and between persons in society in general, and with which religion attempts to deal. Here Kristeva probes into a psychological fourth dimension that is beyond the reach of standard analytical language, a primitive terror of maternal engulfment and devouring that threatens the boundaries of the self almost before they come into being. "A fluid haze," "an elusive clamminess," a "violent nausea,"[10] Kristevan abjection afflicts a troubled and unformed entity that knows itself as an *I* only through the sense of having been thrown out or repulsed from an Other. This trauma precedes the incest struggle and the murderous impulses between child and father both temporally and analytically.

The subjective condition resulting from abjection is one of discomfort, unease, and dizziness. It precedes subject-object relations and is indeed the ground from which they rise. This condition becomes then Kristeva's point of reference for considering the meaning and function of law, defilement, purification, and atonement in the history of religion. Here she seeks, in classic structuralist fashion, to tie the two anthropo-psychological motifs of maternal incest and paternal murder together by a single principle. Abjection, she argues, not only helps to explain certain aspects of religion but enables us also to understand how murder and incest, taboo and sacrifice, individual psychic maturation and the establishment of social cohesion are *linked*. Her ultimate concern here is to demonstrate both how abjection is represented in society and how it is mediated, purged, and healed by the mediations of language—in religious discourse, undeniably, though as it were accidentally and in spite of itself, but more recently and preeminently in art and psychoanalysis.

Freud is useful to Kristeva in this project because he brings together, at least at the start of his discussion, two crucial dimensions of the relationship between the sacred and the abject: the incest taboo and violence. Kristeva reminds us that the controversial myth of origin promoted by *Totem and Taboo* posits a group of sons

10. Julia Kristeva, *Powers of Horror*, trans. Leon S. Roudiez (New York: Columbia University Press, 1982), 6.

who murder the father, and then, seized with guilt, set up an even stronger paternal authority in his wake to regulate sexual access to the women of the family or tribe. Thus, she concludes her summary of Freud, "renouncing the possession of all women in their turn, they establish at one stroke the sacred, exogamy, and society."[11]

In describing this scenario, Kristeva places great stress not only on the violence and sacrifice that lie at the origin of this ordered social life, but on speaking and language as implicated in its drama. As she puts it:

> If the *murder* of the father is that historical event constituting the social code as such, that is, symbolic exchange and the exchange of women, its equivalent on the level of the subjective history of each individual is therefore the *advent of language,* which breaks with perviousness if not with the chaos that precedes it and sets up denomination as an exchange of linguistic signs.[12]

Once this law of naming and exchange is set up, however, the individual knows him- or herself to be violently split, abjected, or decentered with regard to it. The violence of the first sacrifice, which is both patricidal *and* matricidal, perseveres in the violence of abjection the law creates. The power of this law is such that it splits not only the world, but the subject as well, creating simultaneously in those who embrace it a sense of abjection, or exclusion, and a striving for purity, or wholeness. "I hate a divided heart," writes the great psalmist of the law in Psalm 119, "I love your law." But, as Paul knew so well, though Kristeva does not cite biblical authority here, the law is precisely the discourse that reveals and even constitutes the divided heart.

Even as its institution spells violence, however, the law functions in a way to avert, defuse, or defer that violence, helping to constitute a solid identity both for the self and for society by displacements and degrees, rather than through literal sacrifice and murder. Hence it consolidates even as it divides. In recognition of that dual function, Kristeva is able to draw Freud and Lévi-Strauss

11. *Powers of Horror,* 56.
12. *Powers of Horror,* 61.

together and to formulate her own structuralist hypothesis, announced and developed in the central sections of *Powers of Horror*. Its fundamental principle may be formulated in the sentence to which I have given such attention, *Taboo forestalls sacrifice*. Now, however, we can unpack this a little and say that the development and elaboration of a ritual system, eventually encoded into a symbolic paternal Law, takes the place, under some circumstances, of the sacrificial self-mutilation and drastic exclusion of impure elements occasioned by the horror of maternal abjection. It does so in part by allowing for a ritual transgression of taboo that defers or deploys murderous impulses toward the other through a mediating system that removes their sting.

For Kristeva, then, to recapitulate this difficult argument, incest taboo and ritual prohibition institute symbolic exchange, and this, in turn forestalls or mitigates the sacrifices they demand. The Law, then, is relieving as well as painful. Not only does it split the subject into pure and impure, and establish that "he" is not master in "his" own house, but it offers him a way of coming to terms with his disenfranchisement. By acknowledging ourselves as mortal and speaking, as dependent on and recognizing in the breach if not the observance a law that does not stem from our own self but is nevertheless in some kind of parlay with it, we gain the ground for growth and transformation. As Deuteronomy puts it (though Kristeva does not cite this text), "This Law that I enjoin on you today is not beyond your strength or beyond your reach. No, the Word is very near to you, it is in your mouth and in your heart for your observance" (30:11–14). And again, in the words of the Psalmist of Psalm 119, "I run the way of your commandment / For you have given me freedom of heart."

Religion, however, insofar as it mystifies this law and wields it as an instrument of punishment and reward, rather than of internalization and revelation, not only hides from us the violence and sacrifice mediated by religious life but masks the knowledge of the inevitability of death and of our human limitations. This knowledge is vital to our health because it is a presupposition of that maturity which allows us to separate from the eternal mother and know ourselves as distinct beings, at once discontinuous with others and alone in our individual mortality. At the same time we need defenses against its recognition, because to live without a screen from such mortal awareness (which is in any case not the "whole truth") is to risk madness, paralysis, and despair. Hence religion is, for Kristeva, a two-edged sword, capable of the most profound ways of negotiating the basic violence of human maturation and capable as well of infantilizing us to the point where we cannot make use of them properly.

Kristeva's analysis of religion tries to remain structuralist and synchronic with respect to its role in the maturation of the individual and the maintainence of stable communities while moving diachronically in terms of the historical transformation of these structures along a continuum from past to present. For Kristeva, each stage of religious and social formation casts and recasts the factors at work in some perennial human problems of sexual and linguistic maturation, while assuming and transuming the understandings and strategies of the previous stage in new and sometimes progressive, sometimes regressive ways. To sketch this view reductively, it entails seeing, in a rather Hegelian way, a primitive pantheism rife with human sacrifice as superceded by a Judaic monotheistic patriarchy, with its violence deployed along another axis, followed in turn by a tragic Greek drama centered on precisely these contradictions and a Christian transumption in which they are internalized and mediated in a different but perhaps also newly problematic manner.[13]

The culmination of this process and its "way out," Kristeva often seems to imply, is an enlightened secularism, informed by the kind of psychoanalytic and cultural understanding she offers to describe. The resulting subject or identity or work "in progress" will accept otherness, both within and without, both onto- and phylogenic, with the equanimity born of acceptance of personal and cultural self-division. He or she will also greet strangers with the same equanimity and will be encouraged into further and more

13. For the influence of Hegel on Kristeva, see Moi, *The Kristeva Reader*, 2, and Philip E. Lewis, "Revolutionary Semiotics," *Diacritics* 4 (Fall 1974): 28–32. Neither finds Kristeva's appropriation of Hegel simple or uncritical; both acknowledge his centrality to her work.

engaged social practice by the dream of a still-freer and more spirited life, animated by a nonviolent analytic and aesthetic appreciation for all forms of difference, wherever they occur.

There is certainly a degree of enlightened optimism and aestheticism about this project—not to mention a certain parochial faith in psychoanalysis itself—that raises serious questions for ethics and politics, as well as for theology, feminism, and literature.[14] For the moment, however, the most immediate question posed by this project is the question of religious faith and practice and their role in constituting or supporting it. Kristeva's response to this question is both equivocal and ambivalent. On the one hand, she wishes to assert and does assert, again and again, that *for her* religion has been as it were superceded by psychoanalysis and art. "I see psychoanalysis as the lay version," she says, "*the only one*, of the speaking being's quest for truth that religion symbolizes for certain of

14. Dealing with the religious figures of the past as "cases," which retrospective analysis must "treat," is only one of the hazards of Kristeva's position. It is probably also a specific instance of that general imperializing tendency of the psychoanalytic method which Françoise Meltzer's anthology *The Trial(s) of Psychoanalysis* (University of Chicago Press, 1988) has so thoroughly examined. I have discussed this problem in "Love Degree Zero: Kristeva and Madame de Guyon," a paper delivered at the Modern Language Association, December 1990.

For a more general and very cogent critique of Kristevan ethics, see Edith Wyschogrod, *Saints and Postmodernism: Revisioning Moral Philosophy* (Chicago: University of Chicago Press, 1990), 246–51. Wyschogrod argues with respect to Kristeva's work on Céline that "repelled by National Socialist discourse, she is nevertheless led by the ecstatic empirical thrust of her thought to bring this discourse into the closest contiguity with the language of ecstasy or *jouissance* in a way that ultimately renders their discrimination nearly impossible" (246).

For a different view of the possibilities of Kristevan ethics, see David Fisher, "Kristeva's Chora and the Subject of Postmodern Ethics," in Crownfield, *Body/Text*; see also Toril Moi in *The Kristeva Reader*, 18; and Shuli Barzilai, "Borders of Language: Kristeva's Critique of Lacan," *Publications of the Modern Language Association*, March, 1991, 294-305. Those interested in postmodern psychoanalysis and feminist ethics may also wish to consult Elizabeth Grosz, *Jacques Lacan: A Feminist Introduction* (New York: Routledge, 1990), and Ellie Ragland-Sullivan, *Jacques Lacan and the Philosophy of Psychoanalysis* (Urbana: University of Illinois Press, 1987).

my contemporaries and friends. My own prejudice would lead me to think that God is [psycho]analyzable. Infinitely. . . ."[15]

Elsewhere, however, and at the level of general theory as opposed to personal stance, she is not so sure that religion's role in the constitution of new and more mobile subjective and cultural identities can entirely be dismissed. "What discourse, if not that of a religion," she asks in her prophetic and speculative essay "Women's Time," "would support such an adventure?" As Jean Graybeal has pointed out, this question is far from rhetorical, and it can be read in a number of ways. Kristeva could equally be saying that the supportive discourse must *not* be a religion and that, whatever it is, it will in some sense always already *be* one.[16] Even in this case, however, Kristeva is confessing that she cannot found her personal rejection of religion on a principle. Indeed the very force of her own critique of rational secularism and her clinical observation forces her to consider that the religious alternative is an open one—for others, if not for herself. This equivocation opens a space for religion in her work to which we must in a moment turn.

KRISTEVA AND THEOLOGY

Looking now, however, at the second of the two areas where Kristeva's work is important for feminist theology, her attitude toward theology proper, we meet a similar set of openings and closures. Here Kristeva's views are shaped in part by the postmodern critique of theology, a critique according to which it is an oppressive discourse in itself and the model or paradigm or even cause of oppressive discourses elsewhere. Kristeva, however, seeks consistently and sometimes with great success to move beyond the reductive aspects of this critique toward a more open reappropriation of theological insights. For theology, to her, is not just the *locus classicus* of a mystified and power-hungry view of language, but a sometimes very elegant metadiscourse or way of reflection upon

15. "My Memory's Hyperbole," 226 (emphasis added).

16. "Women's Time" is reprinted in Moi, *The Kristeva Reader*, 187–214. See also Graybeal in Crownfield, *Body/Text*.

the religious mediations of psychic and cultural experience. In this sense, theology is to religion as literary criticism is to literature: an analytical and sometimes arid but also refining source of theoretical understanding and practical critique.

Kristeva's understanding of theology assumes a familiarity with the view of it taken in most postmodern thought. That view is a critical one, developed over a period of time from disparate studies in linguistics, philosophy, and the history of ideas, and adumbrated most notably by Roland Barthes, Jacques Derrida, and Michel Foucault. According to their analysis, theology is not only a dated discourse, but the paradigm of mystified thinking in many realms, for it is based on a mistaken assumption about the nature of the linguistic sign. According to this mistaken assumption, sign and signified, word and concept, text and meaning, logos and God, have a natural and friendly link guaranteed in some sense by divine authority. This link allows theology (and any discourse modeled on it) to claim to represent the reality to which it attends in a unique and privileged way. The discourse in question (which can be science, philosophy, or even literature, as well as theology proper) can then assume power and subdue self-reflection and critique in the name of this connection. Derrida calls this assumption and suppression logocentrism; Barthes, the pretensions of the Last Signifier, the arrogant discourse that seeks always to "have the last word" in the colloquial sense; Irigaray, based on her critique of masculinist rationalism, calls it phallogocentrism.[17]

Derrida, Barthes, and Irigaray alike oppose to theology's assumptions and modes a different view of the linguistic sign, one that replaces its friendly relationship with the signified by a hostile, unsettling, and oppositional one, a relationship best seen and deployed in—though not confined to—literature and literary modes of expression. Theology, according to this view, is based on the superceded uncritical assumption of the alliance between sign and signified and cannot function without this assumption; literature, however, can capitalize on its own potential for unsettling this false

17. For a general discussion of the role of theology in postmodern discourse, see my "Fantasy and Art in Aquinas and Kristeva" in Crownfield, *Body/Text*.

equation. It can do so because of its attention to what Barthes calls *textuality* or *écriture*, the material, punning, playful and subversive level of language, according to which the actual trace or mark of the word is forever and comically slightly at odds with the signified, allowing for a difference, sometimes even an erotic and transgressive difference, between the two. To put the emphasis on textuality in literature into play in this way is to do part, at least, of the work of what Derrida calls deconstruction.

Textuality, for Barthes, points then to that in discourse which cannot be reduced to a didactic, moral, or conceptual point, that which resists translation into *exemplum* or dogma or ideology, even the "politically correct" ideologies of liberation or conservatism. Textuality includes word play, the flicker of images, even the accidents of printer's ink and typeface; it includes all that is in excess of the story's moral, all that offers itself to us for a host of responses that are less bound to the binary oppositions of agreement and disagreement, orthodoxy or heresy, correctness or deviance, than to a range of responses moving from mild pleasure to orgasmic *jouissance*. This textuality runs not parallel with but often counter to the rational discourse of the literature in question; and Barthes, like Kristeva, finds its clearest though not its sole expression in the aesthetic practices of the literary (avant garde).

Kristeva presumes this postmodern critique of theology in her own work, and she presumes it thoroughly enough to develop her perspective in a slightly different way, based on her somewhat different and highly original theory of the nature of the linguistic sign. This sign, or the signifying practice in which it is embedded, operates on two levels, the *semiotic* and the *symbolic*. *Symbolic*, for Kristeva, describes the rational, conscious, socially negotiable level of a signifying practice, while *semiotic* describes its corporeal, associative, less conscious, and more drive-patterned other face. (These terms can be very confusing to Anglo-Americans, for whom the term *symbol* carries a good deal of the connotations of materiality, associative meaning, and sensuality that Kristeva would place on the side of the semiotic.) To put this in other terms, the symbolic level of a text lies in its rational, linear line of argument, its moral or *exemplum* or doctrine, while the semiotic level lies in its material aspect, in rhythms or patterns arising from and directed at different, perhaps less conscious, levels of response.[18]

Kristeva's semiotic has deep affinities with Barthes' notion of textuality, but she develops her own term rather than simply appropriating the Barthian one not only to call attention to the textual level of any written work, but to emphasize more strongly its relation to the body and to preconscious, subconscious, and even unconscious factors in signifying practice. She wants above all, in contradistinction to deconstruction, to stress the dynamic potential of the semiotic level of texts for inaugurating change, both at the individual and cultural levels. Kristeva also accentuates more definitively than Barthes the potential violence between symbolic and semiotic modes, or rather more accurately the violence that establishes their difference.

For her, the two levels of signifying practice, semiotic and symbolic, are not simply playfully or mischievously or erotically opposed, but separated and distinguished by what she calls the *thetic cut*, a line between them fraught with danger and potential violence. Negotiating that line, keeping it open or permeable in both directions, is the task of the mobile subject, the *I* of *I am mortal and speaking*, and it involves both the establishment and the transgression of a certain taboo. Walking this line is, for Kristeva, as essential to the preservation of sanity, community, and ethical practice on the one side as it is to the sustenance of bodily drives, needs, and orgasmic *jouissance* on the other.[19]

The thetic cut can be seen diachronically, as the passage from an infantile (largely semiotic) state of connection with the mother into a rational (largely symbolic) one with the father; it can also be seen synchronically, as the relative balance or imbalance in any given discourse of the rhythms, patterns, and impulses of the body over and against the constraints of syntax, form, and logic. Kristeva's critique of theology rests on the assumption that, taken straight, and without the benefit of postmodern reading, it leans

18. Kristeva's concepts of semiotic and symbolic modes are adumbrated in *Revolution in Poetic Language*, trans. Leon S. Roudiez (Columbia University Press 1984), extracted in Moi, *The Kristeva Reader*, 90–136. See also "From Symbolic to Sign," Moi, *The Kristeva Reader*, 63–73.

19. For the thetic cut, see Moi, *The Kristeva Reader*, 98.

so heavily to the symbolic level that it violently represses the semiotic. We then have a mode of signification that seeks to stifle our awareness of the body, and thus of sex, mortality, and our own self-division in the name of a logocentric connection with ultimate reality. Such repressions, in Kristeva's view, serve primarily to buttress institutional, ecclesiastical, and/or individual neuroses and aspirations to power, for these batten on our persuasion that some authority can support our denial of mortality or suspend its operations on our behalf.

Kristeva's alternative to overly symbolic or "theological" discourse in this sense is less Barthes' free textual play (about which French feminism has always wisely had its reservations)[20] than that continuous and mobile negotiation of the line between semiotic and symbolic levels of signification in the construction of an ever-renewed subjectivity. This negotiation allows us to relapse neither into the position of the patriarchal theologian nor into that of rebellious daughter. Rather, it asks us to move *between* the semiotic and symbolic and to do so not, perhaps, without pain, but at least without the violent extinction or sacrifice of one or the other. Such a new identity is hard to imagine, much less establish, but the struggle for it is the struggle for healing, both in the individual and in the collective as a whole.

Kristeva's language theory, her psychoanalytic theory, and her theory of religion come together here, for when the subject can say *I am mortal and speaking*, it can accept itself as a *sujet en procès*, a provisional and flexible self, in both the semiotic and symbolic realms. Likewise, when *taboo* is allowed to *forestall sacrifice*, a culture can manage the violent separation from parents and the desire of

20. This unease often takes the form of a debate over the implications for women of such transgressive and erotic works as those of de Sade and Lautréamont. Many of the essays reprinted in Elaine Marks and Isabelle de Courtivron's groundbreaking but now somewhat dated *New French Feminisms: An Anthology* (New York: Schocken, 1980) deal with this issue. For a summary of the literary critical issues at stake for feminism from an Anglo-American perspective, and a discussion of the question of Barthes and textuality in particular, see Patricia Yaeger's *Honey-Mad Women: Emancipatory Strategies in Women's Writing* (New York: Columbia University Press, 1988), particularly the chapter called "The Bilingual Heroine: From Text to Work," 35–76.

every social organism to purify itself from alien elements through the mediating words of the sacred law, which isolates but also establishes terms on which difference may be negotiated. Both of these stances entail the withdrawal of projections onto the other in the service of a balanced acceptance of alterity, inside and out. But if religion and theology are less reliable than psychoanalysis and art as supports for these open and mobile stances, how precisely are they to be deployed?

Kristeva suggests two practical strategies for the support of the *sujet en procès* and the open and invigorating cultural matrix it necessitates: they are *analytic listening* and *aesthetic practice*. These strategies emerge from Kristeva's love of art, her passion for dialogue, and her training as a literary critic and psychoanalyst. But they also stem from her disillusion with masculinist political and social modes of relationship and with classical left politics-as-usual. They have then, I think, profound implications for the style and manner of feminist theology, as well as for its matter.

"Analytic listening," for Kristeva, is a practice of disciplined attention, psychoanalytically informed but not confined to the analytic situation. It works:

> by recognizing the unspoken in all discourse, however Revolutionary, by emphasizing at each point whatever remains unsatisfied, repressed, new, eccentric, incomprehensible, that which disturbs the mutual understanding of the established powers."[21]

Aesthetic practice is its complement, the practice of speaking or communicating in a way that allows discourse to resonate on semiotic as well as symbolic levels. As Kristeva puts it:

> The role of what is usually called "aesthetic practices" must increase . . . in order to emphasize the responsiblity which all will immediately face of putting this fluidity into play against the threats of death which are unavoidable whenever an inside and an outside, a self and an other, one group and another,

21. In Kristeva's "About Chinese Women," in Moi, *The Kristeva Reader*, 156. This text is about Chinese women only in the sense that Kristeva's travels in China release in her a prophetic meditation about the women's movement and its potential for human liberation.

> are constituted. At this level of interiorization, what I have called "aesthetic practices" are undoubtedly nothing other than the modern reply to the eternal question of morality.[22]

Both analytic listening and aesthetic practices are informed and disciplined by psychoanalysis and literary criticism, but are by no means merely academic in location. Indeed they take place all the time, whenever we weave on the loom of common experience—birth-struggle, passion, epiphany, adolescence, friendship, madness, parenthood, illness, separation, mourning and death—our unique texts of beauty, and pain, power and authenticity.

Psychoanalysis and literary criticism are, however, useful in the development of these practices because they foster an essential element of self-reflection, self-limitation, and self-criticism in their exercise. Above all these reflective disciplines prevent us from erecting new bastions of mystified and privileged discourse in the place of the old ones. Psychoanalysis, for instance, in its attempt to come to grips with the problem of the transference and the ending of the therapeutic relationship, *has* to recognize a self-imposed limit and an ethical responsiblity, for at its best it insists upon a refusal to set up a new master of authority and "truth" in place of the internalized superego which caused the problem in the first place. Literary criticism, too, must among other things remind us of the historical and cultural constraints on texts, constraints which help us to relativize them and to avoid the worst pitfalls of logocentric or "theological" readings in the postmodern sense, as well as drawing attention to their material, playful, and erotic modes. No such attentive, joyful, self-reflective and self-limiting discourse, or at least none so adequate, exists for Kristeva in other alternatives we might consider for social practice: in typical left-wing politics or in feminist separatism, for instance.[23]

22. In Kristeva's "Women's Time," in Moi, *The Kristeva Reader*, 210. This essay may usefully be paired with "About Chinese Women" (see previous note), for both discuss issues of feminism in a broad historical, philosophical and psychological context, and both warn of the danger Kristeva sees in allowing feminism to become a quasi-religion in the pejorative sense of the term.

23. See "My Memory's Hyperbole," 225. For Kristeva's account of her distance from active politics of the sort we would call New Left, see her "Memoire," in *L'Infini* 1 (1983): 39–54.

Kristeva deploys these tactics of analytic listening and aesthetic practice herself, especially with respect to Judeo-Christian religious discourse, where she is often able to prescind from questions of faith and belief in order to hear in this discourse what she calls "another sense (or meaning)." After all, as she points out in her short but rewarding study *In the Beginning Was Love: Psychoanalysis and Faith*, even in psychoanalysis proper there is a persistent experience both in therapy and beyond it, which insists on using the apparently dated language of Judeo-Christian passion and ethics to find articulation, a persistent desire, for instance, to call the ache of transference *love*. Not only does Kristeva admit to this Judeo-Christian note in analysis, she *attends* to it. She discusses both its importance for the theory of the transference, always a difficult point, and its creative and leavening activity in the history of the arts and even to some extent the sciences as well.

Hence much of her work is devoted to close reading not only of the sacred art, literature, and music of the past, but of its sacred texts and theologies, as well, texts such as Genesis, or the Song of Songs, or the Pauline letters, theologies such as that of Aquinas, Duns Scotus, or Meister Eckhart. Nor does she fail to investigate the potential for support of human maturation even in such compromised ecclesiastical practices as confession and communion. As she says in *Psychoanalysis and Faith*:

> In the theme of our discussion is perhaps hidden the suffering of religious discourse as well as that of rationalism, together with one or another more strictly personal malaise or anxiety. Let us simply try to welcome them and to open our ears to another sense [or meaning] (*un autre sens*).[24]

KRISTEVA AND FEMINIST SACRAMENTAL THEOLOGY

There is much here for feminist theology to appropriate and also much to resist. Long before the theoretical questions raised by Kristeva's work are settled, however, its practical applications for

24. *In the Beginning Was Love*, 2. I have slightly altered the Goldhammer translation in light of the original, *Au commencement etait l'amour: psychanalyse et foi* (Paris: Hachette, 1985), 2.

the revisioning of feminist theology will, I believe, be well under way. For as many scholars are coming to see, Kristeva's understanding of suffering, of language, and of the religious dimension of their conjunction is too rich to be tabled until some putative future adjudication of her more general claims has taken place. In no field is this importance more apparent than in that of sacramental theology. For just as the sacraments are at the heart of Christian ecclesiastical tradition, so they are at the heart of Kristeva's psychoanalytic and structuralist account of that tradition. Indeed her own strategies of analytic listening and aesthetic play are seldom more acute than when directed to sacramental practices and their rationales.[25]

Kristeva's interest in the sacraments, like her interest in religion in general, assumes a basic critique. This critique is most succinctly set forth in *In the Beginning Was Love*: *Psychoanalysis and Faith*, and it depends in the first place on her sharp opposition to the deployment of creeds in Western religion and the insistence on their affirmation as "truths" or "matters of faith." (As Sarah Halford has pointed out, Kristeva might do well to borrow an important distinction from religious studies and say "belief" rather than "faith" here.)[26] For Kristeva, insistence on such affirmations creates a false consciousness in which, in a classically logocentric way, a merely verbal formulation is treated as having a privileged connection with ultimate reality and regarded as in itself sufficient, without supplement, the last word, leaving no more to say. This reification of language blocks the mobility that the psychoanalytic process tries to foster. It also places serious obstacles in the way of an effective, engaged, and yet provisional and flexible sense of cultural and personal identity. For Kristeva, as we have seen, psychoanalysis remains a better way than religious discourse for preventing this reification from stultifying and choking the development of a viable subjectivity.

25. Kristeva deals with confession and eucharistic motifs in *Powers of Horror*, in the chapter called "*Qui Tollis Peccata Mundi*," 113–32

26. Halford discusses Kristeva's view of faith and the dangers of her tendency to use this term as a synonym for belief, a distinction well established in religious studies and one that would clarify the many problems in a Kristevan perspective, in her "'Throughout a Night without Images': Julia Kristeva's 'Religious' Rhetoric," unpublished paper.

Furthermore, just as the word *creed* shares a root with *credit* (Kristeva draws here on the philology of the Sanskritist and linguist Emile Benveniste), such emphases on credal formulation and their verbal authority presuppose a kind of economic model of the life of that subject. You invest in a certain belief, a gold standard, so to speak, of signification, substantial and above the accidents of material change, and you receive in return a certain dividend, either in terms of your ability to deny unpalatable realities like sex, death, and the change and decay of body, or your advancement within a particular institution, or your confidence in reaping a deferred reward in heaven.

Both in terms of content and social location, of what we believe and of the context in which we believe it, credal formulae and the confessional assent they require seem then to privilege symbolic, rational, and closed modes over semiotic, dispersed, and open modes of the religious life. And they do so sometimes violently, as in cases of martyrdom, or, less hyperbolically, in cases of the suppression of doubt and critical discourse in catechetical instruction or religious discipline. Creeds and confessions, after all, exist in part to make thetic and sometimes bloody cuts between orthodoxy and heresy, between membership in and exclusion from a given community or ritual practice, as well as to mark, at their worst, the complete capitulation of the semiotic flux to the symbolic law. The establishment of binary oppositions and the maintenance of strong borders is part of their very *raison d'être*.[27]

Yet there is in any culture which enables human maturation a kind of faith or covenant—a kind of implicit affirmation or assent or conviction—a covenant, so to speak, between the semiotic and

27. That there may be a more positive function to the recitation of the creed in the context of sacramental practice is only one of the questions a feminist theology might wish to explore. Such recitations may in part function, at their best, to ensure that the strong emotional appeal of sacramental participation is not allowed to overwhelm rational or conscious assent to its effects as well as its presuppositions. Halford also suggests that Kristeva sees the possibility of another kind of covenant here, though she associates this possibility with the disillusion at the end of psychoanalysis, where the recognition that "trust guarantees nothing in return" is negotiated (see note 26).

symbolic, which fosters rather than inhibits life and creativity. Such a covenant is necessary, Kristeva insists, to the establishment of an open and growing identity-in-process, and it is by no means completely alien to religious discourse, not at least when that discourse is operating at its best. But how are we to name this faith or covenant nonreductively, without returning either to logocentric theology (and thus to the institutional church of the fathers at its most repressive) or to psychoanalytic terms (and thus to endless sessions on the couch)? It is here that Kristeva is led, against her own bias, to try to find a word beyond either conventional theological or conventional psychotherapeutic discourses, but one that will not entirely foreclose their insights and practices either.

One solution, the one she suggests in *In the Beginning Was Love*, is to look to a very different culture and language for a term that will name this affirmation or covenant or trust or faith without necessarily giving it Western logocentric connotations or credal implications. She discovers such a word in Chinese, in the Confucian term *xin fu*, which is often, she says, translated in the West as "faith." But *xin fu*, it seems, is imaged in the Chinese language not as a "credit deal" but as a surrender or marriage, a marriage between the heart or personal energy and the cosmic law or *qi*. This language compact between the heart and the law does not take place in the expectation of a future reward—immortality in return for believing, as Alice in Wonderland said, six impossible things before breakfast—rather, it shows the *yang* joining its energy to the stability of the *yin* in a single moment which is *now*. (The Chinese ideogram associated with this concept, Kristeva suggests, shows a tiger leaping upon the earth.)

Xin fu is a useful if provisional term, from a Kristevan point of view, not least for its ability to allow her to avoid or prescind from the belief question, a question that she answers so equivocally at so many points in her work. Then, too, the strangeness and foregrounded materiality of *xin fu's* typographical manifestation on the page, not to mention its ideogrammatical quality, a quality Kristeva much enjoyed in her own "rudimentary" studies of Chinese, clearly pleases her.[28] These qualities emphasize the textual,

28. In "My Memory's Hyperbole" Kristeva recalls this pleasure from her student days at Jussieu, 233.

semiotic dimension of religious discourse at its best, and the subtext of marriage and of *yin* and *yang* brings an element of sexual difference and even of the erotic into play. *Xin fu* also emphasizes the element of risk in trust or faith, the willingness to risk all on what may well be the fate of an illusion.

Xin fu in this sense, however, might be said, *pace* Kristeva, to speak the language of sacramentality in the West, of faith rather than belief in the credal sense. After all, sacraments, at least from a Thomist point of view, exist precisely to defeat such purely symbolic and instrumental bargaining pacts as Kristeva wishes to scorn by insisting on the signifying function of the body and of fantasy as well as of rational assent in the sacramental moment. *Xin fu*, we might say, resembles more closely Aquinas' concept of sacrament or even the old Roman *sacramentum* or heartfelt oath of personal allegiance than it does the terms *faith* or, better, *belief*, with their emphasis on the cognitive, rational and instrumental levels of human signifying.[29]

Mention of Aquinas here is by no means so far-fetched as it may seem, for not only has Kristeva herself written extensively about his theology of the self and the nature of self-love, but his definition of sacrament seems precisely designed to foreground the issues to which she has devoted her work. For as Aquinas so

29. The term *sacramentum* itself has roots in the Roman sense of oath or contract, in particular a military oath of allegiance. Augustine used it to refer to the recitation of the creed, the Lord's Prayer, and a host of language practices and affirmations of belief at the cognitive level, thus stressing its connection to symbolic as opposed to semiotic levels of signification. Through close association with the Greek *mysterion*, moreover, a sacrament came to signify an esoteric mystery or cultic initiation into a privileged hierarchical relation with truth, a "cover of bodily things," as Isidore of Seville puts it, through which "the divine power works more secretly" or, with Hugh of St. Victor, a "material element set before our senses representing . . . signifying . . . and containing . . . some invisible and spiritual grace." While these definitions continue to privilege an invisible, pre-scriptive truth over a visible signifying trace, they take on, especially in the theology of Aquinas, a material and bodily dimension which inclines them to semiotic as well as symbolic modes of signification. These and other primary texts on the eucharist in Christian theology can be found in *Corpus Christi: An Encyclopedia of the Eucharist*, ed. and compiled by Michael O'Carroll (Collegeville, Minn., Liturgical 1992).

cogently points out, the performance of the sacraments entails and necessitates both a signifying word and a material substance—and indeed seeks to redraw or render permeable the line between them. To put this in more contemporary terms, sacramental ritual implicates both symbolic and semiotic modes of language, and indeed seeks to renegotiate the line between them in a very Kristevan way. Indeed, Aquinas stresses far more than his predecessors the theoretical and practical importance of the *material* level of the sacrament. He also lays great weight on its functional, discursive role in constituting as well as gracing the human subject. For him, a sacrament is a *signum rei sacrae*, a sign or seal of a sacred thing "*in so far as it sanctifies a person*"[30]—or, we might say, creates a *sujet en procès*.

Be this as it may, some such understanding of the potential for signficance and renewal in sacramental discourse is implicit even within Kristeva's own comments on the Judeo-Christian tradition. In her treatment of confession, for instance, Kristeva draws attention to the curious double inscription of sin in this sacrament, which allows the subject to recognize both *I am mortal* (that is, a material body bearing the guilt of violent separation from the mother) and *speaking* (that is, an ordered self able and worthy to speak according to the paternal law, even in the mode of self-condemnation). Kristeva is very acute on the unusual transgressive and healing aspects of this strange conjunction of semiotic and symbolic modes, even when it is encoded and institutionalized in repressive ways. As she puts it, here "this most subtle transgression of law, that is to say, the enunciation of sin in the presence of the One, reverberate[s] not as a denunciation but as the glorious counterweight to the inquisitorial fate of confession." The witness to the liberating effect of confession lies for Kristeva in the aesthetic practices it fosters, the proliferation of religious art, even art depicting highly transgressive actions, and even within the precincts

30. For a postmodern discussion of Aquinas's view of the sacraments, see David Crownfield, "The Seminal Trace," *Journal of the American Academy of Religion* 59 (1991): 361–71; see also John Caputo, *Heidegger and Aquinas: An Essay on Overcoming Metaphysics* (New York: Fordham University Press, 1982), and my "Art and Fantasy in Kristeva and Aquinas," in Crownfield, *Body/Text*.

of sacred spaces. "And these signs shall follow them that believe," Kristeva concludes her analysis of confession, "in my name shall they cast out devils; *they shall speak with new tongues*" (Mark 16).[31]

The double inscription of sin and transgression within a sacred or recuperative space is again operative for Kristeva when it comes to the most important of the Christian sacraments, the one variously called eucharist, communion, and/or the Lord's Supper in different Christian denominations. Here the recognition *I am mortal and speaking* meets her other structural law, *Taboo forestalls sacrifice* in a highly cathected way. In the eucharist as Kristeva sees it, a mortal, speaking subject is reconciled both to the body of the mother and the law of the father by a ritual reenactment of a transgressive and violent act: the act of eating human flesh. The formula "This is my body," Kristeva says, spoken over the elements of bread and wine, "invites a removal of guilt from the archaic relation to the first pre-object (ab-ject) of need: the mother." Hence: "To eat and drink the flesh and blood of Christ means, on the one hand, to trangress symbolically the Levitical prohibitions, to be symbolically satiated (as at the font of a good mother. . . .) and to be reconciled with the [maternal] substance dear to paganism." By the same token, however, this gesture or ritual act that makes speech bodily and semiotic, elevates the body into the symbolic as well. Hence, for Kristeva, in the eucharist "all corporeality is elevated, spiritualized, and sublimated."[32]

As a Kristevan perspective is brought increasingly to bear on the sacrament of the eucharist in religious studies, this reading of the eucharist has begun to be further explored. In David Crownfield's discussion of the eucharist as theorized by Aquinas, for instance, Crownfield argues, along roughly Kristevan lines, that the eucharist is able to remove the sting from the guilt and the violence of this act without suppressing the mortality and self-division implied. He points out, however, that this feat is accomplished only by surrounding participation in the sacrament with taboos which forestall the sacrifice normally called for from those who pollute pure spaces. Nonetheless, there is always some residue, some trace of pollution (in this case the semen of spontaneous

31. Emphasis added; *Powers of Horror*, 131.
32. *Powers of Horror*, 118–20

nocturnal pollution is the example) that resists sublimation and remains leftover, untheorized, and resistant to the full mediations of the sacramental work.[33]

Then, too, there are dangers as well as releases associated with the sacrament. For, as Martha Reinecke has pointed out, the eucharistic moment not only implies a return to the trauma of the connection with the maternal body, where the primitive fear of eating and being eaten is at its height, but it is capable of prompting a regression *into* that trauma, an abjection, a loss of taboo protection, and an ensuing violence as well. Reineke sees this drama enacted on the bodies of late medieval women mystics, who literalized the meaning of the sacrament to the point of anorexia and found the contradictions of its signification inscribed on their own bodies as a result.[34] For either the maternal body, the flesh and blood from which we are formed, is reconciled by confession with the Law of the Father, a reconciliation that both lances and heals the tensions between them, or else that body pollutes the very sanctuary itself, and taboo relapses back into sacrifice, the sacrifice of those who have "profaned" or abused the ritual. This latter relapse and regression into ritual reenactment of the violence of separation from the mother kills rather than establishes the subject, who is indeed "on trial" as well as "in process" in this practice.

So brief a discussion only begins to sketch the relevance of Kristeva's thought for feminist sacramental theology, a field ripe for harvest in terms of her theory of religion, her critique of theological discourse, and her call for a feminine and feminist analytic listening and aesthetic practice. Leaving these issues, for the moment, to further and fuller debate than I can possibly give them here, let me attend in closing to a singular instance of analytic listening and aesthetic practice in our own tradition, Emily Dickinson's poem on the eucharist.[35] In no other single work I know of are the two maxims, *I am mortal and speaking* and *Taboo forestalls sacrifice,* so brilliantly rendered, both at the thematic and at the

33. Crownfield, "The Seminal Trace," 361–71.

34. Reineke, " 'This Is My Body,' " 265.

35. *Complete Poems of Emily Dickinson*, ed. Thomas H. Johnson (Boston: Little, Brown, 1960.), #1657.

textual levels. And no other work captures the resonance of Kristeva's view of theology and the sign quite so accurately, both in tenor and in tone. The poem reads:

> A Word made Flesh is seldom
> And tremblingly partook
> Nor then perhaps reported
> But have I not mistook
> Each one of us has tasted
> With ecstasies of stealth
> The very food debated
> To our specific strength—
> A Word that breathes distinctly
> Has not the power to die
> Cohesive as the Spirit
> It may expire if He—
> "Made flesh and dwelt among us"
> Could condescension be
> Like this consent of Language
> This loved Philology.

For Dickinson, the power to articulate the recognition of our own death, the power to say *I am mortal and speaking,* to be and know oneself as a divided subject, is the defining mystery of human existence, establishing at once weakness, our limit, and our unique mode of being. A word that breathes "distinctly," a logocentric or univocal word, so to speak, lacks the value of that unique pathos. But God defined as the One, as pure abstract immortality, the Last Signifier, the Final Word, cannot make this affirmation; "He" achieves "His" great theological distinction at the cost of a certain unique personhood and communicative strength. To regain that strength, "He" must consent to transgress into mortality and otherness, into that realm of far less privileged and authoritative speech, of struggle with others and with self that we ourselves as human and differently gendered subjects inhabit. Once "He" has done so, the taboo which isolates divinity from death, the eternal mother from the devouring self, must be broken, "with ecstasies of stealth," in a *jouissance* that implies both transgression and delight. Only when taboo has forestalled sacrifice in this way can the *sujet en procès,* with all its unique, provisional quality, be nourished appropriately, that is by the very food "debated" to its own "specific strength."

The ritual enactment of that taboo and sacrifice and of their interdependence to which the poem refers is the eucharist, or Lord's Supper, as Dickinson's tradition called it. But the model for eucharistic incarnation is, for Dickinson, still language, language savored for its very materiality and change, its playful and punning textuality, its subjection to multiple and sometimes oppositional or even taboo interpretations. Her term or figure of speech for the analogy between the eucharist and language is *philology,* the love and study of words, a term that in itself combines semiotic and symbolic levels of meaning in a concatenation of puns. (Dickinson would surely have savored Kristeva's trope of rewriting "in the beginning was the Word" as "in the beginning was Love.")

The analogy between eucharist and philology is not, however, an established but only a potential one. Her poem avoids credal affirmation at every turn (as for instance by use of the subjunctive verb "could"), but it does so without losing the immediacy of what is at hand, "*this* loved philology." Philology is Dickinson's *xin fu,* her sign of the covenant or of sacramental grace, putting a term to the legalistic bargains of logocentrism opening out into the millenial infinitude of loving meanings directed to our unique and specific alterities. Through observation and "tasting" of language, the representation of an established truth in a privileged discourse is translated into the practice of a transitory, mortal and speaking creative word, the practice of what Rebecca Chopp, in her exemplary and inspiring *The Power to Speak,* has called the "perfectly open sign" [36]

Dickinson's poem is here an instance of the analytic listening and aesthetic practice for which Kristeva calls, as well as a brilliant dramatization of Kristeva's central structural and psychoanalytic points about mortality, self-division, sacrifice, and taboo. Furthermore, like Kristeva's own work, this poem opens out beyond its own skeptical and critical perspectives into a feminist theological discourse that takes us into a new world of significations and possibilities, of affirmations as well as denials. This is a different enterprise altogether from either traditional literary criticism or traditional theologizing, and it is one in which both French feminism and American feminist theology are already jointly and joyfully—if sometimes oppositionally—engaged.

36. Rebecca S. Chopp, *The Power to Speak: Feminism, Language, God* (New York: Crossroad, 1989).

—4

Violence and Subjectivity

WUTHERING HEIGHTS, JULIA KRISTEVA, AND FEMINIST THEOLOGY

AMY HOLLYWOOD

I begin with a series of passages from Emily Brontë's novel, *Wuthering Heights*, in order to remind you of the violence of that text.

> Terror made me cruel; and, finding it useless to attempt shaking the creature off, I pulled its wrist on to the broken pane, and rubbed it to and fro till the blood ran down and soaked the bed-clothes. . . .[1]

> You'd hear of odd things, if I lived alone with that mawkish, waxen face; the most ordinary would be painting on its white the colours of the rainbow, and turning the blue eyes black, every day or two. (83)

> You witch! . . . Let me go, and I'll make her rue! I'll make her howl a recantation! (100)

> I have no pity! I have no pity! The more the worms writhe, the more I yearn to crush out their entrails! It is a moral teething, and I grind with greater energy, in proportion to the increase of pain. (118)

> He dashed his head against the knotted trunk; and, lifting up his eyes, howled, not like a man, but like a savage beast getting goaded to death with knives and spears. (129)

1. Emily Brontë, *Wuthering Heights* (New York: Norton Critical Editions, 1990), 20. Further references will be parenthetical within the text.

> The charge exploded, and the knife, in springing back, closed into its owner's wrist. Heathcliff pulled it away by main force, slitting up the flesh as it passed on, and thrust it dripping into his pocket. (137)

> Had I been born where laws are less strict, and tastes less dainty, I should treat myself to a slow vivisection of those two, as an evening's amusement. (205)

It was a little different in the movies. Laurence Olivier may have howled, but the metaphorical evocation of a beast goaded to death is lost in translation, as is much of the physical violence of Brontë's convoluted tale. Whether this translation from the written page to the screen does violence to the meaning of the text is not directly at issue in this essay. In my experience, memories of the book tend to soften and diffuse the violence in the same way that the screen version does. With every reading, the proliferation of scenes of physical and emotional violence, the violent language and imagery (which begins with the title itself), and the complex, time- and order-violating structure of the text are encountered as if for the first time. Yet it is the violence of the text that serves as a primary source of its hold upon readers' imaginations. It is this violence and the fascination it holds for many readers that I address. Through a reading of *Wuthering Heights* informed by certain aspects of the work of the psychoanalyst and literary theorist Julia Kristeva, I hope to articulate the central challenge that I feel French feminist thought offers to contemporary feminist theology with regard to the violence of and in subjectivity, and also to demonstrate that such a challenge comes not only from France (or Bulgaria) but from within the English-speaking world as well.

Like most feminist discourses and theories, feminist theologies are grounded in the joint propositions that women's experience is a necessary resource from which theological reflection can and must begin and that hierarchical structures of power are a form of violence that must be eradicated insofar as that is possible and conceivable.[2] Thus a critique of violence, and in particular violence against women and other oppressed or powerless groups, is central to the projects of feminism and feminist and womanist theologies.

2. See Sharon Welch's chapter in this volume.

This political stance—one that I share—has given rise to readings of *Wuthering Heights* that stress the distortions created in the text by patriarchal power structures and violence. One of the earliest and most influential of these readings is that of Gilbert and Guber in *The Madwoman in the Attic,* in which Heathcliff and the first Cathy are seen as two sides of a gynandrous figure whose violence is a response to the violence they suffer at the hands of the patriarchal Lintons and Earnshaws.[3] More recent readings, particularly in Britain, have given attention to the central role of class and the hints of racial tension in the text, pointing to Heathcliff and Nelly Dean as opposing representatives of the lower classes.[4] The best readings of the text are those that combine these approaches, allowing the interpreters to take account of the great complexities of the text with regard to the issues of class, gender, and history.[5] Despite the usefulness of these interpretive approaches and my own reliance on many of their readings of the text, I believe there is still inadequate attention paid to the joy taken in violence both by the reader

3. Sandra M. Gilbert and Susan Gubar, *The Madwoman in the Attic: The Woman Writer and the Nineteenth-Century Literary Imagination* (New Haven: Yale University Press, 1979), ch. 8. This is the reading followed by Mary Daly in her references to the novel. See *Pure Lust: Elemental Feminist Philosophy* (Boston: Beacon Press, 1984), 8, 192, 382–83. In fairness to Gilbert and Gubar it should be said that they are attempting to formulate a literary reading of *Wuthering Heights* and other nineteenth-century texts in order to avoid "naive" or sociological readings. Such readings lead toward the conclusion that *Wuthering Heights* is a novel solely about wife-beating and leaves us with no adequate understanding of the text's power and continuing appeal. For an example of such a reading, and the problems it raises for the critic, see Sara Mills, Lynne Pearce, Sue Spaull, and Elaine Millard, *Feminist Readings, Feminist Reading* (Charlottesville: University of Virginia Press, 1989), 73–79.

4. There are many examples of such Marxist and class-oriented readings. One of the most interesting, although partial and distorting particularly with regard to the women in the text, is that by Terry Eagleton, *Myths of Power: A Marxist Study of the Brontës* (London: Macmillan, 1975).

5. The study by James H. Kavanaugh is interesting, although theoretically overladen. See his *Emily Brontë* (Oxford: Basil Blackwell, 1985) and the criticism of this book in the much more approachable and ultimately more convincing study by Lyn Pykett, *Emily Brontë* (Savage, Md.: Barnes and Noble Books, 1989), 133–34.

and, partially causing and reflecting the reader's response, by some of the book's central characters, most explicitly Heathcliff, but also the two Cathys, Joseph, and others. Furthermore, the thematic violence within the text mirrors the complex, even tortured nature of the text itself and the proliferation of violent metaphors and language that were as shocking to its first readers as the a- or immorality of its central characters.

All of these factors point to the need for a reading of *Wuthering Heights* that accounts for the role of violence within the text and its relationship to the described subjectivities of its characters. I offer the beginnings of such a reading here, focusing on the narrative and thematic elements of violence rather than the language of the text for reasons of space and clarity.[6] To read the text as a record of "women's experience" Gilbert and Gubar found it necessary to make Heathcliff a woman—an inverted Eve. Such a reading is clearly problematic given Heathcliff's sexuality and the text's marking of him as gendered masculine within the cultural norms of the time. An approach that pays attention to Kristeva's revised psychoanalytic account of subjectivity should enable us both to

6. Kristeva has been praised for her use of psychoanalysis to create a theory of poetic language rather than merely as a diagnostic tool that would reduce the text to the terms of psychoanalytic discourse, as many claim Lacan and others do. Instead of (1) literature in the service of psychoanalysis then, we have (2) psychoanalysis in the service of literature, helping to formulate a theory of the way in which poetic language operates that does not reduce it to conceptual categories. There is, however, another way in which literature functions in Kristeva's work, and that is (3) literature as a resource for psychoanalysis, in which the literary text is subjected to an analysis and in the process teaches the analyst to expand and question her own categories. This type of analysis, which particularly marks Kristeva's most recent work, is what will be attempted here. Like Lautreamont's *Maldoror,* which Kristeva studies in *Revolution in Poetic Language,* the eruption of the semiotic into the symbolic, which is poetic language, and its revolutionary potential are reflected in and in part shape the violence and horror of the narratives within the text. It should also be pointed out that while I will focus on Kristeva's study of horror and abjection, those of love, melancholy, and particularly foreignness would also provide useful points of entry into *Wuthering Heights,* which deals in some way with all of these issues. For a useful introduction to Kristeva's work, see John Lechte, *Julia Kristeva* (London: Routledge, 1990).

understand how Brontë was able to create a male alter-ego such as Heathcliff and to understand his joy in violence and Cathy's joy in him.

The question of Heathcliff's violence and his attractiveness takes on added relevance for us when we recall Brontë's place in the religious world of early Victorian England, pointing us to another major camp in Brontë criticism, which insists on her centrality to a tradition of mystical, religious, or mytho-poetic writing in England. Critics point not only to Brontë's poetry, but also to Cathy's and Heathcliff's understanding of their love as it is expressed in *Wuthering Heights*.[7] Some place Brontë with those who have attempted to map a mythology beyond traditional Christianity. Thus J. Hillis Miller is able to argue that Cathy's pronouncement, "I am Heathcliff, therefore I exist," is "the climax and endpoint of the long tradition making love a private religion in which the loved one is God and there is a single worshipper and devotee."[8] Like the mystic's experience of union with the divine, the nature of this union in love is ineffable.[9] Thus like the mystical writer, Brontë's Cathy is forced to make use of hyperbole, logical contradictions, metaphor, and referential ambiguity to evoke this experience.[10] The

7. Some of the more famous examples in this critical camp are Jacques Blondel, *Emily Brontë: Expérience Spirituelle et Création Poétique* (Presses Universitaires de France, 1955); J. Hillis Miller, *The Disappearance of God* (Cambridge: Harvard University Press, 1965); and Robert M. Polhemus, *Erotic Faith: Being in Love from Jane Austen to D. H. Lawrence* (Chicago: University of Chicago, 1990).

8. Miller, *The Disappearance of God*, 175.

9. Literature on the nature of mystical language is enormous, but see Michel de Certeau, "Mystic Speech," in *Heterologies*, trans. Brian Massumi (Minneapolis: University of Minnesota Press, 1986); Michel de Certeau, *La fable mystique, XVe-XVIIe siècle* (Paris: Gallimard, 1982); Moshe Idel and Bernard McGinn, *Mystical Union and Monotheistic Faith: An Ecumenical Dialogue* (New York: Macmillan, 1989), particularly the article by Michael Sells; and Amy Hollywood, "The Soul as Virgin Wife: Meister Eckhart and the Beguine Mystics, Mechthild of Magdeburg and Marguerite Porete" (Ph.D. Dissertation, University of Chicago, 1991).

10. Unfortunately, I do not have space to demonstrate the use of these operations here. Such a demonstration would be the beginnings of an assessment of Brontë's language along lines mapped by Kristeva in her theory of poetic language. It should be pointed out, however, that my

relationship between mystical and poetic language is too large a subject for this chapter, but it is important to mark this moment in Brontë's novel, for it is not surprisingly a moment of violence. Not only is violence done to logic in Cathy's and Heathcliff's attempts to name their love, but that love itself ultimately destroys both of them, just as some would argue the mystic's love destroys the self.[11] The question of whether such destruction is brought about by their love or by the revenge sparked by the destruction of this love, and of whether such destruction and revenge are avoidable, is one to which we will return. At this point it is merely necessary to point out that such metaphysical readings have a tendency to elide or to ignore gender issues in favor of what are considered to be "larger" issues. Again what is needed is a discussion that will show the coexistence of this metaphysical level with the political dimensions many contemporary readers wish to uncover. As Lyn Pykett and others have argued, the convoluted narrative structure of the novel, with its polyphonous structure, allows for such a layered text and variety of positions and viewpoints to be displayed in it without the necessity of resolution.

VIOLENCE AND SUBJECTIVITY

It is best to begin with as clear an understanding as possible of what I mean when discussing violence. Turning to dictionaries and

---

reading of Brontë's language, while compatible with many aspects of Kristeva's theory, owes as much if not more to comparisons with mystical discourse and the study of mystical language by figures such as Michel de Certeau. The "coarseness" of Brontë's language, in the form of expletives and curses, so shocking to her contemporaries, and the use of dialects that are almost indecipherable to the reader of standard English, should also be pointed to. See Kristeva on Céline's use of slang and bad language in *Powers of Horror: An Essay on Abjection*, trans. Leon S. Roudiez (New York: Columbia University Press, 1982).

11. This is a very complicated issue and there are many different ways in which the claim could be true. See George Bataille, *Eroticism: Death and Sensuality* (San Francisco: City Lights, 1986) and "Emily Brontë and Evil," in *Emily Brontë: A Critical Anthology*, ed. Jean-Pierre Petit, and also in the Bataille collection, *Literature and Evil* (New York: Marion Boyars, 1990).

etymologies, we find that the terms *violent* and *violence* come from the Latin *violatus*, the past participle of the verb *violare*, meaning primarily to violate or dishonor. Sacrilege seems to have been a central context for the term, as well as sexual assault or rape. In Livy's account of the rape of Lucretia by Sextus Tarquinius, her final words before suicide contrast the violation of her body with the innocence of her spirit: *"Ceterum corpus est tantum violatum, animus insons: mors testis erit."*[12] Where the Romans refer to religious or sexual violation as the root meanings of violence, in modern American English the language of rights and justice becomes central, keeping with shifts in modern thought about what can and cannot be interfered with by means of physical force or about what is sacred. As dictionary definitions show, however, not all violence can be spoken of in terms of justice or rights; the forces of nature, for example, cannot be reduced to those terms. This type of violence is linked to other forms by its destructiveness. Yet as another use of the term *violence* shows, not all violence is purely destructive, for in doing violence to the meaning of a text one creates a new meaning that replaces and supplants the "proper" one. It is this supplanting that itself is the act of violence. Finally, one can speak of violent emotions or feelings that are not literally destructive or obviously productive of harm.

It is important to make this point in order to counter the argument that violence must be understood only in terms of harm and morality, for, as I will attempt to show, physical violence and destructive violence are only the most visible manifestations of a much more variegated and prevalent phenomenon. Thus while early psychoanalytic theory taught us to see the central role of sexuality in the formation and maintenance of the human psyche, the later Freud and many of his French followers have emphasized more and more the violent aspects of the formation of the subject. Lacan, with his famous linguistic turn in psychoanalysis, appears to desomatize and make abstract psychoanalysis. Yet at the same time he shows us the violence that language acquisition and the accession to subjectivity do to the infant in breaking him or her out

12. "Although the body has been so violated, the soul is innocent: death will be the witness of this." Titus Livius, *Ab Urbe Condita* I. 58.

of the imaginary, prelinguistic bond with the maternal figure. The irony of the subject's position is never far from us in Lacan's discourse, for once the subject has situated him- or herself in language, any attempt to undo this violent severing of early ties itself becomes an act of violence against the subject—a suicide, following in the path of the Freudian death drive. Thus Lucretia is only able to regain her lost innocence through suicide.

Yet, the question will be asked, can we use Lucretia as an emblem for the Freudian or Lacanian subject? Is it doing violence to these male theorists to speak of the subject of their discourse as either male or female? Or, more pertinently in this context, is it doing violence to female experience that perhaps cannot be encapsulated within the domains of these male-oriented theoretical discourses? These questions have been asked, answered, and asked again by feminist thinkers in North America and Europe (and perhaps beyond), with no clear consensus. I would argue, however, that psychoanalysis provides what is not available through any other body of discourse today: a language that attempts to describe the formation of subjects and of subjects as gendered. While anthropology has provided us with the important distinction between sex and gender, only through psychoanalytic discussions have we been able to begin to account for the way in which subjects are engendered both psychologically and culturally. This is crucial for all feminist theory, grounded as it is in female experience, for without an account of what we mean by female experience and what it means to be gendered, feminist theory is without adequate resources for its critique and construction of social and cultural systems.[13] While Mary Daly, for example, has developed a hermeneutic of suspicion that includes an understanding of the internalization of negative self-images and gendered behavior, her rejection of

13. I would argue for the importance of historically situating any such psychoanalytical discussion. For the importance of history to feminism, see Denise Riley, *Am I That Name: Feminism and the Category of 'Women' in History* (Minneapolis: University of Minnesota Press, 1988); and Joan Wallach Scott, *Gender and the Politics of History* (New York: Columbia University Press, 1988), esp. chs. 1 and 2.

psychoanalysis leaves her with no methodological basis or explanatory theory for how this comes about and how it can be reversed.[14] In point of fact, her work relies much more heavily on Freudian principles than she would probably be willing to admit. By directly acknowledging what has been appropriated from psychoanalysis one is in a better position to correct and criticize that discourse and its account of women's experience and female subjectivity. At the same time, as we will see, contemporary psychoanalytic discourse, particularly the work of Julia Kristeva, challenges some of feminism's most cherished assumptions about the subject (particularly the female subject).

The subject of this volume, the possibilities and problems of bringing together French feminist theories and feminist theology as it has become part of academic and ecclesial communities in North America and England, thus lies—albeit rather obliquely—behind this concern with providing a partial new reading of *Wuthering Heights;* I believe that like the novel, the work of Julia Kristeva, particularly in its middle phase, shows a fascination with violence with which many feminist theorists and theologians are uncomfortable. Theoretically oriented and grounded in philosophical, linguistic, and psychoanalytical discourse, Kristeva attempts to provide a genealogy of certain extreme examples of literary violence, and thus can be helpful in providing a new reading of *Wuthering Heights*. The novel, in turn, by making explicit the religious implications of its poetic language and the proximity of the poetic to the mystical and the sacred, can serve as a critique and illumination of certain blind spots in Kristeva's work. Together, I will argue, they challenge the one-dimensional view of violence predominant in feminist and womanist criticism. At the same time I feel that I myself and all feminist theorists must be suspicious of the fascination with violence that draws us to Brontë and Kristeva. The question to be untangled is: What do the novel and Kristeva attempt

14. For her often trenchant rejections of Freudian theory and other forms of psychotherapy, see Mary Daly, *Gyn/Ecology: The Metaethics of Radical Feminism* (Boston: Beacon Press, 1978), 230, 256, 266–67, 274–76. Yet while Daly clearly rejects Freud's patriarchal theorizing of the unconscious, she seems implicitly to accept his identification of women with that unconscious. See Mary Daly, *Pure Lust*, 358–60.

to show us about the role violence plays in the formation and maintenance of the subject, as well as in its destruction?

A central text on this issue, one that has been subject to criticism by those distrustful of Kristeva's seductiveness, is her study of the French novelist and anti-Semitic pamphleteer, Céline.[15] Taken by some as an apology for anti-Semitism and fascism, it has been read by others as an attempt to provide a genealogy of violence, and, I would say, our fascination with it.[16] More importantly, it is an attempt to see the other side of the revolution in poetic language that Kristeva describes in her book by that title. There, Kristeva is concerned to show the radically egalitarian and nonauthoritarian nature of poetic language itself, marking as it does the rupture of the presymbolic semiotic into symbolic patriarchal discourse and thus putting the subject into process/on trial. Centering on the work of the nineteenth-century poets Mallarmé and Lautréamont, Kristeva attempts to show the revolutionary potential implicit in their seemingly esoteric literary productions. The avant garde, with their daring defiance of linear logic, narrative, and semantic meanings, become true harbingers of political upheaval not explicitly through thematic elements in their work, but rather through the activity of writing.[17] It is in this light that Céline, the avant garde novelist become fascist, becomes a problem for Kristeva. Kristeva is at pains to show how these two apparently contradictory subject positions can be held by the same figure. Her explanation hinges on a reappraisal of the presymbolic semiotic realm and its relationship to subjectivity.

In *Revolution in Poetic Language,* Kristeva argues that the pre-Oedipal semiotic is the first groundwork for and last support of subjectivity, rather than its antithesis. It is through the pulsing drives, the rhythms of the maternal body, and the child's first verbalizations that he or she begins to distinguish him- or herself as subject in relationship to an object. When this split between subject and object becomes definitive the subject is able to speak

15. Kristeva, *Powers of Horror*.

16. Jacqueline Rose, "Julia Kristeva—Take Two," in *Sexuality in the Field of Vision* (London: Verso, 1986).

17. See note 6.

and master symbolic discourse. Kristeva emphasizes both the necessity and the violence of the symbolic and of language acquisition. Later, in *Powers of Horror*, she begins to explore the ambivalence of the semiotic and of the infant's relationship with the maternal figure. As Kristeva acknowledges, acquisition of a subject position within language is absolutely necessary to the survival of the subject within the human community. Thus the semiotic, and the maternal presence that has been historically associated with the semiotic, is a field of great ambivalence. On the one hand, the subject longs to return to that state of undifferentiated union with the beloved that is projected onto the semiotic and given mythological status in the figure of the good mother. On the other hand, the semiotic that will not cede to the symbolic, figured as the mother who will not let the infant go, is destructive and terrifying. This is the root of what Kristeva calls abjection—the subject's inability to recognize the maternal as an object, which ultimately reflects back upon the subject itself. This ambivalence, traced on the level of the individual psyche in part of *Powers of Horror*, is then traced throughout the history of the relationships between Judaism, Christianity, and other religions in an effort to explain the psychological roots of Céline and Western Europe's anti-Semitism. Without tracing Kristeva's entire argument, I would like to point to one moment within it that is particularly useful for our reading of *Wuthering Heights*.

After having given her reading of the history of religions in the West, dependent upon Mary Douglas's work on purity and defilement and her own psychoanalytically informed concept of abjection,[18] Kristeva articulates one of her most telling assessments of the place of religion in history and in the modern world:

> The world of illusions—the world of religions—brings to light or embodies the prohibition that has us speak. Thus, it gives

18. Central to this analysis is the claim that Judaism represents the triumph of the symbolic and paternal realm and the consequent abjection of the mother. Christianity, in turn, marks the internalization of abjection as sin and the symbolic negation of this abjection in the triumph of the virgin mother. There is implicit in the discussion of early societies the claim that sociality can exist without the triumph of the paternal and the absolutizing of the symbolic and the consequent abjection of the mother.

> *legitimacy* to hatred if it does not *invert* it into love. Embodying, legitimizing—today we are too aware of their techniques to yield to them. The worlds of illusions, now dead and buried, have given way to our dreams and deliriums if not to politics or science—the religions of modern times. Lacking illusions, lacking shelter, today's universe is divided between *boredom* (increasingly anguished at the prospect of losing its resources, through depletion) or (when the spark of the symbolic is maintained and desire to speak explodes) *abjection* and *piercing laughter*.[19]

In these lines, I believe, lie the clues to a more adequate reading of Emily Brontë's novel and to the projected aims of Kristeva's own corpus, both of which are attempts to find other methods of resolution for the modern subject deprived of his or her illusions.

Central to Kristeva's thesis on the history of religion is the assertion that religions embody the paternal prohibition—the name/no of the father, the incest taboo, the separation of subject and object signified by the removal of the child from the mother—necessary to establishing the subject in discourse and establishing discourse itself. This emphasis upon the conservative function of religion runs throughout Kristeva's work, although her attitude towards that conservative function changes from qualified rejection to qualified, almost nostaligic, acceptance. Yet in placing religious traditions, in particular Judaism and Christianity, on the side of the symbolic realm, Kristeva acknowledges the ability of that same religious discourse to harbor the language of poetry and desire.[20] The hatred felt for the abject, and for ourselves as abject, is given warrant by religion or it is turned into love, the latter being the route most often taken in Christian discourse. Thus the ambivalence of the subject's relation to its pre-Oedipal realm is resolved. For

---

Thus it is through pollution rituals and acts that the necessary symbolic links and social bonds are maintained. See Kristeva, *Powers*, 77–89. It would be fruitful to examine her description of such societies with reference to *Wuthering Heights*.

19. Julia Kristeva, *Powers of Horror*, 133.

20. See, for example, her discussions of Christian discourses on love in *Tales of Love*, trans. Leon S. Roudiez (New York: Columbia University Press, 1987).

those living in a world without the illusions of religion, this resolution of the tension between the semiotic and the symbolic is no longer possible.

WUTHERING HEIGHTS

It is easy to place the dynamics of *Wuthering Heights* within this theoretical framework, viewing the project of the novel as the legitimizing of hatred and/or the transformation of this hatred into love. Whereas Patricia Yaeger, in her excellent chapter on *Wuthering Heights* as a strong, woman-authored text, reads the comic opening of the novel as an example of the carnivalesque so central for the Marxist orientation of Bakhtin and the early Kristeva,[21] I would argue that the central characters of the novel—Heathcliff, the two Cathys, Nelly Dean—represent forces that are neither pure carnival nor abject. In Heathcliff, the most violent and problematic character in the novel and therefore the one on whom I will focus here, love and revenge are necessarily tied in a way that the hero of twentieth-century abject literature will not or cannot allow. Whereas the abject subject is the one whose disgust for the liminal and the shadowy from which it cannot seem to separate itself becomes disgust and fear for subjectivity itself, Heathcliff is a figure thwarted in his desire to return to the pre-Oedipal realm and to have the object of his desire.[22] He does not reject the symbolic but rather is forced to a role of vengeance within the system that denies him the object of his love.

This reading can be demonstrated by turning to the account of the early relationship between Heathcliff and Cathy and the result of Cathy's turning away from Heathcliff and toward Edgar Linton. Most commentators point to the juxtaposition of two competing worlds in the novel, that represented by the Heights and that found at Thrushcross Grange, the home of the Lintons. The

21. Patricia Yaeger, *Honey-Mad Women: Emancipatory Strategies in Women's Writing* (New York: Columbia University Press, 1988), ch. 6.

22. As we will see, it might be asked how far this explains his attractiveness to modern, abject readers. See, for example, Eagleton's heroic reading of Heathcliff in *Myths of Power*.

problem with such readings, however, is their inability to account for the constant movement, both of characters and of thematic and metaphorical elements, between the two houses. All is not civility at the Grange, and the Heights is only hell to certain characters at certain moments in its history. The novel is much more complex than any simple set of dualisms can contain or suggest. Upon Heathcliff's arrival at the Heights, for example, we see the house inhabited by a "classic" family circle of father, mother, son, daughter, and two servants.[23] It is implied that Heathcliff himself, the dark outsider, is responsible for the disruption of this family unit, yet it is not clear how he is capable of such destructive force. This "gypsy brat" is barely capable of speech:

> I had a peep at a dirty, ragged, black-haired child; big enough both to walk and talk—indeed, its face looked older than Catherine's—yet, when it was set on its feet, it only stared round, and repeated over and over again some gibberish that nobody could understand. (28–29)

Presumably, this gibberish was some foreign tongue—many speculate that Brontë had in mind the influx of poverty stricken Irish workers in Liverpool during the period—yet from the perspective of the Earnshaws and the servant girl Nelly Dean, the child is "as good as dumb" (29) and thus outside of the symbolic realm of language and social order. He is thus seen as threatening to the family. This distrust is initially shared by all of the inmates of the Heights, with the exception of the father who brought him home.[24] The transformation of Cathy's distrust into love is not pictured in the novel, and the narrator Nelly Dean does not attempt to explain what she was not there to see.

23. If, as Nancy Armstrong has argued, Emily Brontë helped to create the literary trope of psychological depth and thus to create the space in which psychoanalysis is enacted, it is also noteworthy that she helps to define the parameters of the middle-class family, although only to disrupt and problematize it with the figure of Heathcliff. See Nancy Armstrong, *Desire and Domestic Fiction: A Political History of the Novel* (Oxford: Oxford University Press, 1987), 186–202.

24. By bringing Heathcliff home, the father also replaced, both in body and in name, his lost eldest son—the first Heathcliff (29). The elder Earnshaw, however, is either unable or unwilling to share his patronymic with his newly found son.

The pre-fall state of love between Cathy and Heathcliff is never directly portrayed within the text. Like the natural world of the moors for which Cathy has so much love, their relationship is only seen in the gaps of the text and retrospectively.[25] Thus in Cathy's makeshift diary entries read by Lockwood at the beginning of the novel, we see a tension between Cathy's literary pursuits and her life with Heathcliff:

> I reached this book, and a pot of ink from a shelf, and pushed the house-door ajar to give me light, and I have got the time on with writing for twenty minutes; but my companion is impatient and proposes that we should appropriate the dairy woman's cloak, and have a scamper on the moors, under its shelter. (17)

We can only assume with Lockwood that they did take this run in the moor, for the next entry in the book tells us of the forced separation of Heathcliff and Cathy by her brother Hindley. Hindley hates the foster son who has usurped his place in his father's affections and he desires revenge. We can usefully see the relationship between Cathy and Heathcliff at this point in the light of Kristeva's theory of poetic language. Cathy has clearly entered the symbolic, her highly verbal nature and desire for mastery having been emphasized by Nelly Dean throughout her narrative.[26] Heathcliff has not, and for Cathy he represents that lost semiotic realm of drives, rhythms, and ties to the natural world.[27] Like the poet and the mother in Kristeva's discourse, Cathy welcomes an alliance with the semiotic, although she does not enact it in writing. The later claims by both Cathy and Heathcliff that they are part of each other and not in fact complete persons alone are given further

25. See Margaret Homans, "Repression and Sublimation of Nature in *Wuthering Heights, PMLA* 93 (1978): 9-19; and *Bearing the Word: Language and Female Experience in Nineteenth-Century Women's Writing* (Chicago: University of Chicago, 1986), ch. 3.

26. When the father departs for Liverpool, Cathy asks for a whip, whereas her brother, the future drunk and tyrant, Hindley, asks for a fiddle. Both gifts are lost or destroyed by the newcomer, Heathcliff (28).

27. This tells us how Heathcliff is understood by Cathy and the others at the Heights. Heathcliff's own relationship to language—his native tongue perhaps—is inaccessible to the reader.

validation by this reading of their relationship, in which the two together do in fact make one complete person. Heathcliff's claim that without Cathy he has no soul is in agreement with a reading that allies Cathy from the beginning of the text with the world of symbolic language.

Cathy's shift of alliance from Heathcliff to Edgar is not, therefore, an uncomplicated move from the semiotic to the symbolic, the maternal to the paternal, or nature to culture, for she has always allied herself in part with the symbolic. Yet in her relationship with Heathcliff, like the poet and the "good" mother, Cathy has been willing to put her subjectivity into process and to allow the semiotic to emerge in and through the symbolic. More importantly perhaps, she has been unhampered by gender identifications of Victorian femininity that serve to restrain her enjoyment of the semiotic. It is crucial to remember Kristeva's insistence on the impossibility of living and speaking entirely outside of the symbolic realm. Cathy's turn away from Heathcliff, with her marriage to Edgar Linton, is not just a turn to the symbolic—she already has allied herself with the symbolic in her love of and use of language—but rather an attempt to gain the stability and patriarchal power that the subject-in-process cannot attain within the symbolic world and that women cannot attain within the patriarchal realm except through such alliances. The choice, however, is not between the violence of nature and the civility of culture, as some critics have felt, nor even between the innocence of nature and the violence of patriarchy, as more politically oriented interpretors have insisted. Brontë, and Kristeva with her, insists that violence exists on both sides of the divide. It is not that violence does not exist on one or the other side, but rather that the nature of the violence changes.

The most startling evidence against a reading of Cathy's early relationship with Heathcliff as one of innocence and uncomplicated union with nature is given by Cathy herself later in the novel.[28]

28. The obliteration of all marks of human habitation and culture by a snowstorm early in the novel (25) succinctly images the danger nature poses for human life and culture. That the victim of this natural event was the cultivated Lockwood, in his attempt to escape the Heights, further underlines this thesis.

Separated from Heathcliff by the latter's departure and her subsequent marriage to Edgar Linton, Cathy is driven to seeming madness after Heathcliff's return to the Heights. Only at this time does Cathy come to realize the incompatility of the two men and the two lives she wishes to bring together. Caught between Edgar's jealousy and Heathcliff's desire for revenge, Cathy starves herself, leading to her death. In a delirium, the feathers in her pillow call to her mind the lapwings she and Heathcliff used to see on the moors:

> Bonny bird; wheeling over our heads in the middle of the moor. It wanted to get to its nest, for the clouds touched the swells, and it felt rain coming. This feather was picked up from the heath, the bird was not shot; we saw its nest in the winter, full of little skeletons. Heathcliff set a trap over it, and the old ones dare not come. I made him promise he'd never shoot a lapwing after that, and he didn't. Yes, here are more! Did he shoot my lapwings, Nelly? Are they red, any of them? Let me look. (95)

The passage itself is ambiguous, clearly pointing to the violence of their days on the moors and to the nature of Cathy's power over Heathcliff. It is unclear to what end Cathy here uses her influence, the power traditionally alloted to the woman in the most prevalent strands of Victorian culture. It appears to be a civilizing function; she keeps Heathcliff from shooting the birds. Yet, implicit in this prohibition is the permission to set traps, leading to the bloodless death of the small birds and the procuring of untainted feathers. In the same passage, Cathy's imagination transforms Nelly Dean, the only available mother figure in the book, into a "withered hag" attempting to hurt the heifers on the moors. For Brontë the maternal realm and the moment of conjunction between the maternal and the paternal are not innocent, nor free from destructive violence. Furthermore, in bringing this pre-symbolic realm into contact with the symbolic, the result is not a lessoning of violence, but rather its masking.

Despite these claims, however, it remains true that the separation of Heathcliff and Cathy, brought about by Hindley, Edgar Linton, and Heathcliff and Cathy themselves, precipitates ever-increasing violence within the work. The important theme of revenge is introduced early in the text, in the dream Lockwood has while attempting to sleep in Cathy's closet bed at the Heights. The servant Joseph, generally read as a comic figure in the novel, has clearly been the inspiration for Lockwood's dream, and I believe that he occupies a much more central place in the novel than has often been acknowledged. His rigid style of Christianity, delighting in doom and revenge, is parodied in the dream's account of Jabes Branderham's sermon, which is a perversion of a text on the inexhaustability of forgiveness in the Gospel of Matthew. Whereas Jesus tells Peter that he must forgive anyone who sins against him not just seven times seven times, but seventy times seven times, Jabes Brandenham's sermon is a vengeful diatribe enumerating the four hundred and ninety sins and the four hundred and ninety-first sin, which will bring down the vengeance of God and the community. Rather than marking the inexhaustible nature of forgiveness, the wealth of sins serves to increase and augment the necessity for punishment and revenge when the time for it finally arrives. Not only that, but the audience forced to listen to this account of sins is tortured with boredom, just as the young Cathy and Heathcliff were tortured by the boredom of Joseph's religious teaching and reading materials.

Joseph, with his gospel of revenge, is apparently both structurally and thematically in opposition to the outsider Heathcliff, yet clearly Joseph's religion serves precisely to legitimate Heathcliff's own lust for revenge by giving voice to the prohibitions of the father God. Thus on one level the text can be read as enacting the progression described by Kristeva from hatred to love, in that the second Cathy and her relationship to Hareton can be seen as an overcoming of revenge through forgiveness and love. The younger Cathy, taught to hate by the cruelty she has been subjected to by Heathcliff (as an act of revenge against her father Edgar), is able to forgive Hareton for his apparent neglect and ignorance. The mechanism of this change is once again passed over in silence. When we first meet the younger Cathy at the opening of the book, she is hopeless, vengeful, yet passively resistant to Heathcliff and all associated with him. Upon Lockwood's return to the Heights at the close of the book, Cathy and Hareton's love has been cemented. While Nelly Dean is able to show Cathy's attempts to win over Hareton and her ultimate success, she does not account for the change of heart undergone by Cathy. The only thing that might explain it is the reintroduction of Nelly Dean at the Heights. While Nelly Dean's absence marked the moment of the first Cathy's and Heathcliff's love, her presence seems necessary to the transformation of the second Cathy and Hareton. At issue, I believe, are the very different types of love that are shared between these characters.

Nelly Dean is one of the most complex characters in the novel; the fact that she narrates much of the tale only increases the difficulties of interpretation, for much that we know about the story is shaped by her. Many early commentators found in Nelly Dean the moral center, and in fact, the only morally acceptable voice within the novel. More recent readers are more likely to criticize the conservative tendencies of much of Nelly's beliefs and actions.[29] Once again, I find Kristeva's theoretical work helpful in explaining the ambivalence surrounding the figure of Nelly. As was said above, Nelly is the only mother figure within the novel who survives for any length of time and plays an active role in the text. Although never biologically a parent, she is clearly a mother to Hareton and the younger Cathy. Furthermore, her ambiguous role as servant in the Earnshaw household finds her caught between maternal, sororial, and servile status. Like a third child, she is promised a present by the elder Earnshaw before his departure for Liverpool. Like a mother, she is the one expected to care for the young gypsy Heathcliff on his arrival at the Heights. But, like a servant, she is cavalierly dismissed from the house when she neglects to carry out this order. Her relationship to Cathy and Heathcliff is marked by ambivalence throughout the work, both because of her early sisterly affection for Hindley and her later allegiance to Edgar Linton. It is crucial to see that Nelly consistently sides with the legitimate fathers and householders in the novel, while at the same time she repeatedly shows a covert sympathy for the outsider, Heathcliff, a sympathy that she just as insistently denies. The one person for

29. The most recent work has tended to try to rehabilitate Nelly Dean as an unambiguously "good" mother. See Pykett, *Emily Brontë*, ch. 7; Homans, *Bearing the Word*, ch. 3; and Kate Ferguson Ellis, *The Contested Castle: Gothic Novels and the Subversion of Domestic Ideology* (Urbana: University of Illinois Press, 1989), Epilogue.

whom she has no clear sympathy is Cathy. Herself an outsider twice over, Nelly's only hope for limited power and voice is through allegiance to those with legitimate power through land and paternity. Unlike Heathcliff, who is able to go off and procure wealth and thus to obtain the Heights, as a woman Nelly is barred from this method of entering into the symbolic. As a servant, however, she is unable to share in the paternal authority through marriage and influence in the way chosen by Cathy. Under the necessity of working for others, she is unable to indulge in the emotional manipulations and power struggles enacted by Cathy.[30] That such a mode of authority is also inadequate to Cathy's needs does not seem to have elicited any sympathy from Nelly Dean, for whom class solidarity appears to have been more compelling than that of gender. While Nelly Dean preaches a message of common sense, Christian forgiveness, and love, in contrast to the gospel of revenge offered by Joseph and its subversion by Heathcliff, she herself has a posthumous vengeance on the figure of Cathy who she seems to have felt usurped her own chances for authority both at the Heights and later at Thrushcross Grange.

Our recognition of this posthumous revenge, together with cultural ambivalence surrounding the figure of the mother as the "phallic mother," account for the difficulties surrounding Nelly Dean's character. Kristeva attempts to explain the psychological roots of the image of the phallic mother, the mother invested with possibly stultifying power over the child. She argues that mothers have traditionally occupied an uneasy alliance with the paternal order. On the one hand, entrance into the symbolic realm and, hence, identification with the father are necessary to the aquisition of subjectivity for mothers themselves and for their children. At the same time, in the experience of maternity the subject is called into question by its own internal splitting and feeling of rhythmic and drive-related union with the infant. As a surrogate mother and servant, Nelly Dean's situation is even more ambiguous. She seems to envy most the older Cathy's experience of pregnancy and motherhood. In fact, she almost completely effaces them from the texts.

30. See Pykett, *Emily Brontë*, ch. 7.

While it might be argued that this elision is merely Victorian prudery, Brontë shows little such circumspection with regard to other matters in the text. Nelly Dean's desire for the experience of motherhood, however, again is two-sided: it reflects a desire for the kind of closeness with the child experienced in pregnancy and the culturally accepted inseparability of mother and child, and the legitimation of her role as mother and the authority given by patriarchy.[31]

This discussion of Nelly Dean's maternal function is crucial for two reasons in any discussion of Heathcliff. On the one hand, Nelly is in many ways a double for Heathcliff, particularly along class lines. At the same time, she marks the point of greatest alterity in Heathcliff's character. While virtually all of the characters in the novel are motherless on the literal level, Heathcliff is the most deprived, refusing even the maternal care of Nelly Dean. His stoicism in illness, Nelly's first experience as a surrogate mother, marks this refusal. It has been remarked that the love relationship between Cathy and Heathcliff resembles that between the believer or mystic and God, with the exception of its equality and reciprocity.[32] However, the point can be taken in another direction by emphasizing the bond between contemporaries as exemplifying the relationship between the pre-Oedipal semiotic and the symbolic. Such a relationship is akin to the mother-child bond, but without its hierarchical structure. The destruction of this relationship is thus brought about by the abandoned child's equal, thereby changing the dynamics of the reaction. Within Kristeva's theory, the infant must be helped to separate itself from the mother, often by the mother herself, in order to attain subjectivity. A failure on the mother's part to allow the subject autonomy is experienced as abjection, just as a too-forcible rejection by the mother causes psychic damage and the specter of the phallic mother. On one level, Heathcliff is saved from this dilemma by his equality with Cathy, which forces

31. Thus Nelly shows great sorrow over her enforced separation from her two most beloved foster children, Hareton (69) and the second Cathy.

32. Miller, *Disappearance of God*, 174. It should be pointed out, however, that many Christian mystics use the image of love between men and women for the relationship between God and the soul precisely to point to such an equality existing between them.

him either to share the blame with her or to see others as primary agents in their separation. Only when he hears Cathy voice her apparent feelings of superiority to him does he expand his revenge to include her. Yet he himself ultimately sees that this solution was based upon a misunderstanding of Cathy's words and of the forces of patriarchal and symbolic language that shape their lives. While the following sections of the novel leading to Cathy's death are a continued debate between the two characters over who is destroying the other, Heathcliff finally comes to acknowledge, at the close of his life, that his attempt to find the fitting object of revenge always ultimately misses the mark. Having aided in the destruction of the one he did love, he acknowledges that there is no satisfaction in any of his acts of revenge, for the ghost of his former love and happiness with Cathy in childhood will always return to haunt him.

What is most powerful and haunting about Heathcliff is his refusal to sublate his desire for revenge into love. Having acknowledged the inability of revenge to give him satisfaction, he choses to die rather than forgive. Forgiveness, it is implied, would no more help Heathcliff than did revenge. Rather he must return to Cathy in the only way available to him, the mingling of their dust and remains in the earth of the moor and the communion of their spirits in nature. The reversal of this story of love and revenge in the account of the love between the second Cathy and Hareton cannot supplant the impact of Heathcliff's end. As the moviemakers knew, we are fascinated by the specter of undying love and fidelity, for which we are willing to forgive Cathy and Heathcliff a multitude of sins and acts of violence. While the self-immolation of Heathcliff is necessary to the movement from hatred to love in the novel (for without his removal from the novel Cathy and Hareton's love would have met with an obstacle beyond the influence of forgiveness), there is no hint of a logical progression in this movement. Heathcliff's position has not been superceded, but remains as a ghostly alternative to the vision of bucolic happiness pictured in the closing chapters of the novel. Cathy and Heathcliff both die with the conviction that death will allow them, in some way, to return to the childhood happiness from which they had fallen. Neither has interest in the afterlife of Christianity or any restoration of innocence.

Rather it is a life with nature and each other, with all of the violence and self-dissolution that this implies, to which they wish to return. Death is a struggle, yet one that both Cathy and Heathcliff in some way appear to chose, refusing to eat and thus precipitating their ends. Again we see the religious element at work in Brontë's novel, attempting to offer a mythology of immanent, or this-worldly, transcendence to supplant the Christian myth. Presented as though it were a pagan antecedent to Christian love and forgiveness, on another reading it is clearly a post-Christian revision of Methodist Christianity's message of damnation and revenge.[33] For Brontë, it is not God who should enact vengeance upon humanity for sinning, but rather human beings who must demand vengeance against the God who has taken from them their happiness. Innocence or guilt is not at issue, for we are all children of nature and share in the amoral violence of nature. Innocence and guilt can only become issues when we have entered the human world of language, laws, and the symbolic. Heathcliff is willing and desirous of being an outlaw in that system because of his need for revenge against a God and a system that have taken his happiness from him.[34]

NEGOTIATING VIOLENCE IN FEMINIST SUBJECTIVITY

Like Kristeva over a hundred years later, Brontë offers a picture of the violent underside of all of our subjectivities, as well as providing a compelling counter-myth to the prevalent Christian discourse of innocence, fall, guilt, and redemption.[35] Like the poet Emily Dickinson, Brontë rejects the divine vengeance preached by her Evangelical relations and poses instead the issue of divine and cultural

33. This is of course only one aspect of Methodist Christianity's message. For Brontë's own religious background and its influence on her writings, see Winifred Gérin, *Emily Brontë* (London: Oxford University Press, 1971).

34. The only character spared from his revenge, except when she goes too far in protecting his enemies, is Nelly.

35. It could be argued that Kristeva attempts to provide such a counter-myth, particularly in *Tales of Love*, in which psychoanalysis might be seen as the site of an atheological religion.

guilt.[36] This reading in many ways agrees with that of Gilbert and Gubar, with the crucial distinction that while some of the hatred in Heathcliff (and Cathy and other characters within the work) is sparked by the forces of classism and sexism in his society, much of it is directed against the process of socialization itself. As Kristeva attempts to show, a distinction must be made between the system of patriarchy, its distortions and abuses, and the realm of symbolic language, which for Kristeva is merely referential language itself. We must differentiate ourselves as subjects in order even to exist in the linguistic world, and this necessity is the occasion for both an act of violence and the curbing of the violence of the drives. It is how we negotiate and control violent drives and our need for freedom that must be subject for discussion, rather than how to do away with violence entirely, an impossible task that can lead to the worst kinds of oppression. Readers have felt love for and fascination with the figure of Heathcliff in part because of his faithfulness to a childhood experience that lies beyond good and evil. The force of his emotional and physical presence, in an age marked by increasing feelings of vascillation and dis-ease with the self—in point of fact, abjection—is a source of mythological fascination for some Victorian and many modern readers. Willing to explore the depths of violence and evil in his faithfulness, Heathcliff goes beyond the Romantic Satan in that he acknowledges violence as violence, evil as evil, and *still* finds them preferable to the cultural world that has taken his love from him.[37] It is thus that Heathcliff can be read as emblematic of what Kristeva argues is the most important stake and process of discovery within contemporary feminism, "*the interiorization of the founding separation of the socio-symbolic*

36. On Dickinson, see Cynthia Griffen Wolff, *Emily Dickinson* (New York: Knopf, 1987), 66–104.

37. Isabel, who marries Heathcliff, serves to warn the reader against a Romantic reading of Heathcliff's character. As Cathy tells her, he is not a diamond in the rough (80). It is also important to note that upon learning, too late, the truth of Cathy's assessment, Isabel alone among the women in the novel responds with active, other-directed violence (140). She is quickly banished from the story, showing the persistance of gender stratification even in this often revolutionary text. Women may not actively destroy, only passively destroy or, better yet, self-destruct.

contract." It is only through this interiorization, Kristeva argues, that we will escape the process of scapegoating that has marked all of our cultural foundings and replace it with "the potentialities of *victim/executioner* that characterize each identity, each subject, each sex."[38]

To return briefly to the model of the raped Lucretia with which we began our discussion of violence, it must be said at this point that she ultimately fails as an emblem for Kristeva's psychoanalytic discourse, not because of her gender but because of the patriarchal and symbolic assignment of values upon Lucretia's body and her mind. Her desire is not for Kristeva's amoral, presymbolic realm, but rather for that imaginary and ideal realm posited by the subject upon its entry into language according to Lacan's theory. For the latter, any attempted return is clearly an illusion, for such prelinguistic innocence is itself illusory. Within this system Lucretia becomes precisely the scapegoat who lies at the basis of a new cultural formation, and whose physical suffering is elided in the name of that culture. Kristeva, by denying that such a realm is one of innocence, reasserts its reality. Yet to return, except through the mediation of writing and thus of the symbolic, leads the subject to death, which for Kristeva appears to be final.[39] While Brontë's novel enacts this eruption of the semiotic into the symbolic, the hope for some actual reattainment of the loss of boundaries and freedom that is one face of death remains in the figures of Cathy and Heathcliff, as does a belief in the transcendent power, not of God, but of fidelity.

All of the characters in *Wuthering Heights* are resisting states of unhappiness, of captivity. The nature of this captivity and the

38. Julia Kristeva, "Women's Time," in *The Kristeva Reader,* ed. Toril Moi (New York: Columbia University Press, 1986), 210, emphasis in original. Again, it must be stressed that this does not deny the workings of patriarchy against the female sex within the text of *Wuthering Heights,* marked particularly by the differences between Cathy's and Heathcliff's ways of responding to their situation. For insightful comments on the danger of denying the existence of violence in women, see Adrienne Rich, *On Lies, Secrets and Silence: Selected Prose 1966–1978* (New York: W. W. Norton, 1979), 122.

39. More should be said of Kristeva's ambiguous and repeated comments about the infinite. See Lechte, *Julia Kristeva,* 114–18.

modes of resistance used by each are easily explained, particularly with regard to the central characters. Thus the first Cathy is in revolt against the gender identifications that have straitjacketed her in her quest for power through marriage. She wishes to retain her ties with Heathcliff, the other side of her girlish self, but her only way to work toward this desire is through "feminine" modes of emotional manipulation and influence, modes that ultimately fail and lead to her death. The death itself is both Cathy's only chance of returning to her girlhood and its freedom and an ultimately successful method of punishing Edgar and Heathcliff for their inability to share her. Her daughter is more successfully socialized within the ideals of a certain feminine tradition in Victorian England, for she has a mother figure in Nelly Dean, who has introduced her into a role of moderate independence and femininity. While not the emotional and cultural straitjacket experienced by her mother, it keeps her from ever experiencing the kind of childhood freedom known by her mother. The result is that she is able to respond to Heathcliff's cruelty with a passive and verbal resistance, but when physical violence threatens she is helpless. Hareton, even when socialized by Cathy, is unwilling to use his violence against the man he has learned, however wrong-headedly, to love. Ultimately, the happy resolution of the plot depends upon the death of Heathcliff, who cannot be circumvented in any other way.

There is, however, a sustained model for active resistance in the novel, although it is not immediately apparent because he is presented as the enemy within the text. Heathcliff is willing to destroy anything that he feels comes between him and Cathy. It is only at the close of the novel that he realizes that all of his revenge has not brought him any closer, yet in his single-mindedness there is neither the time nor the necessity for remorse. The figure of Heathcliff and the reemergence of the ghosts of Cathy and Heathcliff at the end of the novel have repeatedly been read as the return of the repressed into the apparent psychological and cultural resolutions represented by Cathy and Hareton. What we must see is that the repressed is not just sex (if it is that at all), but also the violence of the drives, or violence itself, either that primordial violence represented by nature or the more cultivated and hence perverse violence of revenge. For Heathcliff, the breaking of the final boundary between himself and Cathy is the only solution. The fidelity and the violence that drive him demand the breakdown of all boundaries in a search for freedom, regardless of how destructive that freedom might be. Many critics have argued that Heathcliff is an impossible, inconsistent, and flawed character. I would argue, however, that he is not a character, but rather a representation of the strength and violence that exist in all of us, although masked, weakened, or perverted by cultural and in particular patriarchal socialization. The return of the repressed in Brontë's novel is not just a threat, but also represents a hope and a promise, the attempt to inscribe a new pre- and post-Christian mythology that would help shape a new and powerful subjectivity. The ambivalence, however, between threat and promise always remains, for as the novel shows us, such power and violence are both liberating and destructive.

It is here, finally, that Brontë's novel helps us to move beyond the impasse between Kristeva's psychoanalytic theory and the aims of much feminist theology, while at the same time working together with Kristeva to critique such feminist theologies. In the quotation from *Powers of Horror* cited earlier, Kristeva voiced her assumption that religion and the realm of the sacred were illusory, precisely because they were involved in offering solutions to unresolvable ambiguities in the human situation. In later works, Kristeva points to the importance of psychoanalysis and artistic practice in offering realms for fictive resolutions of these tensions, resolutions that recognize themselves as fictive and hence avoid the taint of illusion. What Brontë offers us in *Wuthering Heights* is an understanding of sacrality, and even of limited transcendence, that does not resolve tensions but rather continues the ambiguities of life in death. As such the "ghosts" of Cathy and Heathcliff serve as sources of power and force, without illusion and without offering false resolutions to the conflicts of subjectivity and of life on earth. Such a fictive or mythopoetic position offers an alternative to the secularizing and demythologizing views of traditional psychoanalysis. Yet at the same time it shows the dangers inherent in those feminist theologies that are equally concerned with the smooth resolution of tension and ambiguity, refusing to see the violence inherent in all subjectivity. Such a tendency clearly exists in those who wish to maintain a traditional Christian eschatological frame[40] but is also, and perhaps even more apparent, in the work of such post-Christian thinkers as Mary Daly. With her rejection of psychoanalysis, Daly has also rejected any account of the subject as split or rendered problematic by anything other than patriarchal perversions. In her post-Christian, feminist world, the violence is all on the side of men and patriarchy; it exists in women only insofar as they have been harmed by that false system.[41] Such a position is not only untrue, I think, to experience; it also undermines the true vitality of that realm before and beyond Christianity that Daly herself, together with other Christian and post-Christian feminists, is attempting to create.

40. Many who heard or read this paper were puzzled by this allusion, apparently because of the rejection of traditional Christian eschatologies by many feminist theologians, from Rosemary Radford Reuther to Sharon Welch. That such theological rejection is not the norm among nonacademic Christians, including many who consider themselves feminist, however, seems to justify this reference. The central point is that the rejection of such an other-worldly eschatology does not mitigate—but perhaps even excacerbates—that fear of ambivalence under discussion.

41. In her earliest work of post-Christian philosophy, Daly argued that "the power of sisterhood is not warpower," although she does not deny that conflict will remain. See Mary Daly, *Beyond God the Father: Towards a Philosophy of Women's Liberation* (Boston: Beacon Press, 1977), 198. It can be argued that her claims become significantly less nuanced in later works, such as *Gyn/Ecology* and *Pure Lust*.

5

This God Which Is Not One

IRIGARAY AND BARTH ON THE DIVINE

SERENE JONES

Anyone familiar with the writings of Luce Irigaray and Karl Barth will most likely be surprised by—if not also a little suspicious of—an essay that intends to discuss the two of them together. Given their vast differences, it is hard to imagine what they could possibly have to say to one another. Irigaray is a French psychoanalyst and philosopher; she writes as a feminist and her theological reflections are far from "traditionally Christian." Barth, on the other hand, is a theologian deeply rooted in the German intellectual tradition; he is somewhat of a Marxist but definitely not a feminist; and he refers to his theology as "dogmatic." What could the two of them possibly share, particularly with regard to theology and the nature of the divine?

In this essay I intend to illustrate that they actually share a good deal and that their similarities subsequently make a discussion of their differences quite interesting. Furthermore, it is precisely

I want to thank Kathryn Tanner, Kalbryn McLean, Margret Homans and Lisa Cartwright for the valuable conversations and critiques they contributed to this essay. I also want to thank participants in the Women and Religion Section of the American Academy of Religion, where I first presented these ideas in 1988.

because of their similarities that a comparative analysis of Barth and Irigaray can provide a good model for exploring how contemporary theologians might fruitfully use French feminist theory in interpreting and critiquing more traditional Christian texts. Likewise, these similarities make it possible to explore the various ways in which a Christian theologian may challenge and even deepen the theological insights of French feminist theory. Thus, in the following pages, using Irigaray and Barth as my guides, I hope to demonstrate that French feminist theorists and Reformed Barthian theologians not only hold some rather surprising assumptions in common but also have a good deal to learn from one another, especially when one attends to the different contexts in which they develop and play out these assumptions.

The similarities upon which I shall be focusing are fundamentally twofold. The first concerns the interesting parallel between Irigaray's critique of "phallocentricism" and its "logic of the same" on the one hand and Barth's critique of "liberal theology" or "natural theology" and its subjective narcissism on the other. The second concerns the parallels between their constructive attempts to secure the identity in difference of "the other": the other who for Irigaray is "woman," and who for Barth is "God." I will also explore the crucial points at which their positions on these questions sharply diverge. However, before I turn to a more indepth discussion of these parallels and differences, I want briefly to underscore a parallel that has to do with genre and form, a parallel rooted in their shared understanding of the position they occupy as authors and the rhetorical ends toward which their writing moves.

Students of both Irigaray and Barth have commented often on the difficulties confronting any attempt to summarize neatly their positions. This difficulty stems from the fact that although they are both extremely systematic thinkers, they refuse to offer the reader a nicely packaged "system" or a tightly coherent "theory." This refusal is grounded in their belief that systems and theories inevitably impose false closure upon subjects that are, in reality, fractured, fluid, mysterious, and discursively open-ended. Thus, instead of presenting their readers with theories and systems to be analyzed and critiqued, they engage readers in another kind of rhetorical enterprise, an enterprise best understood as a kind of training or discipline in which one is introduced and called to participate in a different "way of thinking." Margaret Whitford captures this dynamic in Irigaray's writing when she suggests that the best way to approach Irigaray is to begin by asking "what does she make it possible for us to think?"[1] George Hunsinger makes a similar observation when he suggests that in order for one to engage Barth's theology, one must become practiced in the interweaving "thought forms" or "patterns of thinking" that structure his theology.[2]

In the following analysis of both Irigaray and Barth, I try to honor this dimension of their writing by resisting the urge to systematize them rigorously. Instead, I let the unwieldy character of their work stand and impose only the loosest kind of order, an order that emerges if we return again and again to the question, "What are they trying to make it possible for us to think?" Such an approach, I believe, is not only appropriate to the genre but also necessary to the task at hand. Why? Because it is only when one learns their "ways of thinking" and thereby enters the strange worlds of Irigaray's essays and Barth's *Church Dogmatics* that one can begin to sense fully the powerful undercurrents that draw their positions "near to one another" and then forcefully pull them apart.

THE LOGIC OF THE SAME

What does Irigaray make possible for us to think? In answering this question, it is useful to begin where Irigaray herself begins, namely with *Speculum of the Other Woman*, an early text in which she develops her critique of Western philosophy and the broader patterns of Western thinking it "rules."[3] It is helpful to begin with this text because Irigaray's later writings assume the reader's familiarity with the basic logic of this critique. Furthermore, I will be

1. Margaret Whitford, *Luce Irigaray: Philosophy in the Feminine* (London: Routledge, 1991), 4.

2. George Hunsinger, *How to Read Karl Barth* (New York: Oxford University Press, 1991), 29.

3. Luce Irigaray, *Speculum of the Other Woman*, trans. Gillian C. Gill (Ithaca: Cornell University Press, 1985).

referring to this text at length when I later compare Irigaray's critique of philosophy to Barth's critique of natural or liberal theology.

Speculum of the Other Woman consists of a collection of essays in which Irigaray analyzes a series of texts that hold canonical status in the field of Western intellectual history. These texts range from fragments of Plato, Aristotle, and Descartes to the psychoanalytic theories of Freud and Lacan. Within this spectrum of texts, she also includes an essay on the Medieval mystics, Kant, and Hegel. In analyzing these texts, Irigaray follows a rather unusual procedure, a procedure that in its very deployment challenges a more traditionally analytic approach to philosophical interpretation: positioning herself as a kind of Talmudic storyteller, Irigaray reads between the lines of these texts in order to excavate primal scenes, plots, and characters that history has buried and hence centuries of interpreters have missed. Although the specifics of these excavated plots and characters vary significantly, according to the text she is reading, the thematic unity of *Speculum* lies in Irigaray's skillful ability to demonstrate the deep similarities between these diverse subtexts. On the basis of her rereadings, it becomes evident that the philosophers, psychoanalysts, and mystics of Western culture all bury in the crevices of their texts the same story. Or, as Irigaray would put it, they all tell "the story of the same." As she excavates this story, Irigaray artfully deploys a series of rhetorical devices designed to evoke in the reader the recognition that this "story of the same" not only inhabits the canons of Western literature, but also subtends the reader's own habits of knowing as well.

What is the plot and who are the characters populating this subterranean "story of the same"? Before answering this question, one must understand the basic plot and logic of the story within which this sub-story is buried. Again, the particular features of the surface story vary according to author and era, but Irigaray highlights for the reader certain thematic regularities that appear in all the texts she analyzes. The first of these regularities can be summarized as the philosopher's quest to establish identity. This "quest for identity" simply points to the fact that historically Western philosophy has seen as its primary objective the establishment of an internally coherent and noncontradictory definition of its chosen subject matter. Whether the topic at hand is God or the cosmos or the nature of the good or the essence of the human subject, philosophers use their tools of critical analysis for the purpose of securing a static definition of a central principle or truth. A presupposition that undergirds this quest for identity and definition is the assumption that reality, be it material or ideal, actually consists of stable forms that can be analyzed and then categorized in this manner.

A second thematic regularity that Irigaray highlights resides in the tendency of Western philosophers to generate elaborate conceptual systems that serve to bolster or support this quest for identity. These systems may consist of a series of formal or logical axioms, or they may be constituted by a developed ontology, cosmology, or epistemology. The important point for Irigaray is that these systems revolve around a central principle which rules and thereby consumes all the elements within the system in order to keep ambivalence or ambiguity to a minimum. This tendency within philosophy can be summarized as a proclivity for monadic totalization. A third thematic regularity, closely related to the second, resides in the tendency of Western philosophers to achieve definition by situating the central principle in relation to its binary opposite. Through the use of binary opposites, definition is won by marking the boundaries that separate the conceptual space occupied by a given identity from the space of nonidentity or negativity that surrounds it. Irigaray refers to this proclivity within Western thought as the conferring of identity though "the play of difference." A fourth thematic regularity that structures the patterns of Western philosophy is the presupposition that within these systems, the central principle—whether it be God, the first principles of reason, or the ideal form—assumes legislative authority over all other elements within the system because it is nonderivative, self-generated, necessary, and thereby *a priori*.

After identifying these four thematic regularities, which drive the surface story of Western discourse, Irigaray makes two "disruptive" observations about their logic. First, Irigaray demonstrates that although each of the philosophers she analyzes wants to claim that there is room for true difference between the various elements within their system, they have set their projects up in such a way that the admission of real difference is impossible. Given the legislative power of the system's central principle, all elements that systematically accrue around this principle have their identity conferred only to the degree that they stand in relation to the organizing center. The quest for identity, when combined with the proclivity for monadic totalization, minimizes difference by demanding that all elements within the system come to identity only insofar as they mimic the primal identity attributed to their legislative master. This tendency to reduce difference is most apparent when one takes a closer look, as Irigaray does, at the procedures that structure the play of binary oppositions. While it may seem, at one level, that identity thrives in its encounter with the other (its binary opposite), Irigaray argues that this other is only a negative reflection of the center or the one. The "other" or the "opposite" finds its being or nonbeing, its shape and form, its meaning and function conferred only to the degree that it either mirrors back the attributes of the center or, in its negativity, provides the center with the edge that marks its defining contours.

On the basis of this analysis of Western philosophy's obsession with the identity of "the one" and the subsequent exclusion of all difference, Irigaray claims that the logic underlying these systems is a "logic of the same." She then complements this observation/critique with a second, even more "disruptive revelation." As she reads between the lines of the philosopher's story, she uncovers a secret, namely, that although a philosopher may claim that his or her central principle is nonderivative, the construction of its identity is a function of its interaction with the other; for without its other, the contours of its shape would be endlessly fluid. However, in order to protect the stability and *a priori* status of the central principle, philosophers have refused to acknowledge openly the productivity of this play of difference, for if it were admitted, the legislative authority of the center would be threatened. Irigaray refers to the sleight of hand whereby philosophers hide generative difference as the "blind spot" of Western discourse. This "blind spot" refers to that logical moment within discourse that is repressed for fear that the very pillars of discursive coherence might crumble if it came into view.[4]

4. The term *blind spot* first appears in Irigaray's essay "The Blind Spot in an Old Dream of Symmetry," *Speculum*.

In addition to these two disruptive observations about the logic of Western discourse, Irigaray excavates yet one more layer of the subtext that undergirds the workings of philosophy. Through the combined forces of her skills as a literary critic and psychoanalyst, Irigaray uncovers the gendered character of the philosopher's project. Attending to the imagery and rhetoric of these texts, she exposes the traditionally "masculine" characteristics that accrue around the philosopher's central principles and the traditionally "feminine" nature of the "other" which serves to define the center. Using the tools of psychoanalysis, she delves even deeper into the subtext of philosophy and reveals that the "logic of the same" is directly linked to the expansive and yet unconscious workings of a culturally constructed Western "imaginary." In general terms, the "imaginary" refers to the phantasies of images and dynamics that both structure and fund the most basic movements of thought. According to Irigaray (and here her psychoanalytic orientation becomes most obvious), the imaginary of the dominant culture "bears the morphological marks of the male body," and the manifestations of this morphology show forth clearly in the logic that structures philosophical discourse.[5] Just as the phallus is one, unitary, singular, and linear, so too is the dominant Western rationality, which seeks unitary identity and order and which is fundamentally teleological in character. Similarly, just as the phallus needs the hand or another body to know itself, so too Western philosophy assumes that an "other" is necessary for attaining knowledge and definition of its central principles. This "other," however, earns its identity only in so far as it serves the phallus, or in the case of philosophy, in so far as it serves the central, unitary, and stable principle of identity.

What becomes of woman in this phallic economy of relations? She is the "other." As binary opposite of man, she plays the role of the flat reflecting mirror that confers his identity (or the identity of the central principle—figured as masculine) by means of her ability to reflect him back to himself. Thus, she is sometimes conceived as "this little man." She also serves him in her negativity: as he relegates her identity to a space that is no space, she secures

5. Whitford, *Luce Irigaray*, 54.

the borders of his subjectivity by her absence. In this sense, she is portrayed as "nothing," as "the mysterious dark continent," as the one who "lacks." She is also the reproductive ground or "mother" whose difference generates *his* identity; but in this role she is repressed and silenced. She becomes a "blind spot" that must disappear in order for Western discourse to maintain the non-derivative, self-evident status of the phallus, the central principle. In each of these roles, Irigaray notes, woman has no identity of her own. She is destined always to be "the same" as him. It is this disturbing insight into the role of the feminine in discourse which leads Irigaray to assert that within the logic of Western discourse, there is no sexual difference. There is only the economy of the phallus and its systematic servants.

It is important to note at this point that Irigaray's articulation of the role played by the masculine body in the Western imaginary does not function as either a causal explanation of the construction of gender relations or as a kind of biological reductionism that links anatomy to social relations of power.[6] Instead, she seeks to offer suggestive if not jarring descriptions—descriptions that expose the interconnections between general tendencies within Western thought and the power relations that presently define the contours of sexual difference. The points of interconnection reside in the fact that in each instance the "other" (woman) conceptually and materially serves the "one" (man); the "other" is reduced to "the same" and hence given no autonomous identity; and finally, insofar as her difference is necessary for establishing his identity, woman's "otherness" is repressed and silenced, exiled into the blind spot of discourse. Although Irigaray is neither historian nor political theorist, it is not difficult to "imagine" the role that such an ideological construct has played in the history of the oppression of women.[7]

6. Elizabeth Grosz, *Sexual Subversions* (Sydney: Allen and Unwin, 1989), 112–14, 132.

7. In the last four chapters of *This Sex Which Is Not One,* trans. Catherine Porter (Ithaca: Cornell University Press, 1985), Irigaray makes several comments that suggest that she is open to making links between her theoretical reflections on language and material relations of power that have historically existed between women and men in the West. However, Irigaray privileges the category of gender in her reflections on power by

THE FEMININE IMAGINARY

Having episodically exposed the phallocentric "logic of the same" that undergirds Western rationality, Irigaray next asks and attempts to answer the question, "What is to be done?" Are there discursive avenues that might take us beyond this crippling phallocentricism? In *This Sex Which Is Not One* and a number of other essays, Irigaray struggles to answer this question in the affirmative. In this section, I summarize some of the central features of "what Irigaray makes possible to think" when she enters the realm of constructive philosophy in search of the grounds for this affirmation.

The first thing to be noted about Irigaray's constructive proposals is the extreme caution she exercises as she steps into the realm of constructive philosophy. This caution is precipitated by her recognition that one cannot simply jump out of the discursive world of Western thought and land in a space free from the taint of its phallocentric logic. To do so would be tantamount to jumping out of language itself, which is impossible given the constitutive role played by language in the construction of the human subject. It is at this point that Irigaray decisively parts ways with the projects of Hélène Cixous and Mary Daly, both of whom embrace the idealist's assumption that the critic can break free from the strictures of cultural formation by means of physical or psychic separation.[8] Irigaray instead admits that she cannot help but stand firmly within the very symbolic order from which she has been conceptually (and materially) exiled as a woman. Her stance within this order, however, is far from complacent. Quite to the contrary, it is restless, disruptive and, most importantly, imaginative.

---

virtue of the fact that she makes no mention of race, economic class, ethnicity, or sexual orientation as contexts in which discursive and historical "others" have been exploited and repressed by the rhetoric and institutions of the dominant culture.

8. Hélène Cixous and Catherine Clément, *The Newly Born Woman*, trans. B. Wing (Minneapolis: University of Minnesota Press, 1985). Mary Daly, *Gyn/Ecology: The Metaethics of Radical Feminism* (Boston: Beacon Press, 1978), 313; *Pure Lust: Elemental Feminist Philosophy* (Boston: Beacon Press, 1984).

One of the disruptive strategies used by Irigaray is simply to assume, in exaggerated form, the very role that she has been ascribed in the phallocentric order.[9] By intentionally performing the feminine, Irigaray unveils and exploits the "excesses" internal to the discursive system of phallocentricism. She reveals the illusion of sexual difference by assuming the position of mirror, and she uncovers the "blind spots" by laying bare the feminine ground upon which phallocentric identity is built but which it quickly represses. The constructive potential of this strategy lies in the fact that under the weight of her performance, the system self-destructs. Or, as Irigaray describes it, "the theoretical machinery is jammed."[10]

When she follows this strategy, Irigaray adopts a kind of Derridean posture, deploying the tools of deconstruction.[11] In assuming this posture, she also comes close to promoting the kind of mimesis more recently suggested in the work of Judith Butler.[12] However, Irigaray's work makes clear that she would be content with neither. While she admits that such tactics may be strategically useful, she worries that this approach finally does not get one very far. Although "assuming the feminine" may collapse the logic undergirding the construction of a male subjectivity, this mimesis contributes nothing substantive to the creation of spaces of enunciation in which women's subjectivity and agency may be affirmed in their difference.[13] Thus, to open Western discourse to the possibility of female subjectivity, she moves beyond the space of mimicry and steps into the arena of constructive ontology.

When Irigaray steps into this arena, however, she occupies it in a rather peculiar way. To gain critical leverage against the phallocentric morphology of the imaginary that funds and structures

9. Irigaray performs this mimicry in the essays that comprise *Speculum*. She reflects on this activity most explicitly in her essay, "The Power of Discourse," *This Sex Which Is Not One*, 68–85.

10. "The Power of Discourse," *This Sex*, 78.

11. Jacques Derrida, *Of Grammatology*, trans. G. C. Spivak (Baltimore: Johns Hopkins University Press, 1976); *Positions*, trans. Alan Bass (London: Athlone Press, 1981); and *Margins of Philosophy*, trans. Alan Bass (Chicago: University of Chicago Press, 1982).

12. Judith Butler, *Gender Trouble: Feminism and the Subversion of Identity* (New York: Routledge, 1990), 25, 128.

13. See Irigaray, "Sexual Difference," *French Feminist Thought: A Reader*, ed. Toril Moi (Oxford: Basil Blackwell, 1987), 118–19.

Western rationality, Irigaray posits an alternative morphology that draws its principle features from the female body. She describes this morphology as follows:

> Woman has sex organs more or less everywhere. She finds pleasure almost anywhere . . . the geography of her pleasure is far more diversified, more multiple in its difference, more complex, more subtle than is commonly imagined.[14]
>
> In order to touch himself, man needs an instrument, his hand, a woman's body, language. . . . And this touching requires at least a minimum of activity. As for woman, she touches herself without any need for mediation, and before there is any need to distinguish activity from passivity. Woman "touches herself" all the time . . . for her genitals are formed of two-lips in continuous contact. Thus, within herself, she is two—but not divisible into one(s)—that caress each other.[15]
>
> She is indefinitely other within herself.[16]

The alternative story that Irigaray draws from a morphology of the feminine runs counter to the phallocentric narrative at a number of points. First, instead of giving precedence to order, oneness, and autonomous identity, the imaginary of the feminine embraces fluidity, multiplicity, and the open play of difference. Second, rather than using "the other" simply for the purpose of defining one central principle or identity, female morphology is internally "other" to itself. For this reason, "the other" cannot be repressed or exiled without destroying the very economy of female pleasure. Third, in contrast to the phallocentric imaginary, "the other" of the feminine imaginary cannot be reduced to "a logic of the same" without simultaneously denying the fundamental and irreducible difference structuring her body. Finally, and perhaps most importantly, Irigaray suggests that this alternative morphology is so diffuse and multiple that it resists definition. One cannot determine or delineate "what it is" because in doing so one would simply be reenacting the logic of phallocentricism, which is driven by the search for stable forms.

14. *This Sex*, 28.
15. Ibid., 24.
16. Ibid., 28.

In her later works, Irigaray uses a variety of metaphors and images to elaborate the economy of relations represented by the "two-lips." One question that continues to occupy the attention of her critics and students, however, concerns the status of this alternative morphology or vision. Does she begin walking down the dangerous path of essentialism the minute she steps into the field of constructive ontology? Perhaps she does. As Diana Fuss suggests, "the risk of essentialism may have to be taken," if only momentarily, to derail strategically the coursings of a phallocentric logic that gives to woman no essence of her own.[17] Or perhaps, as Naomi Schor argues, Irigaray is constructing "an essentialism which is not one."[18] This would seem to be the case if one takes seriously Irigaray's claim that she does not wish to produce a "theory of woman," nor does she intend for her image of the "two-lips" to define "women's experience" by reference to her genital anatomy and pleasure.[19]

In terms of assessing the status of her constructive proposal, I find it useful to bracket the question of essentialism and take a more pragmatic approach to analyzing her project.[20] This pragmatic approach (and here I betray my sympathies for the North American pragmatist tradition) requires that one inquire into the social and conceptual function these constructive metaphors serve. While Irigaray remains unclear on the question of essentialism, her position

17. Diana Fuss, *Essentially Speaking: Feminism, Nature and Difference* (London: Routledge, 1990), 1–22, 55–72.

18. Naomi Schor, "This Essentialism Which Is Not One: Coming to Grips with Irigaray," *differences: a journal of feminist cultural studies* 1 (1989): 38–58.

19. *This Sex,* 159. "What I want is not to create a theory of woman but to secure a place for the feminine within sexual difference." In light of these comments, it would appear that her "essentialism" (if she has one) is not the same kind of essentialism ascribed to her in the critical evaluations of Toril Moi and Monique Plaza. See Toril Moi, *Sexual/Textual Politics: Feminist Literary Theory* (New York: Methuen, 1985), 147–49; Monique Plaza, " 'Phallomorphic Power' and the Psychology of 'Woman,' " *Ideology and Consciousness* 1 (1978): 5–36.

20. This pragmatic approach is very similar to the approach taken by Diana Fuss, who argues that for political and social reasons the path of essentialism has strategic usefulness at this particular historical moment.

on this issue is more obvious. Her practical objectives appear to be primarily twofold. First, by positing an alternative morphology, she is attempting to pry open and loosen the strictures of phallocentricism in order that we might begin to imagine new and different futures. In this sense, her constructive project is strategically parasitic upon her assessment of our present limitations and her desire to push us to think beyond them. Second, the future she opens is not posited as a finished product; rather, it is a future that emerges as an ongoing collective creation.[21] In this context, Irigaray's constructive gestures serve as "general directives" or "signposts" that point toward this future without restrictively defining its outcome. And these directives are really quite simple. She urges us into a future in which "woman" no longer functions as a mirror of "man" but has an agency of her own and a subjectivity as multifaceted and richly textured as the real differences that exist between and among women. As such, it is a future that nurtures difference, in all its multiplicity and irreducible otherness. Finally, it is not a future of relativized, amoral pluralism but rather one in which the discursive as well as political repression of the "other" is eclipsed by an ethic and politic that seeks and applauds the presence of the incommensurable other(s).[22]

IRIGARAY'S "GOD"

After this introduction to Irigaray's work, we can now turn to her reflections on the nature of theological discourse and the role of the divine. Deciphering what Irigaray has to say about theology and God poses a challenge because her reflections on religion appear in widely dispersed fragments and her references to such things as angels, Mary, the Trinity, and Jesus Christ are often quite elliptical. However, the fact that her remarks on theology are scattered and enigmatic does not imply that Irigaray has only a casual interest in issues of a theological nature. Throughout her writings,

21. Whitford, *Luce Irigaray,* 139.

22. Both Whitford and Grosz have excellent discussions of the "ethic of difference" developed by Irigaray: Whitford, *Luce Irigaray,* 149–68; Grosz, *Sexual Subversions,* 140–45.

she returns again and again to the question of "God"; and she does so with such rigor and persistence that one cannot help but sense that this particular question stands at the very heart of her project.

For the purpose of summary, Irigaray's theological reflections divide into roughly two categories; those that critique the thoroughly phallocentric character of Western Christianity and those that explore the positive role a notion of divinity might play in the formation of a nonphallocentric subjectivity. With regard to the first of these categories, it is easy to imagine the contours of her critique of the phallocentricism that runs through the history of traditional Protestant and Roman Catholic theology. As one might expect, she reveals the thickly gendered subtext undergirding classical theologies that gender God as male, as the absolute, static center of order and subsequently, as the principle term over and against which the feminine assumes its assigned identity (or nonidentity) as chaos, fluidity, and margin. Similarly, she reveals the workings of the "logic of the same" in traditional theological discourse, a logic in which truly incommensurable difference remains only illusory. And she likewise exposes the "blind spots" of theology. These "blind spots" consist of those theological sleights of hand that repress or hide the generative role played by the feminine as the ground or body in which divinity originates. This repression, Irigaray argues, results from the fear that an acknowledgment of her originating productivity might undermine the legislative authority of the supposedly static, self-originating One who rules.[23]

23. There are three "types" of theological texts to which she applies these criticisms. First, in her essay "Cosi Fan Tutti," *This Sex,* 86–105, she explores the role ascribed to God in the classical metaphysical tradition. Second, in her essay "La Mysterique," *Speculum,* 191–202, the rhetoric of Medieval Christian mystical experience serves as the text that she rereads in order to expose its phallocentric moorings. Here, Irigaray gives a haunting account of the violent mutilation "feminine subjectivity" undergoes as it seeks union with the masculine divine. Most recently, in her article "Equal to Whom," *differences*/1 (1989): 59–76, Irigaray highlights the process whereby the Christian tradition has repressed the role played by the female body in the Incarnation, and has constructed in its place a trinitarian economy of male relations that serves to affirm the reign of the Father and the masculinity of the Son. The effect of such a construction, Irigaray argues, is to void the narrative possibility of establishing the identity of a divine daughter as well as negating a genealogy of mother-daughter relations.

Irigaray, however, does not only depict the divine as the master trope of phallocentricism or as the law of the phallus writ large. There is another side to her critique, a side in which she argues that God ultimately plays a role not unlike that of woman. Although traditional theology may assert that God is truly an objective other, who stands over-against the created order, and is in this sense really different, Irigaray points out (as have many feminist theologians) that this God is in fact only an imagined screen against which man projects his own identity and thereby secures the perimeters of his own subjectivity. Viewed from this perspective, it becomes evident that like woman, God has no identity independent of the phallomorphic economy which posits "Him." Subsequently, God is not that which is truly different or incommensurably other. Quite to the contrary, "He" is just another instance of the same and, like woman, just another victim of phallocentricism's consuming drives. This understanding of God will play an important role in my analysis of Irigaray's relation to Barth's doctrine of God.

While it is clear that Irigaray is highly critical of religious discourse that simply replicates the "logic of the same," this critique does not lead her to dismiss all religious rhetoric as inherently phallocentric.[24] Quite to the contrary, she argues that even if she desired to do so, the religious dimension of culture could not be excluded or repressed because it serves a crucial (essential?) social function.[25] As to what this crucial function is, Irigaray offers a strangely phenomenological answer. I say "strangely" because up to this point in her work, Irigaray appears to have been exceedingly careful not to adopt any founding or grounding set of anthropological claims, given their tendency to universalize human experience at the expense of eliminating true difference and hence to annihilate any subjectivity that is not a reflection of the same/man. In her discussion of the necessity of "religion," however, she takes a radical change of course. Both Ludwig Feuerbach and Emmanuel Levinas enter the picture, and foregoing her usual searing critique of Western philosophy, Irigaray freely draws upon their works to

24. She would admit that religious discourse is inherently phallocentric to the degree that all language is phallocentric.

25. Grosz, *Sexual Subversions*, 151.

defend her claim that religion plays a critically important role in the construction of cultural identity[26] She argues, in short, that religious discourse represents the process whereby human persons project an ideal self or subject into the future as that goal towards which they move in the dialectic of becoming. Religion, in this scenario, is necessary because it provides the discursive horizon of being within which identity is both given shape and drawn into the infinite plane of the future. To put it in slightly different terms, for Irigaray, along with Feuerbach and Levinas, God functions as the "other" or "the form of alterity" which both constitutes and affirms the human.[27]

Having laid this phenomenological foundation for her discussion of "God," Irigaray then proceeds to explore the possible role the divine might play in constructing or imagining female subjectivity. As I explained above, she admits that in its traditional Western form, religion has been thoroughly phallocentric. The alterity it projects has been singularly rooted in a phallic morphology. As such, it has thwarted the development of subjectivities that are different from the "same," which is "man." As a way of responding to this problem, Irigaray is interested in exploring ways in which "divinity" can be used to undermine the "logic of the same" and subsequently carve out a space for woman. In her article "Divine Women," she explains, in very Feuerbachian terms, why a notion of divinity is needed to complement the aims of her constructive project:

> If women lack a God they cannot communicate, or communicate among themselves. The infinite is needed, they need the infinite in order to share a little? Otherwise the division brings about fusion-confusion, division and tearing apart in them/her, between them. *If I can't relate to some sort of horizon*

26. Granted, she does critique Feuerbach and Levinas for having posited a masculine God. But what she does not question in relation to both are their underlying assumptions about the phenomenon of human subjectivity, which requires religious symbols and myths. It seems to me strange that her critique does not cut as deeply as it usually does when it comes to assessing other universalizing projects within philosophy.

27. Grosz, *Sexual Subversions,* 152.

> *for the realization of my genre,* I cannot share while protecting my becoming. (Emphasis added.)[28]

Along the same lines, she writes:

> Only a God can save us and guard over us. The feeling or experience of a positive, objective and glorious existence for our subjectivity is necessary for us. Such a God who helps and guides us in our becoming, *who holds the measure of our limits*—women—and our relation to the infinite, which inspires our endeavors. (Emphasis added.)[29]

At a very pragmatic level, Irigaray argues that given our human predisposition to posit "divinity," women need to disrupt the male imaginary by actively imagining an alternative divinity. This alternative "God" is conceived as an infinite *horizon* which serves as *the measure of their/women's limits* in a way that does not reduce women to a reflection of men. Thus, for Irigaray, "God" can and should function as the alternative "political, ethical and aesthetic ideal" of the emerging female subject.[30] What content does she actually give to this divinized ideal? Not surprisingly, this God takes a form ruled by the same general directives that guide Irigaray's other constructive metaphors. This God is an ideal whose economy of relations are open to difference, whose internal relations are fluid, unstable, changing, and active, and whose external relation to the human person parallels these same internal dynamics. This God is also a God who beckons us into the future, calling us to find pleasure in difference and to seek our own divinization in all its expansive possibilities:

> [God] shows a way. It is the engine of a more perfect becoming. It is the vector, the bowstring, the horizon extended between the farthest past and the farthest future, the most passive and the most active—permanent and always in tension. God holds no obligation over our needs except to become. No task, no obligation burdens us except that one: *become divine, become*

28. Irigaray, "Divine Women," trans. Stephen Muecke (Sydney: Local Consumption Occasional Papers 8, 1986), 4. Quote taken from Grosz, *Sexual Subversions*, 159.

29. Irigaray, "Divine Women," 9.

30. Grosz, *Sexual Subversions*, 159.

> *perfect,* don't let any part of us be amputated that could be expansive for us. (Emphasis added.)[31]

BARTH AND IRIGARAY

With this overview of Irigaray's work, it is now possible to explore the similarities and differences between her position and the theology of Karl Barth. It must be stated from the outset that Irigaray would be highly critical of Barth's adoption of phallocentric notions of sexual difference, particularly as it appears in his infamous account of the hierarchical relation between men and women.[32] On this matter, it seems to me Barth and Irigaray have nothing constructive to say to one another, and Irigaray would be completely correct in exposing and denouncing his explicit misogyny. Having said this, however, I believe that there are several points at which they could enter into constructive conversation, and the first of these points concerns their respective critiques of the dangerously totalizing and repressive logic that undergirds much of Western philosophy. Having explored Irigaray's position on this matter, let me briefly recount Barth's own analysis of the relation between philosophy and theology.

Barth begins the first volume of the *Church Dogmatics* with an extensive discussion of theological methodology, a discussion that immediately raises the question of the role modern discourses of philosophy and science should play in theology.[33] He asserts that theology, like any other critical discipline, should follow a "path" or "way of knowledge" that is appropriate to its subject matter,

31. Irigaray, "Divine Women," 9; Grosz, *Sexual Subversions,* 160.

32. Karl Barth, *Church Dogmatics,* vol. 3, part 4, ed. G. W. Bromiley, T. R. Torrance, trans., Harold Knight, G. W. Bromiley, J. K. S. Reid and R. H. Fuller (Edinburgh: T & T Clark, 1961), 157. For a critical analysis of this discussion see Jacquelyn Grant, *White Woman's Christ and Black Woman's Jesus: Feminist Christology and Womanist Response* (Atlanta: Scholars Press, 1989), 71. Also see Joan Romero, "The Protestant Principle: A Woman's-Eye View of Barth and Tillich," in *Religion and Sexism,* ed. Rosemary Ruether (New York: Simon and Schuster, 1974), 319–40.

33. Barth, *Church Dogmatics,* vol. 1, part 1, trans. G. W. Bromiley (Edinburgh: T & T Clark, 1975), 3–44.

which in the case of theology is God. Having established this common ground between theology and the other sciences, Barth then proceeds to denounce sharply theologians who have employed methodological procedures borrowed from other disciplines for the purpose of defining the path of knowledge suited to an inquiry into knowledge of God. Given that the conceptual "systems" of these disciplines are constructed around certain organizing principles that determine or legislate the terms under which identity is conferred upon all elements within it, Barth argues it is dangerous to use their systems of analysis to determine the identity and nature of God. Why? Because when God becomes one of the elements within such a system, the identity attributed to God is one that draws its defining borders from the rules governing science and philosophy. The resulting theological analysis simply reflects the logic internal to a system whose procedural rules are not governed by the subject matter of theology, God. When this occurs, the distinct identity of God as the self-generating, self-motivated subject is repressed and replaced by an identity appropriate to the systematic mastery of the founding and yet foreign conceptual scheme.

Barth further develops this critique in volume 2:1, in his diatribe against "natural theology" or "liberal theology."[34] According to Barth, the majority of Enlightenment theologians have made a serious methodological error in analyzing the character and nature of our knowledge of God. In an apologetic effort to render God intelligible to the modern person, they have taken the experience of the subject as the starting point of their theological reflections. The problem with adopting such a starting point, Barth argues, is that once again the identity of the divine is ruled and circumscribed

34. Barth, *Church Dogmatics*, vol. 2, part 1, trans. Parker, Johnston, Knight, Haire, (Edinburgh: T & T Clark, 1957), 3–254. For Barth's critique of natural theology, also see his debate with Emil Brunner in *Natural Theology* (London: Centenary Press, 1946). For his critique of the nineteenth-century liberal theology of Friedrich Schleiermacher, see Barth, *The Theology of Schleiermacher*, ed. Dietrich Ritschl, trans. G. W. Bromiley (Grand Rapids: W. B. Eerdmans, 1982). On twentieth-century liberal theology, see *Karl Barth—Rudolf Bultmann Letters, 1922–1966*, ed. B. Jasper, trans. G. W. Bromiley (Grand Rapids: W. B. Eerdmans, 1981).

by a conceptuality that originates elsewhere; and the results are theologically disastrous. In an argument that closely parallels that of Feuerbach's analysis of religion as the projection of human desire upon a falsely inscribed divine screen, Barth claims that any theology that commences with subjective introspection inevitably ends with a Word of God that is nothing more than a reflection of the same. Thus, to use Irigaray's language, these liberal theologians engage in an enterprise ruled by a logic of mimicry. However, in this case, the position occupied by the feminine in phallocentric discourse is now occupied by God, the mirror that simply reflects the narcissistic gaze of the theologian. Similarly, this liberal theological enterprise has it own "blind spots." To render its own subjective reflections divine, it represses or hides, by sleight of hand, its own projective moment. In doing so, it falsely attributes an objective otherness to a divinity that in fact wears the face of its generative subject, "man."

On the basis of these parallels, one can begin to appreciate the interesting points of confluence between Irigaray's critique of philosophy and Barth's critique of natural theology. They both agree that the logic of philosophy (or any totalizing cultural framework) systematically excludes the possibility of admitting true difference and hence excludes the possibility of identifying subjects that are incommensurable with philosophy's central principles. As such, the philosopher's tool can never render an identity of either woman or God that is not finally reducible to the identity of "man."

In addition to this shared critique, another interesting parallel between Barth and Irigaray emerges when one analyzes their reasons for exposing the problematic working of Western rationality. Both engage in a critique of the "logic of same" for reasons that extend beyond a playful interest in dissecting and exposing the instabilities inherent in Western philosophy or natural theology. In this sense, they are compelled by motives that differentiate their projects from similar critiques of philosophy and theology developed by poststructuralist theorists and postmodern philosophers of religion.[35] In contrast to the disinterested and apolitical projects

35. This difference becomes apparent when one compares the theological motives that drive Barth's critique of natural theology to the philosophical interests that undergird the work of Mark C. Taylor, *Erring: A Post-Modern A/Theology* (Chicago: University of Chicago Press, 1984); and *Altarity* (Chicago: University of Chicago Press, 1987).

of these thinkers, both Irigaray and Barth are driven by their commitment to communities whose very identity has been colonized and distorted by a culture that profits from the play of this "logic of the same." Thus, both recognize that the stakes in the "old game of symmetry" are high and, even more importantly, they recognize that the cost to its losers is profound. For Irigaray, the violence endemic to the old game of philosophy costs women their voice, their agency, their very identities as subjects whose incommensurability resists the phallomorphic economy imposed upon them. For Barth, the violence of the liberal game so deafens one's ear and blinds one's eyes that the true identity of God, the incommensurable other, is lost at great cost to the creature. In terms of social cost, Barth believes that it is precisely this "logic of the same" which allowed liberal German theologians to embrace the genocidal policies of German nationalism during the Second World War.

Barth and Irigaray not only share an explicit acknowledgment that their critiques emerge out of a particular set of communal/political commitments, they also both share in the belief that the knowledge lost or repressed by the "old game" is communally/politically *redemptive* knowledge. For Irigaray, the knowledge sacrificed is one that admits women's voice, their presence, their identity(ies). For Barth, it is a knowledge of the One who loves in freedom and thereby invites the creature into noncoercive and reciprocal communion. Thus, for both, this eclipsed but redemptive knowledge requires recognition of the incommensurable difference of the "other." In Irigaray's case, this redemptive difference "lets women be women" in a multiplicity so fertile that even the notions of "being" and "woman" break open and dissolve. It is also a difference that, in Barth's case, "lets God be God" in a freedom and a love that originates in God's own self and thereby subverts and displaces old philosophical and subjectivist notions of being and God.

Because of these commitments, Barth, like Irigaray, incorporates his critique into the framework of a broader constructive theology.[36] Once again, there are interesting similarities between

36. Just as *Speculum* issues into *This Sex,* so too, Barth's *Commentary on Romans* issues into the *Church Dogmatics*. Barth, *The Epistle to the Romans,* trans. Edwyn C. Hoskyns (London: Oxford University Press, 1933).

the reasons they each give for moving into the constructive realm. As I explained earlier, Irigaray intentionally moves beyond the poststructuralist critique of Derrida and others because she recognizes that although they may have succeeded in exposing the pretensions of "man" as the master trope of philosophy, they still posit this deconstructed trope as the center of their reflections and hence leave the exiled "woman" in exile.[37] In his early work, *The Epistle to the Romans,* Barth first launches his critique against liberal theology by claiming that contrary to the subjectivist attempts to colonize the identity of God, the God one meets in Christian scriptures is a God who is "known as the unknown," the God who is not "man."[38] As a form of what he calls "dialectical theology," this work primarily consists of a radical critique of our ability to know God and hence a radical critique of the theological mastery of God by "man." However, in the *Church Dogmatics,* he moves away from the position of pure critique and begins to make constructive theological claims about positive knowledge of God. This move is grounded in his realization that while dialectical theology may expose the pretensions of "man," it still takes this "arrogant man" as its starting point and therefore leaves the exiled God in epistemic exile.

To move beyond this impasse, Barth boldly marches into the realm of constructive theology and struggles to carve out a space that frees the "Word of God" from its liberal prison. Yet Barth proceeds with a caution similar to Irigaray's. It is born of his recognition that although language, with its systematizing proclivities, inevitably reduces God to a cultural projection, the theologian cannot simply step out of language and enter the constructive sphere untainted. However, this recognition is for Barth, as it is for Irigaray, not finally disabling. Rather, it presents him with a challenge, namely, the challenge to situate oneself within language in such a way that it breaks open and internally subverts the traditional rules of reference that ground the "logic of the same." Barth accomplishes this "breaking open" in several ways.

37. See Irigaray, "Sexual Difference," *French Feminist Thought: A Reader,* ed. Toril Moi (London: Basil Blackwell, 1987), 118–19.

38. *Epistle to the Romans,* 96.

On a strictly conceptual level, Barth demystifies the way that theological language works by claiming that the Christian's God-talk refers to God by means of *analogia fidei* (analogy of faith) rather than *analogia entis* (analogy of being). In traditional accounts of theological language, images and symbols taken from the natural order and human experience are able to refer to God by nature of their analogous correspondence "in being" with the One to which they point. This assumption of ontological parity runs the risk, Barth argues, of once again attributing to God a description, "in being," that is simply a reflection or projection of the natural order. To avoid this confusion, Barth suggests that theological language refers to God's reality only insofar as the logic of faith governs its rules of reference. In this sense, the power of language to point to God resides not in its natural ability to refer but rather in a distinct set of communal norms and linguistic practices that legislate its terms of reference. For Barth, these norms for reference include the confession that it is through the power of the Holy Spirit that God is able to deputize and use language to convey a presence that does not adhere "naturally" within it. Thus, this shift from analogy of being to analogy of faith functions to undermine the notions of identity and natural presence that haunt classical linguistic theory and hence the theology of those who adopt it. It thereby exposes one of theology's traditional "blind spots" by making it clear that the uncritical deployment of images and symbols does not automatically ensure the presence of God's identity. Once again, this parallels Irigaray's claims that "woman" is not automatically made "present" by the workings of a phallocentric language which claims to have identified her.

Barth adopts another strategy for breaking open language that is similar to Irigaray's notions of "jamming the discursive mechanisms." Given that Barth recognizes that theology must and inevitably will use concepts and images drawn from philosophy and from the broader culture, he freely deploys such images throughout the *Church Dogmatics,* as for instance, in his use of Buber's famous "I-Thou" scenario and in his use of Bloch's materialist notion of "being in act." However, he uses these concepts in such a way that no one philosophical framework is adopted in its entirety. Instead, he draws bits and pieces from a variety of conceptual frameworks, deploying them in an *ad hoc* manner which is chaotic enough to jam the discursive workings of any one system. Thus, without presuming to have stepped outside the mediated structures of thought, Barth subverts the systematic mastery of philosophical language by playing one master off another.

In addition to these parallels between Barth's and Irigaray's critiques of philosophy's "logic of the same" and the conspicuously disruptive manner in which they occupy their own positions of enunciation, the actual contents of their constructive proposals share a number of similar features. Just as Irigaray's elaboration of the "two-lips" represents her attempt to counter the phallomorphic imaginary of Western discourse, Barth elaborates a doctrine of the Trinity that serves as an identifying description of God that, in being true to God's own incommensurable otherness, resists the colonizing proclivities of the liberal theologians. How does it resist such colonization?

Barth commences his discussion of the doctrine of God with the argument that God's being is in God's act, that God's very essence is comprised of the work that God does.[39] To describe the act that is God's essence, Barth turns to traditional trinitarian language. In relation to the creature, God's action is threefold. God is the originating one or "Father" from whom the "Son" comes and with whom the "Son" is One. And the "Son" shares in the "Father" through the "Spirit" through which the "Son" also shares in the life of the creature. This description of the economic Trinity, then, becomes for Barth the basis for understanding the immanent Trinity, the being of God in Godself. In terms of the immanent Trinity, Barth describes God as being internally and eternally self-relating, always other to God's own self. Thus, for Barth, God's very reality is radically multiple, radically relational, and infinitely active.

Barth stresses this point with great emphasis in his well-known attack on various forms of trinitarian modalism that he claims define God's being as residing essentially in a prior and static unity or oneness. This static metaphysic of being, according to Barth, denies the essential threeness and hence relationality of God

39. For Barth's discussion of "being in act," see *Church Dogmatics*, vol. 2, part I, 257–321.

by reducing God's threeness to discrete actions or *personae* that emanate from the static One. In opposition to this kind of trinitarian imagery, Barth recalls the language of the Cappadocians, who argued that God's true being does not consist of a static oneness but rather of multiplicity, of three in the constant activity of self-relating. Here one finds corollaries to Irigaray's constructive proposal. On the one hand, this description of the Trinity cuts against Western discourse's phallomorphic preference for static identity and ontic stability. On the other hand, just as Irigaray claims that woman's pleasure is not one but multiple, diffuse, infinitely open to the other, one might say that this triune God's pleasure is diffuse, multiple, and open.

The analogy with Irigaray's description of the "two-lips" goes even further. For Barth, it is precisely because God is internally other to God's own self that God's relating to the human creature cannot and should not be understood as a relating in which God seeks the human creature for the purpose of God's self-knowledge. God does not need the creature in order to know or to actualize Godself because God is eternally self-knowing. To use Irigaray's language, God is autoerotic and not phallomorphic because God's identity runs counter to the phallomorphic imaginary, which assumes that in order to know himself man (or God) needs an other such as language, his hand, or the female body. Given that God is always already other to God's own self, God's relation to the creature is not born of a necessity that devours the other for self-knowledge; it is instead a relating that is free, unwarranted, and grounded in unconditional love. It is love for the sake of love, a love which leaves the one loved free to be truly different, free to be other in a real and substantive sense and not simply a mirror that reflects the self back to the self.

Barth works out the anthropological and ethical implications of this description of God in the third volume of the *Dogmatics*.[40] Here Barth uses this trinitarian doctrine of God as the basis for developing his doctrine of the human person. The true essence, purpose, and being of the human person, he claims, resides in

40. Barth, *Church Dogmatics*, vol. 3, part 2, trans. and ed. G. W. Bromiley, T. F. Torrance (Edinburgh: T & T Clark, 1960), 55–324.

one's relations, in one's relation to God and to fellow human beings. This relationality, for Barth, defines the very being of the creature. As with God, being is in act for the person, and it is the act of relating that constitutes one's essence. For this reason, Barth rejects traditional doctrines of the human person, which posit a substantive essence or a structural ontology which seeks to define persons as having a static or monadic being. Furthermore, this relating should not be a relating that, in the Hegelian sense, serves as the foundation for self-knowledge, a relating in which the other becomes mirror. No, this relating should be noncoercive, free, loving, and open to the radical difference of the other. In terms of relating to God, then, this relating does not attempt projectively to consume God. Rather, it acknowledges that God as Other comes to the person. Similarly, in terms of our relationships with other persons, our interactions should reflect the same respect for difference by resisting the urge to consume the other and instead opening ourselves to the multiplicity and complexity of "the neighbor." In this sense, the essence of the human person is always eschatological; it is always coming into being through the acts of relating that constitute personhood. Again, the parallels with Irigaray's essentialism are interesting, for Barth's essentialism is an essentialism which is not one. It is multiple, as multiple as its relations, and it is always an essentialism of the future.

POINTS OF CONFLICT AND CHALLENGE

My analysis of Irigaray and Barth has focused thus far on the similarities between their projects. However, the commonalities that I have outlined represent only a portion of the issues that emerge when one considers Irigaray and Barth together. There are also many points at which sparks fly, at which conflict erupts, points at which the two discourses move in opposing directions. In this final section, I want to touch briefly upon several of these points in an effort to illustrate the ways in which each challenges the other.

Let me begin with the challenges Irigaray might put to Barth. The first of these challenges has to do with the depth and scope of Barth's critique of philosophical and scientific discourse. Although Barth is adamant about the misuse of these discourses within the realm of theology, he is fairly uncritical of their discursive usefulness when they stay within the perimeters of their designated disciplines. Irigaray, in contrast, critiques the workings of philosophical and scientific discourse in general. She argues that their dangerously colonizing proclivities come into play regardless of the specificity of their disciplinary location. On the basis of this assessment of Western discourse, Irigaray would most likely critique Barth for limiting his account of the "logic of the same" to the field of theology. While Barth might respond by claiming that he limits his critique to theology because theology is his primary subject matter, Irigaray could point to distinctly theological consequences of his failure to apply his critique beyond the bounds of his own discourse. On this score, she might argue that he has no basis for analyzing the corruptive proclivities of the bits and pieces he borrows from other disciplines because his critique of the discourse of philosophy and science does not run deep enough.[41] In this sense, Irigaray's compelling assessment of the dangers of discourse in general could serve to strengthen the normative criteria a theologian like Barth might use to determine the usefulness of culturally borrowed concepts and images.

Second, Irigaray would most certainly call into question the phallocentric remainders that adhere in Barth's theology, remainders that run much deeper than the overt sexism displayed in his assessment of "men and women." This phallocentric remainder appears first in his critique of natural or liberal theology. Although Barth argues that the consequence of the liberal enterprise is the construction of a God who simply reflects the subjective experience of "man," he assumes this "man" encompasses humanity in general and hence he never acknowledges the gendered character of the "man" whose reflection genders God as male. This "oversight" is

41. For instance, if Barth had been more critical of philosophy's "phallocentrism," he may have been less enthusiastic about borrowing Buber's famous notion of the "I–Thou" relationship to depict the interaction between God and persons. The difficulties that Irigaray could point to in this "I–Thou" scenario rest in its implicit concession to static notions of being.

particularly glaring given that Barth is enough of an historicist to recognize that the "liberal man" he critiques is not just a universal man, but the bourgeois man of late nineteenth- and early twentieth-century Germany. The fact that he recognizes the role played by class and national identity in the construction of this "man" but refuses to acknowledge the social construction of this "man's" gendered identity points to a blind spot in his own critique. Thus, his theology hides a gender essentialism that prevents him from cutting as deeply as he needs into the heart of the problem undergirding the project of the liberal theologians. In this sense, one could move beyond Barth, and from a feminist perspective use Irigaray to deepen and expand a critique of the liberal project and natural theology in such a way that its gendered subtext is exposed and its distinctively phallocentric blind spots revealed.

Third, Irigaray would be highly critical of the phallocentric remainder that haunts his constructive proposal as well. While she is not critical of God-talk in general—in fact she claims that women need a God to save them—she makes it clear that the doctrine of the Trinity, in its presently gendered form, cannot provide this salvation. In her essay "Equal to Whom," she argues that the economy of relations instantiated by the doctrine of the Trinity privileges the relation between Father and Son and represses the productive ground of woman.[42] Thus, within this masculine economy of relations, there is no woman, there is no mother, and there is no model for mother-daughter relating. Subsequently, there is no "horizon" within the Trinity that beckons "her" to become. For this reason, women cannot be saved by the male Christ event. At this point, she might also critique Barth on his own grounds by pointing out that his uncritical embrace of a masculine economy of relations

42. Irigaray, "Equal to Whom," *differences* 1 (1989): 59–76. In this article, Irigaray is more concerned with the economy of relations inscribed within the scriptural narratives than she is with the economy of relations formulated in traditional doctrines of the Trinity, although her critiques of the narratives can easily be brought to bear on these doctrines as well. In fact, her differences with Elisabeth Schüssler Fiorenza might have been better focused if Irigaray had recognized the conceptual distinctions in kind that exist between the New Testament narratives and the doctrine of the Trinity.

carries him into the dangerous waters of liberal and natural theology insofar as he, like his opponents, projects his own identity as "man" upon the Godhead. This critique, however, should not be interpreted as suggesting that Irigaray believes a female Godhead would solve the problems of theological phallocentrism. Quite to the contrary, she argues that "Goddess language" can incorporate the "logic of the same" and its totalizing and dominating proclivities as easily as a masculine divinity.

For these reasons, Irigaray would argue that the phallocentric character of Barth's doctrine of God is not confined to his explicit gendering of the Trinity. It is manifest also in the fact that for Barth, God stands as the privileged term in the binary opposition between God and creation. As such, Barth's God still occupies the position of master trope, the Law, the Logos, the central principle of identity. And even though Barth maintains that this God is multiple and relates to the creature in a noncoercive and free manner, this God is clearly not the equal of humanity. This God is Sovereign Other, the Providential Ruler, the One who confers identity by virtue of "His" relation to the creature. As such, the relation between God and humanity is hierarchicalized, with privilege conferred upon the first term. Thus, despite the affinities between his Trinity and Irigaray's "two-lips," the presence of hierarchy in Barth's theology radically separates the two.

Given that Irigaray still wants to speak of "God," it is important to ask how she defines divinity without falling into such a hierarchical scheme. As I discussed earlier in my analysis of Irigaray's remarks on theology, she accomplishes this by getting rid of the first term, by getting rid of the notion that God is objective other and by asserting that the God that will save women will be a God of their own creation, their own projection of all that is divine within them. In this scenario, God is no longer the transcendent other or the one who bears the marks of an irreducible ontological difference. Thus, between God and woman, there is no hierarchy because there is no difference. This raises another point that distinguishes Barth and Irigaray on the question of God. For Barth, God is an objective reality that exists quite apart from human imaginings. In this sense, God is truly an incommensurable other whose being is ontologically real and not merely the projection of more perfect becoming.

This last point leads directly into my discussion of the challenges that Barth would present to Irigaray. Despite all his phallocentric shortcomings, Barth clearly wants to maintain the incommensurable otherness of God, the irreducible difference of the One who in freedom loves the creature. Given Irigaray's interest in preserving the incommensurable otherness of woman, it would seem that a similar respect for difference would appear in her doctrine of God. However, it does not. God, for Irigaray, is the idealized, projected other of women's emerging subjectivity. God's otherness is thereby reduced to a function of the idealized role God fills. From Barth's perspective, it would appear that Irigaray, like the natural theologians and the phallocentric philosophers, is simply reenacting the very logic of the same that she formerly denounced. Granted, it is the multiple and indeterminate female subject, not the unitary male, who projects; but as far as the "other" (God) of theology is concerned, there is finally no room for true alterity. To use Irigarayan language, it would seem that female desire has consumed God. Caught once again in the old game of symmetry, God is merely the screen necessary for self-knowledge, the mirror that reflects the narcissistic gaze of the subject, the hand that must touch the phallus (or her lips) for the purpose of self-identification.

This reduction of God to the "ego ideal" specific to the subjectivity of women, Barth might add, is not only problematic in relation to her doctrine of God; it also has destructive consequences for Irigaray's project as a whole. Although Irigaray maintains that Western thought must embrace an understanding of true, incommensurable sexual difference in order to allow true difference in human relations to flourish, her model of the God-human relation moves in the opposite direction. The question then arises, how can Irigaray maintain an ethic of difference in human relations if the normative model of the God-human relation is one in which difference is reduced to a function of the subject and thereby dissolved as true difference? If theology actually carries the high degree of normative cultural power that Irigaray suggests it does, then what are the social consequences of figuring God as a purely aesthetic, ethical, and political ideal? The consequences would seem to be the reinscription, at the theological level, of the very idealized "logic of the same" that Irigaray correctly identifies as having repressive social consequences when it serves as the norm for the movement of thought in general.

How is it that Irigaray gets entangled in this seeming inconsistency? A partial answer to this question lies, I believe, in her atypically uncritical adoption of Feuerbach's critique of religion. In her early works, Irigaray was scrupulously careful not to make constructive use of any form of general epistemology, metaphysics, or phenomenology of identity or action. She resisted using such general philosophical frameworks because they inevitably universalize the notion of subjectivity and its structure and thereby rule out the possibility of taking difference, in all its historical particularity, into account. It seems that when she turns to the topic of God, however, she lets her guard down and incorporates the phenomenology of religion suggested by Feuerbach. In doing so, she allows his critical apparatus to form the definitive *locus* for imagining the relationship between the human and the divine. The unfortunate consequences of such a capitulation are obvious. First, she implicitly commits herself to a set of anthropological claims that are ideal, general, and seemingly immune to history and the social construction of identity. By anchoring her anthropology in this manner, Irigaray leaves herself vulnerable to the criticism that her understanding of subjectivity is no longer as open-ended as she claims it should be. Second, as I have previously stated, she commits herself to a notion of religion that is equally ideal and hence unable to admit the possibility of God as the real, incommensurable other.

Irigaray's fall into phenomenology, however, offers only a partial explanation for the theological problem in which she becomes entangled. The other, and perhaps more compelling explanation for her idealization of the divine lies in her recognition that although women need a God, this God must not be posited in such a way that a hierarchical dualism is reinstantiated. To avoid the dangers of granting privileged status to one term over and against the other, she quite intentionally dissolves the dualism altogether. It is here that we find her and Barth standing at sharpest odds, for

Barth relentlessly seeks to protect the difference, the otherness of God who is and remains the One who cannot be reduced to mere subjective projection. However, Barth's theology represents a prime example of why Irigaray resists such a move. To protect God's otherness, Barth embraces a hierarchical dualism that reproduces the very model of social relations that Irigaray anticipates it will. For Barth, just as Christ is head of the church, so too man precedes woman: he initiates, she follows. And so the "old game of symmetry" begins.

What is most striking about this standoff between Barth and Irigaray is the degree to which they share a common goal. They are both concerned "to make it possible for us to think" about subjectivity, agency, history, and God in a new way. And they challenge us to think anew by setting up a model of relationality in which real difference can be thought, in which knowledge of the other does not require that the other be devoured in subjective self-reflection. They likewise share a concern that our understanding of human persons not be encrusted with unexamined layers of philosophical speculation but that it instead remain open to an understanding of essence found only in relationship and only in the future tense—in the continual coming into being through relationships with other persons and with God. As such, they set for us a vision of identity in which difference is recognized as irreducible, a vision that can seriously embrace not only the difference between creature and creator in Barth's theology, or sexual difference in Irigaray's case, but difference also with regard to class, race, ethnicity, sexuality, and the unlimited differences that fragment even these categories themselves. But in this shared vision, they leave us caught in a confounding theological tension. How does one, on the one hand, affirm the otherness and difference of God and persons without reinvoking destructive hierarchies? On the other hand, how does one challenge this dangerous dualism without falling into a theological monism that finally cannot account for divine-human difference and in turn risks undermining the celebration of difference between persons?

The answers to these questions, I believe, lie somewhere between Barth and Irigaray. In terms of an understanding of God, Irigaray's analysis of the social dangers inherent in a theology that reinscribes a hierarchicalized dualism needs to be regarded with utmost seriousness. If one does not heed her warnings on this issue, then no matter what gender or relational substance one attributes to the Godhead, this Godhead will ultimately devour difference by virtue of its privileged position. However, Irigaray's theological reflections must be challenged on the issue of difference as it exists between persons and God. Fending off hierarchy by dissolving difference at this point seems to be not only unnecessary but, in the long run, dangerous. For if the difference between God and humanity cannot be affirmed, then how can difference between human persons be fully embraced? It seems that theology, truly to challenge its phallocentric moorings, at the very least must grant to God the same integrity and recognition of incommensurable difference that it grants to human persons.

When we place Irigaray and Barth "near to" one another, the complex spectrum of reflections and refractions that emerge from their interplay may leave one a bit dazzled, a bit frayed and disoriented, and it most certainly leaves one without clear-cut answers to the questions they raise. The interplay does, however, illuminate a direction in which contemporary theology is called to move if it takes seriously the challenges raised by both French feminists and postliberal Barthians. It is a direction that, if followed, promises adventure and risk, and most importantly, conflict. Its signposts are not clear and its ending is not predetermined. What is clear, however, is that the God confessed by each is, contrary to traditional metaphysics, a God who is not One but multiple, active, and relational. And if this God is truly to meet humanity in a relationship of mutuality, then this God must also be respected as incommensurably other, as a sign as well as an actual event of true alterity.

6

Questioning "Woman" in Feminist/Womanist Theology

IRIGARAY, RUETHER, AND DALY

ELLEN T. ARMOUR

One of the principal issues facing feminist theology today involves coming to terms with the diversity of issues and perspectives that need to be and are addressed in the name of 'woman.' Often this means we feminists are called to account. Critiques of feminist theology by women of color argue that feminist theology speaks from and to the concerns of white women. The experience of living at the intersection of racism and sexism leads womanist scholars such as Delores Williams to criticize the *substance* of white feminist analysis at two major points: (1) "women's experience" in white feminism reflects white middle-class women's experience, but not that of women of color and/or of other classes; (2) the feminist claim that patriarchy is the root of all other forms of oppression is inadequate and again reflects the experiences of white women with white males and white male-dominated institutions.

Williams criticizes the feminist critique of patriarchy—understood *either* as direct male dominance over women *or* as a socioeconomic pyramidical system of graded dominations with white men at the top and lower-class women of color at the bottom—on three grounds: (1) it fails to name accurately the distinctiveness of *racist* oppression experienced by women of color and their families at the hands of white-controlled American institutions; (2) it threatens to cover over the benefits that white women and their families receive at the hands of these same institutions; and (3) it threatens to obscure racism as it is perpetuated intentionally or unintentionally by white women, including white feminists.[1]

These criticisms come as something of a shock to white feminists. Most of us would say, in our defense, that our intentions with regard to "inclusiveness" (and this in itself points to a problem) have been good. However, we would have to admit that these criticisms reveal, at the very least, our failure to get to know the full range of the constituency for whom we claim to speak and to come to terms with our own history as white women in this country. I am going to argue in this essay that womanist criticisms of feminist theology *also* indict deeper "realities" at work in our thinking, writing, and speaking as Euro-Americans, which structure in a certain blindness to differences. Exposing these structurings takes us beyond the level of our intentions, good or bad, to unquestioned presuppositions that govern our texts. Feminist thinking/writing/speaking does not emerge *ex nihilo* from our minds/pens/mouths, but bears the marks of the discourse within which it resonates, the discourse of Western culture. I use this term to name a composite of patterns of thinking that recur throughout Western history. This pattern is so ingrained in its fabric of Western culture that it structures our discourse in ways we take for granted. Some of these structures include the hierarchical oppositions of good/evil, spirit/nature, white/black, male/female. They also include such concepts as being, unity, and an essential human nature (characteristically

1. See Delores S. Williams, "The Color of Feminism," *Christianity and Crisis*, April 29, 1985, and "The Color of Feminism: Or Speaking the Black Woman's Tongue," *Journal of Religious Thought* 42:1 (Spring/Summer 1986). For other criticisms of white feminist thought and practice, see *Home Girls: A Black Feminist Anthology* (New York: Kitchen Table Women of Color Press, 1983), especially Barbara Smith's introduction to the collection and Bernice Johnson Reagon's contribution to it. See also *This Bridge Called My Back: Writings by Radical Women of Color*, Cherríe Moraga and Gloria Anzaldúa, eds. (New York: Kitchen Table Women of Color Press, 1983). For details regarding the history of relations between white and black women activists, see Paula Giddings, *When and Where I Enter: The Impact of Black Women on Race and Sex in America* (New York: Bantam Books, 1984).

understood as a self that constitutes itself by making autonomous decisions about who and what it wants to be). These structures have not governed the history of Western thinking uniformly and without coming into question, as even a brief survey of scholarship from this century reveals. The work of Jacques Derrida and Michel Foucault has awakened us in recent times to the ebb and flow of historical forces in the production of ideas. Derrida's work in particular reveals that the reign of these structures throughout the centuries of Western thinking has been marked as much by resistances to them as by their triumph.[2] Freudian, Marxist, and Foucauldian analyses have undercut the notion of an autonomous self. Several of those who have mounted critiques of sexism and racism, for example, have been especially critical of hierarchical dualisms as well as of the notion of an essential nature that all human beings share.[3] However, I am going to argue that these discursive structures—particularly the structure of an essential humanity (or, in these cases, femininity)—continue to function in feminist thinking to the detriment of its dealings with issues of race and class. Insofar as these structures are implicated in the criticisms of feminism raised by womanists, for example, they need to be unearthed and, in some way, exorcised. I view this task as one that attempts part of what womanists call feminists to do, namely, to investigate for ourselves ways in which we feminists are part of the problem rather

2. See, for example, *Dissemination* (Chicago: University of Chicago Press, 1981), esp. "Plato's Pharmacy," and *Margins of Philosophy* (Chicago: University of Chicago Press, 1982), especially the essay entitled "The Ends of Man," 109–36.

3. For example, this critique is central to the work of the two feminist theologians featured in this paper, Rosemary Radford Ruether and Mary Daly, as well as a number of other feminist and womanist thinkers. See, e.g., Ruether's *Sexism and God-Talk: Toward a Feminist Theology* (Boston: Beacon Press, 1983), chaps. 2 and 3; Daly's *Gyn/Ecology: The Metaethics of Radical Feminism* (Boston: Beacon Press, 1978); and Daly's *Pure Lust: Elemental Feminist Philosophy* (Boston: Beacon Press, 1984). See also Sallie McFague's two recent books, *Metaphorical Theology: Models of God in Religious Language* (Philadelphia: Fortress Press, 1982) and *Models of God: Theology for an Ecological Nuclear Age* (Philadelphia: Fortress Press, 1987), especially chap. 1. Cherríe Moraga's article "La Guera" and Doris Davenport's article, "The Pathology of Racism" also feature such criticisms (see both pieces in *This Bridge Called My Back*).

than the solution in order that we might be better able to embody the solidarity we claim to desire. In the first portion of my essay, I will follow the trajectory of issues of race and class through the writings of two centrifugal feminist theologians, Mary Daly and Rosemary Ruether, to find out what these trajectories reveal about subterranean discursive structures at work in these writers' texts. In the second half I will explore the work of the French feminist psychoanalyst, philosopher, and linguist Luce Irigaray to discern ways in which her writings can be helpful to feminist theology as it grapples with these issues.

QUESTIONING "WOMAN" IN FEMINIST THEO/ALOGY: MARY DALY

Womanist critiques suggest that we feminist theologians have assumed that all women share a common female identity. If women are all at bottom, the same, and the oppression we suffer differs only in quantity (depending on our race and/or class and/or sexual orientation), then we can name our common enemy or oppressor as the same: patriarchy. This assessment of where feminist theology finds itself is borne out in the work of two of our most significant feminist thinkers, Mary Daly and Rosemary Radford Ruether.

Mary Daly is arguably one of the most creative and powerful voices in feminist theo/alogy today. The feminist critique of patriarchal Christianity has never found a more eloquent voice than Daly's in her groundbreaking works, *Beyond God the Father* and *The Church of the Second Sex*. In *Gyn/Ecology* and *Pure Lust*, Daly's passionate desire to eliminate the pain women suffer and to envision new possibilities for their lives funds an unhesitating critique of whatever she sees that hinders, represses, or oppresses women. However, disturbing difficulties emerge when one examines her recent work in light of criticisms of feminist thinking raised by womanist scholars. In *Gyn/Ecology* and *Pure Lust*, Daly targets worldwide patriarchy in some of its most horrible manifestations. In *Gyn/Ecology*, she undertakes powerful critical examinations of the structures of patriarchal thinking that make Chinese footbinding, Indian *suttee*, African genital mutilation, and the practice of American gynecology possible. She is fully prepared to defend herself in the event that men well-versed in cultural relativism should accuse her of racism and imperialism. However, when faced with the charge of racism from a woman of color such as Audre Lord, her response exhibits tensions and resistances that are much more problematic than productive. In "An Open Letter to Mary Daly,"[4] Lord praises Daly for her creativity and courage and obvious love for women, yet criticizes the locus granted to women of color in *Gyn/Ecology*. Non-Western women, she argues, appear only as victims and preyers upon each other in this text. Nowhere do they appear as examples of love, goodness, or of divine or human power to resist oppression. This "dismissal" of women of color obliterates the distinctiveness of racist oppression and continues what Lord and other womanist writers argue is the standard pattern of relationship between white women and women of color.

Though never explicitly named, this exchange (or others like it) leaves traces in Daly's next book, *Pure Lust*. On one hand, Daly seems to have listened to criticisms like Lord's and has attempted to broaden the scope of her analysis of women's oppression to include their experiences of racism and poverty. In the Introduction to the book, Daly names racism as one of the "man-made racetracks" of phallocratism and insists that, as such, it should be a target of confrontation by Lusty women. Daly makes repeated references in this book to the multiple problems faced by women of color and poor women. She also uses novels by Toni Morrison and Alice Walker to illustrate the kind of female bonding she wants to promote. However, racism and classism, which are subsets of misogynism in Daly's scheme, serve to triple the *amount* of oppression faced by women. Daly does not address racism or classism as *distinctive* oppressions. As for relations between white women and women of color, Daly places at least a share of the responsibility for white women's racism in our laps (especially those of our slaveholder ancestors). However, she attributes white women's perpetuation of racism to patriarchy. Patriarchy has so separated us from our true Selves, (which would, by implication, be loving and nonoppressive) she argues, that we act in accordance with patriarchal

4. Audre Lord, "An Open Letter to Mary Daly," in *This Bridge Called My Back: Writings by Radical Women of Color*, 94–97.

values rather than our truest values.[5] Daly also uses the same strategy to remove feminism from womanist critiques. In the Foreground to the First Realm Daly condemns "women who have chosen to call themselves feminist and lesbian" who "irrationally conver[t] terms such as *racist*, *classist*, and *elitist* into labels that function to hinder rather than foster the Movement/Race of women" (67). Calling these complaints by women of color against feminism "horizontal violence," she writes, "Instead of Naming the *active perpetrators* of the social evils they claim to oppose, they choose the cowardly device of scapegoating women" (68). Audre Lord (along with any others who might criticize feminism's racism) has truly been "dismissed" from Daly's text and, in fact, from "feminism" itself.[6] This anonymous "they" who accuse other feminists of racism are letting themselves be used as tools of patriarchy and failing to place blame where it finally belongs: in the hands of the fathers. Although Daly says later in *Pure Lust* that women should be held accountable for their conscious racism, her discussions of the dynamics of relationships between women across boundaries of culture and/or religion (Jewish and Arab, Northern and Southern Ireland, for example) always blame any divisions caused by one or the other camp's racist rhetoric on patriarchy's use of these women as tools. Thus, I would argue, women who knowingly or unknowingly perpetuate racism are, in the final analysis, excused by Daly. Her interpretation fails to take seriously the complexities of the

5. Mary Daly, *Pure Lust*, 70–72, for a full elaboration of her critique of this "horizontal violence." See pp. 80 and 143–45 for descriptions of what women would be like beyond the reaches of patriarchy. Further reference will be parenthetical within the text.

6. Admittedly, the intended recipients of this criticism are not named in any way in the text. Sharon Welch tells me that such accusations have been used destructively within women's communities in the Northeast and she argues that Daly's charges here refer to that dynamic. If so, it would be helpful for Daly to *name* that as the target of her criticism (e.g., cite some examples) and/or make it clear whether she thinks charges of racism within and among women can be legitimate. Would Daly see dealing with such charges constructively as *necessary* to "foster[ing] the race of women"? An acknowledgment by Daly of the constructive impact criticisms like Lord's appear to have had on her own work would be an important counterpoint to this otherwise problematic refutation.

legacy of the intertwining of race and gender issues. The history of the women's suffrage movement, if nothing else, reminds us that one can be both a feminist and a racist. When, for example, Susan B. Anthony argues for women's suffrage on the grounds that granting the vote to black men "dethroned fifteen million white women . . . and cast them under the heel of the lowest orders of manhood,"[7] she is just as culpable for her racist ideology as any man. Contemporary women of color continue to find working with white women problematic. Dismissing both their criticisms of us and our complicity with racism as effects of patriarchy fails to carry us very far toward eradicating these difficulties.

I would argue that the stage for this *aporia* in Daly's work is set by the structure of essentialism that operates unquestioned and even celebrated around "woman" in Daly's work. I am not referring here to what many have criticized as a biological essentialism in which women are by nature good and men by nature evil. I read Daly's gender categories as applying to men *in their concrete social incarnations within patriarchy* rather than *in esse*. Under patriarchy, Daly argues, men are the agents of its evil in ways women are not.[8] Whether men are redeemable is a moot point for Daly. Her concerns are exclusively with arousing the Spark of divine goodness in women. Daly wants to promote female self-identity, unity with the power of Be-ing, and the final cause.[9] She calls women forward to claim their true Selves and their true position in the cosmos. Though situated within a fabric woven from words used to hurt women but now reclaimed by Daly, this call is cast largely in the discourse traditional to Western philosophy. Human being (in this case, female human being) is aligned with Being itself, with a *telos* as its

7. Quoted in Giddings, 66.

8. In *Gyn/Ecology*, Daly describes women as "token torturers" in the practices of *suttee*, genital mutilation, and footbinding. Women are often the agents of these practices, but only because they want to do what men find pleasing. Thus, men are the real agents, in Daly's eyes, because they determine women's desirability. See chaps. 3, 4, and 5.

9. Of course, Daly's appropriation of these traditional philosophical concepts is neither wholesale or uncritical, by any means. She distinguishes feminist first philosophy/ontology from traditional ontology on various grounds. My argument here is that this recapitulation of our philosophical heritage keeps too much that is problematic for women in play.

essence—as what it truly and most fundamentally is.[10] Moreover, what "woman" most truly and fundamentally is, according to Daly, turns out to be the free, autonomous and whole human being familiar to us from Western discourse.[11] For all its powerful radicality, Daly's Spinning, Sparking Crone remains bound by the construct of a free, self-constituting whole liberal-woman whose *essential* sameness will eventually bind her to herself and others like her in an unproblematic and undisturbed unity.[12]

QUESTIONING "WOMAN" IN FEMINIST THEOLOGY: ROSEMARY RUETHER

When one follows the intersecting paths of race, class and gender analysis through the feminist theological writings of Rosemary Ruether in light of the critiques raised by womanist scholars, one finds issues of racism and classism interwoven with gender oppression throughout her work. Of her feminist writings, *New Woman/New Earth*[13] gives the most fulsome account of the interplay among these oppressions. She traces the history of the development of women from prehistoric times to the industrial revolution arguing that, as economic life increased in complexity, women were moved farther and farther away from control over the means of production. Our locations within the capitalist economic system have hardly been symmetrical, according to her analysis. For example, the pedestal on which perched the Victorian ideal of womanhood rested on the backs of women of the lower classes who worked in sweatshops and as domestic servants, thereby freeing the upper-class woman for her role as ornament. The similar position accorded to slave-owners' wives in the Old South depended

10. See, for example, the Introduction to *Pure Lust*, esp. 2.

11. For examples, see 3 and 87 of *Pure Lust*. See also Sheila Greeve Davaney's article, "The Limits of the Appeal to Women's Experience" in *Shaping New Vision: Gender and Values in American Culture*, ed. Clarissa W. Atkinson, Constance H. Buchanan, Margaret R. Miles (Ann Arbor: UMI Research Press, 1987), for a similar assessment of Daly's hidden ontology.

12. For example, see 26–27, 87, and 176 of *Pure Lust*.

13. Rosemary Radford Ruether, *New Woman/New Earth: Sexist Ideologies and Human Liberation* (New York: Seabury Press, 1975).

upon slave women's enforced domestic and sexual servitude. Ruether also attends to the speckled history of relations between white and black women since the days of the abolition movement and recognizes that this legacy shapes our interactions in the present. However, Ruether, like Daly, places the blame for this situation not on white women's racism *primarily*, but on patriarchy's strategy of divide and conquer.

In the first chapter of *Sexism and God-Talk*, Ruether lays out the method, sources, and norms that will govern this more systematic incarnation of feminist theology. She names "women's experience" as the norm governing her claims. The differences between women that were so much a part of her analysis in *New Woman/New Earth* mark this text as well. Ruether writes, "Feminist theology makes explicit what was overlooked in male advocacy of the poor and oppressed, that liberation must start with the oppressed of the oppressed; namely, women of the oppressed."[14] This articulates both a critique and an embrace of other theologies of liberation. Ruether also goes on to acknowledge that, like men of oppressed groups, women of dominant classes will find *their* blind spots challenged by those whom *they* oppress. Thus, she recognizes that "women's experience" may vary depending on one's socioeconomic location.

Race and class concerns also figure prominently in one of her later works, *Women-Church*.[15] The collection of powerful and eloquent rituals that Ruether offers as resources in the second half of the book include several that intertwine criticisms of racism, classism, sexism, and homophobia.[16] In the narrative description of the

14. Ruether, *Sexism and God-Talk*, 132.

15. Rosemary Radford Ruether, *Woman-Church: Theology and Practice of Feminist Liturgical Communities* (San Francisco: Harper & Row, 1985). Future references will be parenthetical in the text.

16. The baptismal rite includes a rite of confession of ways in which the individual has been a victimizer or has benefited from acceding to oppression (129). The Rite of Reconciliation includes a rite of repentance from horizontal violences between middle class white women and poor women of color (133ff). Also two rituals for the Easter season are directed toward the intersection of oppressions. The Ash Wednesday liturgy includes a section on sins against racial minorities (247). The Stations of the Cross liturgy consists of a walk through Washington, D.C., that stops at places that symbolize issues of injustice in our world today (119).

women-church movement, which comprises the first half of the book, Ruether describes briefly and appreciatively the impact on the Chicago woman-church conference by the diversity in culture and class of its attenders. However, when she does finally speak in detail of ways in which diversity threatens divisiveness in communities struggling for liberation, blame for that divisiveness is accorded differently to male theologians of liberation and to feminists. Male liberation theologians are held directly accountable for their hostility to women's issues (See 54-55). Similar problems within women's groups are described quite differently, if not glossed over altogether. Ruether recognizes that race and class differences erect barriers between women, but the blame for this divisiveness is, as it was in *New Woman/New Earth*, diverted from the shoulders of possibly hostile or ignorant feminists to the broader shoulders of patriarchy. In fact, what proves divisive enough in African-American and Third World theological communities to be termed an "explosion within an explosion" (Mercy Amba Oduyoye) hardly makes a ripple on the smooth surface of Ruether's feminist theology.

I am not disputing Ruether's contention that our society's value system is in some sense to blame for racist and classist attitudes among white middle-class women. I am suggesting that it does not seem equitable to place the blame on society *only* for *white* women's racism but not for men of color's sexism. Or, on the other hand, to hold male liberation theologians accountable for their failures to recognize the validity of women's issues while granting a kind of general amnesty to white middle-class women for their failures to take issues of race and class seriously.

We should applaud Ruether for always keeping before us the interconnectedness of race, class, and gender oppressions. However, could it be that something in Ruether's texts shapes the trajectory according to which they interact in her texts? Could it be that Ruether's texts, despite explicit intentions to the contrary, are structured by an assumed feminine identity of some description to which distinctions of race and class are additions that serve primarily to triple the *quantity* of oppression on working- and underclass women and women of color? Could it be that, for this reason, patriarchy takes the role of the "father" of oppression whose children, racism and classism, serve to further subject and divide the objects of "his" attention, women?

Like Daly, Ruether's texts are marked by traditional discursive structures even as she calls these same structures into question. Throughout the three texts discussed in this essay Ruether employs a critical typology of feminist thinking. The first type, liberal feminism, argues that women are just as ____ (fill in the blank) as men (i.e., we share the same essential humanity). We should, therefore, have access to the same opportunities and benefits that men have in our society. The second type, romantic feminism, accepts and celebrates society's definition of woman as aligned with nature, emotion, and so forth and argues that what needs to change is society's valuation of these attributes. Often, romantic feminists' dissatisfaction with society leads them to adopt separatist strategies. Ruether is critical of both types of feminism. Romantic feminism's separatist path ghettoizes women's concerns, effecting little or no change in the system of male privilege. In *Women-Church,* Ruether roundly criticizes the philosophical tradition of liberal humanism on which liberal feminism is modeled because it has "devised a variety of ways of keeping gender, class, and racial hierarchies intact, despite its claims of establishing universal human rights" (52). Liberal feminism at least tacitly approves of the structures that support male privilege and often settles for token individual achievements rather than systemic change.

Ruether's constructive positions attempt to find a way between liberalism and romanticism. However, liberal-woman continues to mark the boundaries of these positions. In *Sexism and God-Talk,* the romantic/liberal typology figures most prominently in the chapter on theological anthropology. A liberal feminist anthropology defines woman as equal to man (who is associated with society's "goods": intelligence, spirit, culture). A romantic feminist anthropology defines woman (aligned with emotion and nature) as good. Ruether suggests a different equation, wherein the subsets of both man and woman come together to form "good" *and* to equal human being. While her definition of woman/human being could be said to incorporate the best of *both* liberal and romantic feminism, the philosophical structure underpinning her constructive position is very much a free, self-constituting, whole and essential human subject. The attributes that Ruether brings together to constitute human being make up a smorgasbord from which individual men and women choose those most appropriate for themselves. In its female incarnation, Ruether's ideal human being is liberal-woman.

The discursive structures of liberal-woman and her enemy, patriarchy, inscribe both the rituals and the narrative portion of *Women-Church* in such a way as to submerge differences of race and class. Let me cite two quotations from the narrative section:

> Although undoubtedly third world women have to *contextualize feminism* in terms of their own situation, greater communication between women of the two worlds would undoubtedly reveal they have many issues in common. (55, Empasis mine)

The encounters of cultures and classes at the women-church conference confirm this expectation:

> Communication between women across the divisions of class and race drawn by patriarchy is not insurmountable if women of resources reach across the divisions and provide the means while, at the same time, really allowing the space for disenfranchised women to define their own experience. (68)

The boundaries between women are, as in Daly's work, the responsibility of patriarchy. Crossing the boundaries requires action on the part of "women of resources" who reach and allow space (what do the disenfranchised do, by contrast?). Once the boundaries are crossed, space is made, and the ground of unity appears—"feminism" which, even when contextualized, remains "common to all women."[17]

The same structures of patriarchy, as "father" of oppressions and of liberal-woman, inscribe the goals of women-church praxis

17. I am not suggesting that women from different social backgrounds cannot find common ground. We do indeed *forge* such ground, but Ruether's rhetoric here suggests it pre-exists and that its name is "feminism." Nor am I arguing that the women of the women-church gatherings should have taken different roles (i.e., that the women of resources should not have provided the means or allowed the space and that the disenfranchised women should not have defined their own experience). I am leaving that question aside to push to an underlying problem. I am trying to point out that the way power is allocated between those who have "resources" and those who are "disenfranchised" occurs in and through discursive patterns as well as economic and political structures.

for both the individual and the community. The communitarian goal of women-church is to bring into existence true church; namely, "a community that seeks to overthrow patriarchy as the root expression of oppressive relationships between men and women, between generations, between the powerful and the weak" (64). Patriarchy is the fundamental problem under which other oppressions are subsumed. The purpose of coming to terms with ways in which patriarchy has affected our own psyches is to "come to a firm ground of autonomous humanity as a female who can continually resist and refuse the snares of patriarchy without confusing this with the humanity of males. . . . [We] have to be able to affirm the humanity of males behind the masks of patriarchy" (60). Clearly this ideal woman resembles the liberal philosophical ideal of essential human being both in her autonomy and in her ability to see truly to the genuine male hidden behind the masks of patriarchy.

I noted earlier that several of the rituals in *Women-Church* intertwine critiques or confessions of participation in gender, race, and class oppression. Is it merely "accidental" that, in the rite of Reconciliation, the repentance of horizontal violences against working- and under-class women of color is included under the heading "Rite of Mind-Cleansing from Sexism?" (133). Certainly, the main biases informing instances of violence across ethnic or class lines are those of race and/or class, yet here they are subsumed under the flag of patriarchy. What are we to make of Ruether's suggestion that "U.S. Americans and Latin Americans" may want to commemorate the martyrdom of Archbishop Romero and others on December 6 while "other nationalities" may want to focus on South Africa? (117). Where, for example, are African-Americans to locate themselves according to this suggested agenda?

I want to make it clear that I am leaving aside any question of either Ruether's or Daly's intentions as authors of these texts. The attention they both give to issues of diversity suggests that they intended to write feminist thea/ologies that addressed the multiplicity of concerns facing women. My questioning is directed toward what courses below authorial intentions, good or bad; I am trying to expose the workings of a "text" beneath the text, so to speak. The traditional discursive structure of liberal-woman inscribes/prescribes/proscribes both thinkers' writing about women in such a way as to preclude full acknowledgment of the substantial differences among women. To the degree that such differences occur in both thea/ologian's works, they seem all too easily to resolve/dissolve into an untroubled unity of "women."

QUESTIONING "WOMAN": LUCE IRIGARAY

So how is Luce Irigaray helpful in finding another path through this morass? Let me first acknowledge that, in some ways, Irigaray is just as vulnerable to the criticisms raised by womanist scholars as Daly and Ruether are (or most of the rest of us, for that matter). The fundamental problem, in her analysis, *is* that of sexual difference, and she does not sufficiently address the impact of race on women's issues. However, Irigaray's work carries criticisms with which we are familiar to new depths: those of the discourse of Western thinking. Her critical work thus deepens and furthers questions raised by feminist theology and offers possibilities for alliances with womanist theology. The constructive work that emerges from her stance of critical engagement does not reinstate the discursive structures she exposes as antithetical to women, but rather attempts to write and think otherwise. Whatever woman/women "is/are" in Irigaray's writing, she/they are not essentially the same, but bear difference and pluraling in/between her/them. Thus, in both critical and constructive ways, Irigaray offers American feminist theology an important resource for grappling with the implications for the discursive structures that womanist critiques bring to light. Irigaray's insights can help us unearth resistance, on the part of what we might call the "textual economy" of Western culture, to differences and the role that resistance plays in rendering recognition of genuine alterities extremely difficult.

The complexity and density of Irigaray's writings present a significant barrier to American readers—even with able translations of two of her major works, *Speculum of the Other Woman*,[18] and *This*

18. Luce Irigaray, *Speculum of the Other Woman*, trans. Gillian C. Gill (Ithaca: Cornell University Press, 1985).

Sex Which Is Not One.[19] I hope—by shedding a little light on *what* she does, *why* she does it, and *why* we should take note of it—to begin an exploration of an important intersection between American feminist and womanist thinking and French feminism.

The background against which Irigaray writes is a distinctively French convergence of psychoanalytic theory (Sigmund Freud via Jacques Lacan), the traditions informing philosophy from Plato to Jacques Derrida, and Marxist analysis. This convergence is somewhat foreign to American thinking with its roots in pragmatic philosophies of various sorts, its suspicion of Freudian psychoanalysis and Marxism, and its relatively recent (and no less suspicious) acquaintance with Derrida, in particular. It may be helpful to understand why she works at this particular convergence. Like some American feminists, Irigaray finds that all three streams of thought shed some light on the situation of women; yet the question of woman also brings to light their limits. That is, all three streams of thought share a common inscription in and by what Irigaray calls the "general grammar of Western culture" and its "economic" system, which is built on sameness. And they all call each other's inscription in and by that larger "text" to our attention and into question.

The philosophical tradition comes into question for Irigaray because, as the master discourse, it lays down the rules for other

19. Luce Irigaray, *This Sex Which Is Not One*, trans. Catherine Porter and Carolyn Burke (Ithaca: Cornell University Press, 1985). The secondary literature on Irigaray has grown to comprise a substantial body of work. However, as I shall argue later in this paper, much of it perpetuates serious misreadings of Irigaray's thought. Elizabeth Grosz attempts a strong defense of Irigaray against these misreadings, yet they seem still to affect her own reading. Nonetheless, her work on Irigaray and the divine is particularly of interest to theologians. See Elizabeth Grosz, *Sexual Subversions: Three French Feminists* (Winchester, Mass.: Unwin Hyman, Inc., 1989), especially chap. 4, and *Jacques Lacan: A Feminist Introduction* (New York: Routledge, 1990) especially chap. 6. Margaret Whitford's recent book, *Luce Irigaray: Philosophy in the Feminine* (London, New York: Routledge, 1991) is the refreshing exception to the trend of misreadings. Her careful attention to Irigaray's multilayered writing illuminates the subtleties and complexities of Irigaray's work in extremely helpful ways for the reader unfamiliar with it.

discourses. The bulk of *Speculum* consists of careful, subtle readings of several major philosophers from Plato to Kant. A reader will find some familiar criticisms of what philosophers have had to say about women in these essays. However, Irigaray's questioning of the tradition does not stop with these philosophers' explicit statements about women. Irigaray simultaneously exposes coincidences between the trajectory of the tropes that describe woman in their texts and those that describe, for example, the relationship of matter and form in Plotinus' *Enneads* or the relationship of subject and world in Kant and Descartes. This coincidence exhibits philosophy's inscription in the larger text that is the ultimate target of her critiques, the "general grammar of Western culture."

Freud is most valuable, in Irigaray's view, for opening the door to the dynamics of the unconscious, to forces at work in us that call into question philosophy's assumption that the subject is the master of "his" discourse. Her reading of Freud also sounds some familiar criticisms. Irigaray's account exposes his theories as both inscribing and inscribed in what she calls an "economy of the Same." Freud's account of sexual difference reduces to sameness because the standard of value that governs his account of femininity is the phallus. For example, Freud's focus on the clitoris (the deformed penis) and the vagina (the replacement for the little boy's hand) to the exclusion of any other erogenous zones in female sexuality suggests that male sexuality provided a hidden lens through which Freud viewed female sexuality. She writes:

> The opposition between "masculine" clitoral activity and "feminine" vaginal passivity, an opposition which Freud—and many others—saw as stages, or alternatives, in the development of a sexually "normal" woman, seems rather too clearly required by the practice of male sexuality. . . . In these terms, woman's erogenous zones never amount to anything but a clitoris-sex that is not comparable to the noble phallic organ, or a hole-envelope that serves to sheathe and massage the penis in intercourse: a non-sex, or a masculine organ turned back upon itself, self-embracing.[20]

20. Irigaray, *This Sex Which Is Not One,* 23. Future references will be parenthetical within the text.

American feminists have, on similar grounds, tended to dismiss Freud out of hand. Irigaray, on the contrary, still finds him quite useful. She finds his accounts of femininity quite powerful *as descriptions* of the status quo. When Freud turns description into prescription, she finds him problematic.

However, even as Freud opens the door to this other "realm," so to speak, Irigaray exposes his own inscription/prescription/proscription by it. The phallocentrism evident in Freud's texts is not simply or even primarily a matter of his authorial intention or of his own personal beliefs. Rather, the phallocentrism of psychoanalysis reflects/reveals the phallocentrism of the larger text in which Freud and philosophy are inscribed: the general grammar of Western culture and of Western society.

Irigaray brings Marxist analysis into play because it offers a path of inquiry left unexplored by Freud (the material conditions that produce "normal" femininity) and because it challenges philosophy's claim to be free of material interests and influences. Marxist analysis has its limits, however. "Women" make a difficult object for it to pursue because we do not form a discrete class. Our racial differences further complicate matters. Irigaray's reading of Karl Marx and of women's status through Marx appears in the essay "Women on the Market." She argues, first, that women are commodities on an exchange market in which their value is determined by men's desire. For example, the institution of bourgeois marriage arises out of our economy, in which a woman's value is measured by her ability to attract a man and then to bear *only* his children. Her reading of Marx does not stop with what his writings expose about the material conditions which produce "normative" femininity. The economic features of women's oppression reflect the "economy" of the Same, which structures Western discourse and its "economy" in the strict sense. Her reading of Marx also reveals that the workings of capitalism itself (for example, the idea of "commodity"), as he analyses them, reflect this same sexual economy in which the standard of sameness is the phallus.

Irigaray collects the characteristics of this general grammar as exposed by the convergence of Freudian, Marxist, and philosophical thinking in the term "scopic economy" in *This Sex Which Is Not One* and "specular economy" in *Speculum*. The logic of this economy is photo-logic, she writes in *Speculum*. Its system of values and of argumentation is dominated by sight, light, and the gaze. In Irigaray's text, one sees both what we feminists already knew (the equation of man with mind, spirit, idea, logos, subject while woman equals body, nature, matter, object) and something more. We come face to face with an uncanny connivance of the dominance of presence, form, and the visual with the definition of woman as lack. She writes:

> [Woman's] entry into a dominant scopic economy signifies, again, her consignment to passivity: she is to be the beautiful object of contemplation. While her body finds itself thus eroticized, and called to a double movement of exhibition and of chaste retreat in order to stimulate the drives of the "subject," her sexual organ represents *the horror of nothing to see*. . . . This organ which has nothing to show for itself also lacks a form of its own. And if woman takes pleasure precisely from this incompleteness of form which allows her organ to touch itself over and over again, indefinitely, by itself, that pleasure is denied by a civilization that privileges phallomorphism. (26)

This collusion of Freudian, philosophical, and Marxist discourses is not a grounding made possible by some participation in a deeper reality; rather it is a series of reflections of phallocentrism. The phallocentrism of Western discourse is reflected in/reflects the phallocentrism of sexual difference, the sexual "economy" of Western society in which only the phallus has value in and of itself. The phallocentrism of the sexual practice and theory of Western thinking reflects/is reflected in the phallocentrism of the economy in its narrower sense (job market, monetary system, etc.). In our phallocentric economy, women are commodities evaluated and defined in terms of their use or exchange value "in the eyes of" the subjects of this economy, those in possession of the phallus-equivalents.

Just as Irigaray has taken the exposure of structures implicated in the oppression of women to new depths, the profound level of the discourse that constitutes Western thinking, so also her strategies for unearthing and overcoming it take feminist critical and constructive work in new directions. The options available for "practical" or "theoretical" resistance to this discursive economy's inscription of woman through its institutions, methods of analyses, or its job markets, are circumscribed by phallocentrism's pervasiveness. In fact, her assessment of these options in *This Sex Which Is Not One* runs parallel to Ruether's typology of feminisms. Women can, on the one hand, demand access to the same opportunities and benefits that men have (what Ruether labels the liberal feminist agenda). On the other hand, women can withdraw from phallocratic culture and establish their own society (Ruether's romantic feminist agenda). Like Ruether, Irigaray finds both options to be problematic, though necessary as stages. Adopting a strategy of development—perhaps securing places for women on a par with men—leaves the phallocentric economy in place. Nonetheless, women must "continue to struggle for equal wages and social rights, against discrimination in employment and education, and so forth" (165–66) yet always keep in mind that this alone is not enough. While she advocates temporary separatist moves, "tactical strikes," as she calls them, as "necessary stages in the escape from . . . proletarization on the exchange market," she rejects total withdrawal because such a strategy threatens, in Irigaray's words, to "correspond once again to the disconnection from power that is traditionally theirs." She asks, "Would it not involve a new prison, a new cloister, built of their own accord?" (33). Retreating to this cloister, even though it would allow women the space necessary for exploring their differentness and would remove them from the commodities market, is not itself the answer. If such a move were undertaken with the goal of reversing the economic order as it now stands, "history would repeat itself in the long run," Irigaray asserts, because the economy would revert to sameness: a different kind of sameness but phallocratism nonetheless because it would again be based on identity. As long as an economy of the same is in place, even if femaleness replaced maleness as normative model, "What I am trying to designate as 'feminine' would not emerge. There would be a phallic 'seizure of power' " (130).

The "options" available to women in terms of theory are similarly problematic. In fact, the practical options listed above are undergirded by parallel courses in theory. Liberal versions of feminist activism are based on the concept of woman's equality with man. "She" partakes from the same smorgasbord of human characteristics that "he" does. Romantic versions of femininist activism accept the definition of woman current in culture but reverse its valuation. As we have seen, the texts of both Daly and Ruether remain bound by the discursive structure of an essential woman. And I have argued that this structure is implicated in critiques of feminist thinking raised by womanist thinkers. What does Irigaray pose as an alternative?

The answer is not a matter of charting corrective courses in Freudian theory, Marxist analysis, or philosophical anthropology. Such theoretical corrections leave in place the text in which these systems of thought are inscribed. To speak about woman is to keep her in the role of object even if a woman speaks as the Subject most knowledgeable about that object. In opening her mouth to speak (or picking up her pen to write) in one of these discourses, a woman is always already perpetuating her own oppression. These theories are inscribed by the discourse of Western thinking. Because it is structured by phallocentrism, the "power" or ability of women *sexualized as female* to speak this discourse is limited—even denied. Phallocentrism does not allow "woman" as such to speak as a subject. To speak and be heard one must speak according to the rules, that is, in accordance with the structures of this discourse. By definition, speaking "woman" cannot be "subject," have "ideas," or even "speak her mind."[21] Irigaray writes:

> In other words, the issue is not one of elaborating a new theory of which woman would be the *subject* or the *object*, but of jamming the theoretical machinery itself, of suspending its pretension to the production of a truth and of a meaning that are excessively univocal. Which presupposes that women do not aspire simply to be men's equals in knowledge. That they do not claim to be rivaling men in constructing a logic of the feminine that would still take onto-theo-logic as its model, but that they are rather attempting to wrest this question away from the economy of the logos. (78)
>
> So for woman it is not a matter of installing herself within this lack, this negative, even by denouncing it, nor of reversing

21. This does not mean that a woman cannot assume the position of Subject or speak as Subject. It means that this position is a male position because of the phallocentrism of our discourse (not because men are "natural" subjects and women are "natural" objects).

> the economy of sameness by turning the feminine into *the standard for "sexual difference"*; It is rather a matter of trying to practice that difference . . . Is it possible that the difference might not be reduced once again to a process of *hierarchization? Of subordinating the other to the same*? (159)

Rather than either creating a realm of the feminine completely outside phallocentric discourse *or* articulating a theory *about* woman within that discourse, Irigaray wants to make a place for the feminine—genuinely other, genuinely different—within phallocentric discourse. By "make a place for," I do not mean create a space within the enclosure of phallocentric discourse; I mean rather, set in motion a disruption in that discourse that will open it up for a different discourse, that of the feminine imaginary. To borrow a phrase from Derrida, Irigaray "uses against the edifice the instruments or stones available in the house"[22] to deconstruct it. She wields the speculum of the specular economy on behalf of woman through her strategy of *mimétisme*. She writes:

> To play with mimesis is thus, for a woman, to try to recover the place of her exploitation by discourse, without allowing herself to be simply reduced to it. It means to resubmit herself—inasmuch as she is on the side of the "perceptible," of "matter"—to "ideas," in particular to ideas about herself, that are elaborated in/by a masculine logic, but so as to make "visible," by an effect of playful repetition, what was supposed to remain invisible: the cover-up of a possible operation of the feminine in language. It also means "to unveil" the fact, if women are such good mimics, it is because they are not simply re[ab]sorbed in this function. *They also remain elsewhere*. . . . (76)

Mimétisme works in her readings of Freud, Marx, and the philosophers in much the same way that *différance* and other undecidables work in Derrida's readings of texts. *Mimétisme* lets loose a "disruptive excess" that phallocentrism attempts to cover over. As *différance* exceeds systematization, so *mimétisme* shows that "woman" exceeds attempts to tame or circumscribe it.

22. Jacques Derrida, "The Ends of Man," *Margins of Philosophy*, trans. Alan Bass (Chicago: University of Chicago Press, 1982), 135.

Through the jamming logic of *mimétisme*, a "place" is made *in Irigaray's discourse*—not in some reified metaphysical space or language—for the feminine imaginary to speak/write itself. This aspect of her writing gives rise to the primary controversy that surrounds evaluations of Irigaray: is her project, perhaps despite its best intentions, itself bounded by essentialism?

Those who read her as an essentialist (and they are numerous; the bulk of the secondary literature on Irigaray follows this line of interpretation) read the feminine imaginary as a construct that posits an essential difference in how women think that is grounded in their autoerotic experience.[23] One can see where such readings get their impetus. In *This Sex Which Is Not One*, Irigaray spends a great deal of space describing the plurality of the erotic areas of a woman's body (28ff), the continuousness of genital stimulation that women experience, and so forth (24). She even seems to assert that this plurality of woman's autoeroticism is reflected in her thought patterns, yielding a uniquely feminine form of rationality:

> "She" is indefinitely other in herself. This is doubtless why she is said to be whimsical, incomprehensible, agitated, capricious . . . not to mention her language, in which "she" sets off in all directions leaving "him" unable to discern the coherence of any meaning. Hers are contradictory worlds, somewhat mad from the standpoint of reason, inaudible for whoever listens to them with ready-made grids, with a fully elaborated code in hand. For in what she *says*, too, at least when she dares, woman is constantly touching herself. . . . One would have to listen with another ear, as if hearing an "other meaning" always in the process of weaving itself, of embracing itself with

23. Chris Weedon's assessment exemplifies such readings. Irigaray "produces a radical theory of the female libido based in female sexuality and autoeroticism which celebrates the female body. . . ." Weedon, *Feminist Practice and Poststructuralist Theory* (London: Blackwell, 1987), 56. For other examples, see Andrea Nye, *Feminist Theory and the Philosophies of Man* (London: Croom Helm, 1988), especially 148–64; Janet Sayers, *Biological Politics: Feminist and Anti-Feminist Perspectives* (New York: Tavistock, 1982), 131–32. Toril Moi, in *Sexual/Textual Politics: Feminist Literary Theory* (London: Routledge, 1988) offers a much more appreciative reading of Irigaray but concludes (I think, wrongly) that Irigaray "falls" into essentialism against her will (see 127–49).

> words, but also of getting rid of words in order not to become fixed, congealed in them. (28–29)

She continues:

> But if the female imaginary were to deploy itself, if it could bring itself into play otherwise than as scraps, uncollected debris, would it represent itself, even so, in the form of *one* universe? Would it even be volume instead of surface? No. . . . (Re)-discovering herself, for a woman, thus could only signify the possibility of sacrificing no one of her pleasures to another, of identifying herself with none of them in particular, *of never being simply one.* A sort of expanding universe to which no limits could be fixed and which would not be incoherence nonetheless. . . . (30–31)[24]

I would like to propose three arguments to counter essentializing readings of both these texts and Irigaray's work as a whole. First of all, even if one reads the quotation about the feminine imaginary as, in some sense, a normative claim about femininity, it is difficult to see how "never being simply one," being always elsewhere, and so on, could describe an essence in its usual sense of permanently enduring features of woman regardless of location. A plural, always differing/deferring, decentering, moving essence seems to me to be an oxymoron.[25]

Second, it also seems to me that some essentialist readings of Irigaray fail to take into full consideration the significant differences in readings of Freud on the two sides of the Atlantic. In America, we tend to read Freud as positing a biological cause (anatomy) for the intrapsychic dynamics his patients exhibit. Thus, his

24. Toril Moi seems to miss this "essential" plurality in her discussion of Irigaray's criticism of the desire at work in phallocentrism. Irigaray argues that this economy is structured by a desire for same; *hom(m)osexualité* (a desire for same/male) in which woman serves as mirror of that sameness. She reads Irigaray as arguing that woman's *own* desire for same is repressed in this economy (*Sexual/Textual Politics*, 135). It is clear that, whatever "woman's desire" would mean for Irigaray, it would not be a desire for same. That would be a reinstatement of phallocratism.

25. Naomi Schor also suggests this may be the best defense against essentialist readings of Irigaray. See Schor, "The Essentialism Which Is Not One: Coming to Grips with Irigaray," *differences: a journal of feminist cultural studies* 1 (Summer 1989): 38–58.

account of femininity would be drawn from and pertain to women's anatomical differences from men and the often tragic course this sets for their lives. Essentialist readings of Irigaray follow the same trajectory. This particular kind of misreading of Irigaray correctly reveals her mimetic relationship to Freud. Yet I would argue that the trajectory of Irigaray's work in fact mimes a different Freud. In France, Freud is read via psychoanalyst Jacques Lacan as an articulator of a cultural discourse that courses below distinctions between anatomy/biology and psyche/society.[26] This discourse *inscribes/prescribes/proscribes* such distinctions. Irigaray's writing is *l'écriture feminine* in contrast to *l'écriture masculine,* which is the general grammar of Western culture. Irigaray's reading of Freud in the first essay in *Speculum* reveals the phallomorphism of his account of femininity to be both a reflection of and reflected by the phallocentrism of the Western discursive and financial "economies." These "economies" inscribe Freud's own reading of femininity. In writing the feminine imaginary, Irigaray is attempting both to inscribe and be inscribed by an "economy" which is repressed by but "appears" in the gaps of the economy of the Same, one which privileges difference rather than sameness and plurality rather than unity. She finds *one* reflection of this economy in a different "accounting" of women's bodies. She is not claiming that her account of women's sexuality is finally how women *really* are or how we *really* experience our bodies. This is not a literal description. She is rather opening up another possibility for reading/writing woman's body/women's bodies. Anatomical differing/deferring figures/reflects a pluralism of sexual *jouissance,* economic *jouissance,* political *jouissance,* etc. Thus she encourages women to "find the struggles that are appropriate for each woman, right

26. cf. Andrea Nye's *Feminist Theory,* chap. 5. She contrasts the biologism of American psychoanalysis (117) with Lacan's reading of Freud, which moves away from "regressive references to anatomy or instinct" (137) to the ways thought and language engineer sexual difference. She recognizes that, in Lacanian theory, men and women can take up either male or female positions, "which shows how little any physical reality is the determinant. . . ." (137). Oddly enough, this reading of the relationship of body, gender, and discursive positions does not carry over to her reading of Irigaray.

where she is, depending upon her nationality, her job, her social class, her sexual experience, that is, upon the form of oppression that is for her the most immediately unbearable" (167).

It is also crucial to understand just what Irigaray means by the feminine *imaginary*. For this, one has to turn to the work of Jacques Lacan, the premier French psychoanalytical theorist (with whom Irigaray studied and who subsequently kicked her out of his institute for writing *Speculum*).[27] The three central constructs of Lacanian psychoanalytic theory are the Imaginary, the Symbolic, and the Real—and they, like Irigaray's *l'écriture feminine*—must be understood through the *French* Freud (for whom Lacan is somewhat responsible). These are not *simply* different stages of the individual's psychic development. Rather, they are more like a collective psyche—a text that inscribes both our psychic *development* from infancy to early childhood *and* our adult lives. The symbolic is the realm of society and subjectivity. It is governed by the Law of the Father. Our entrance into subjectivity comes via submission to the prohibition against incest, which is the primal command of the Law of the Father. This breaks the union of mother and child, but our desire for reunion with the mother continues to be constituted in us as lack. Thus, for Lacan, the subject is perpetually split. The imaginary "predates" the split from the mother and persists with us as the realm of that Other that constitutes us. But our access to the imaginary comes only through its inscription in the gaps and margins of the symbolic. Insofar as this applies to our "psychological" development, the imaginary is both blocked and made present in its absence by the prohibition. Insofar as the imaginary is a cultural subtext, our access to it comes only through reading its inscriptions in our symbolic discourse. Irigaray's reading of the trajectories of woman/matter/nature in philosophical texts exhibit this inscription. Thus, the imaginary is not a "place" of absolute anteriority or exteriority, as some of her critics would have it.[28]

27. For helpful secondary readings on Lacan, see Nye, chap. 5; Toril Moi, 99-101; and Mark C. Taylor, *Altarity* (Chicago: University of Chicago Press, 1987), chap. 4.

28. Toril Moi, for example, reads Irigaray as accepting and valorizing the place "outside" the symbolic that has been relegated to woman. Since there is nothing outside the symbolic but psychosis, she reads Irigaray as proposing that women *should* babble incoherently and leave logic to the men (see Moi, *Sexual/Textual Politics*, 100).

Irigaray's reading of Lacan parallels her reading of Freud. As description of the status quo, she finds it powerful. Her readings of philosophical texts, of the "economy" in the strict sense, of her analysands' lives confirm that the symbolic that writes society is dominated by a specular logic which, in privileging the phallus, identifies order with the Law of the Father. Her concern, however, is with the disastrous consequences of this inscription on women's lives. To break the hold of phallocentrism on discourse requires, in Irigaray's view, exacerbating the already-"present" play of the imaginary in the symbolic, thereby exposing the "other" (economy and sex) it represses.

Even if I have managed to convince you that an essentialist reading of Irigaray is misguided and that feminist theology needs to let loose in our texts the questioning of essential femininity that Irigaray espouses, you *still* may be wondering what impact engaging in this kind of feminist thinking will have on the "realities" of the multiple oppressions that are so determinative of women's lives. The question as stated assumes a split between language and "reality" that, I have argued, Irigaray challenges. Irigaray describes the political stake of her work as having to do with "the fact that women's 'liberation' requires transforming the economic realm and thus necessarily transforming culture and its operative agency, language" (155). The discourse/text of the specular economy is the "ether" in which all Western institutions—the family, the economy in its strict sense, the political sphere, the church, the academy—are embedded and spoken. I have argued that feminist theology's own inscription by this discourse sets a hegemonic trajectory for its dealings with differences among women, one that runs counter to its goals of resisting all oppressions that limit women. This hegemony is not limited to ways we write and think but carries over into our interactions, our attempts to embody solidarity with women from cultures other than white Euro-American culture. As Derrida notes in an essay entitled "The Ends of Man," the relationship between "linguistic" violence (the quotes are his and suggest the irony of reading this as referring to "mere language") and what we usually think of as violence (economic and sexual exploitation, rape, spouse abuse, the daily violations of self that children of color suffer in white-dominated schools) is complicated and difficult to trace. Nonetheless, he insists (as does Irigaray) that these violences are in "structural solidarity" with one another. The lines from the deconstruction of phallocentrism in books to the "deconstruction" of the political, economic, and psychological systemic violence it makes possible (and which perpetuate it) will probably also be difficult to trace. However, I hope that this essay has shown that to attempt attacks against women's oppression *without* attending to the systemic violence at work in the discourse that speaks the institutions and individuals we hold responsible for oppression—*and ourselves*—is to risk following false exits that either leave the system in place or reinstate it on new ground.

7

Sporting Power

AMERICAN FEMINISM, FRENCH FEMINISMS, AND AN ETHIC OF CONFLICT

SHARON D. WELCH

What would happen if one woman told the story of her life? The world would split open.

—Muriel Rukeyser[1]

This crime has been committed not once, but 100 times told. It began when I was but a young girl. As you see, I have now grown quite old. It is not a crime that you have recorded in your volumes trimmed with gold. I do not speak [only] of the rape of my body, I refer to the rape of my soul.

—Willie Tyson[2]

We are, I am, you are
by cowardice or courage
the ones who find our way
back to this scene
carrying a knife,
a camera

1. Muriel Rukeyser, from "Käthe Kollwitz," *Out of Silence: Selected Poems*, ed. Kate Daniels (Evanston, Ill.: TriQuarterly Books, 1992), 132.

2. Willie Tyson, from "The Ballad of Merciful Mary," *Full Count* (Lima Bean Records), as cited by Mary Daly, *Gyn/Ecology: The Metaethics of Radical Feminism* (Boston: Beacon Press, 1978).

a book of myths
in which
our names do not appear.
—Adrienne Rich[3]

Contrast the promise and pain of these words—the passionate commitment to facing our suffering, our courage, the defiant celebration of the ways in which women throughout history have struggled, endured and thrived in spite of patriarchal oppression—with Nancy Miller's rueful, honest observation: "The move from women's studies to gender studies which is everywhere around us keeps pushing us further and further away from anything separatist. In fact, it has become a positive embarrassment [even] to talk about women."[4] Marianne Hirsch and Evelyn Fox Keller acknowledge the paradoxical state of feminist theory and practice in the United States: there is a "disintegration of the representative subject of feminism" and a "continuing need for a coherent voice with which to articulate political demands on behalf of the group called 'women.' "[5]

We live in a society in which the "two-gender system," the rigid demarcation of masculine and feminine identities, is being reinforced in a frenzy of cultural, sociological, and physical control.[6] While the distinctions and power imbalances of gender are being violently enforced, it has become the norm for feminist theorists to avoid, as essentialist, the appeal to women's experience as a criterion of theoretical and political work.

3. Adrienne Rich, from "Diving into the Wreck," cited by Mary Daly, *Gyn/Ecology*, 74.

4. Nancy K. Miller, Jane Gallop, Marianne Hirsch, "Criticizing Feminist Criticism," in Marianne Hirsch and Evelyn Fox Keller, eds., *Conflicts in Feminism* (New York: Routledge, 1990), 351.

5. Marianne Hirsch and Evelyn Fox Keller, "Conclusion: Practicing Conflict in Feminist Theory," in *Conflicts in Feminism*, 379.

6. Ethan Bonner in 1991 reported an "apparent paradox": "While women enjoy greater equality and power than ever before, reported acts of violence against them have risen steeply, with rapes in 1990 reaching an all-time high." Ethan Bronner, "Senate Panel to Address Rising Reports of Rape," *The Boston Globe*, Thursday, April 11, 1991, 3.

Sheila Greeve Davaney provides an extremely helpful summary of the present conflicts in American feminist theology in her essay "The Limits of the Appeal to Women's Experience." Davaney summarizes the basis of this critique as follows:

> They [women of color] have argued that white women have made a mistake parallel to that committed by white men: the assumption of common experience and hence the false universalization of what is in fact only the experience of a particular group. . . . Although white feminist theologians have attempted to respond to this challenge by incorporating class and race analysis within their definition and critical interpretation of patriarchy, many women of color remain skeptical about the applicability of white feminist theology to their situation.[7]

Davaney, herself a white woman, argues that the appeal to women's experience by Mary Daly, Elisabeth Schüssler Fiorenza, and Rosemary Radford Ruether has been counterproductive. Their appeals have led to the "universalizing of white women's experience," the devaluation of the "radical difference between individuals and groups," and "the depreciation of women whose experience is different."[8] Her response to the critique of white women by women of color is to disallow "claims to universal female experience."[9] She concludes from the critique of women of color that "no particular form of experience, including that of women, will be able to claim ontological and epistemological privilege."[10]

The narrative set forth by Davaney is simple and damning: white middle-class women, appealing to women's experience as a basis for criticizing male oppression of women, reinforce the privileges of class, race, and the constitution of women as fundamentally different than men. In this essay I offer another narrative account of the fate of the "appeal to women's experience," another interpretation of both the limits and the continued power of that appeal.

7. Sheila Greeve Davaney, "The Limits of the Appeal to Women's Experience," in *Shaping New Vision: Gender and Values in American Culture*, edited by Clarissa W. Atkinson, Constance H. Buchanan, Margaret R. Miles (Ann Arbor: UMI Research Press, 1987), 32.

8. Ibid., 44.

9. Ibid., 48.

10. Ibid., 45.

I find Davaney's interpretation of the limits of the appeal to women's experience extremely helpful. Davaney points to what appears to be a logical flaw in feminist discourse: a particular set of women's experiences is described by feminist theologians and used as the basis of critique and constructive work. I find Davaney's critique persuasive if we look at the appeal to women's experience only as an intellectual claim within texts and ignore the discursive function evoked by that appeal. Davaney's article reminds me of the complexity of charting out the relationship between textual coherence—what would seem logically to be the political impact of a text—*and* the actual political and cultural impact of any given text or textual strategy. From a reading of the texts of feminist theology, Davaney concludes that the appeal to women's experience has functioned to exclude and devalue the experiences of working-class women and women of color. I will argue that the contrary is the case. Far from silencing women who are "different," the appeal to women's experience, as a discursive strategy, has elicited and validated the voices of women from a continuously expanding range of contexts and social locations. It has elicited and welcomed the critiques of women of color. Feminists who appeal to women's experience are making a hermeneutical—not a metaphysical—claim. We are referring to a process, a discursive strategy, not a fixed content, an assumed "universal female experience."

THE POWER OF THE APPEAL TO WOMEN'S EXPERIENCE

Davaney summarizes the critique that women of color have made of white women's work. Her conclusions, however, differ radically from the conclusions of many women of color. Many women of color in the field of religion do reject as partial the work of white feminists. They do not, however, reject the appeal to women's experience. On the contrary, they turn to the force and legitimacy of such an appeal as the motivation of their own critical and constructive work. This connection can be clearly seen in a number of textual and political events. I will mention three and focus on one in detail: the proliferation of writings by women of color within the field of feminist theology; the support of work by women of color in the women's section of the American Academy of Religion; the claims made by women of color.

My narrative account of the *success* of the appeal to women's experience is initially grounded in the writings of women of color who state that this hermeneutic leads them to describe their own experiences and the complex relationship between their experiences and those of other women. Such a claim is clearly expressed in the book *Inheriting Our Mothers' Gardens: Feminist Theology in a Third World Perspective*, edited by Letty Russell (Euro-American), Kwok Pui-Lan (Chinese), Ada María Isasi-Díaz (Hispanic), and Katie Geneva Cannon (African-American).[11] Note that this appeal is intrinsically dialogical: the editors assume that "digging in your own garden," recounting your "own experiences and stories," will lead to a better understanding of the lives of others. The "appeal to women's experience," as practiced by these authors, is not the end of theological work but the beginning of conversations about theology:

> For doing theology in a holistic way requires us to include not only our own experiences and stories but also a critical analysis of the effect this has had on our lives, so that we are prepared to understand the stories and the social, political, and historical analysis of those whose lives are quite different from ours, and especially those whose lives are shaped by oppression. The beginning of partnership in dialogue is "digging in your own garden," so that you know what gifts you can bring to the global table talk with your sisters and what parts of your life might be harmful to others. Once we have understood the oppressive and liberating social structures of our own reality more clearly, we are better able to understand the social structures that affect other people's lives.[12]

Many women of color claim that the appeal to women's experience has moved them to explore the theological, political, and cultural significance of their own experiences. Kwok Pui-Lan, for example, claims that "ironically, it is my commitment to feminism

11. Katie Geneva Cannon, Ada María Isasi-Díaz, Kwok Pui-Lan, Letty M. Russell, *Inheriting Our Mothers' Gardens: Feminist Theology in a Third World Perspective* (Louisville, Ky.: Westminster Press, 1988).

12. "Introduction," *Inheriting Our Mothers' Gardens*, 14.

that leads me to a renewed interest and appreciation of my own cultural roots."[13] Rather than being silenced by the appeal to women's experience, Kwok Pui-Lan embraces it as a hermeneutic, as a discursive strategy and finds in it the authorization for challenging the canons, methods, and doctrines of Christian theology. The appeal to women's experience has elicited challenges to the adequacy of earlier descriptions of what it means to be constituted as woman, what it means to challenge oppressive constructions of female identity. Ada María Isasi-Díaz, for example, points to the racism of Anglo feminists. She does not conclude, however, that it is foolish to appeal to women's experience. She asks rather, that the understanding of women's experience be *enlarged* to include the experiences of Hispanic women: "Hispanic feminists' understandings must be included in what is normative for all feminists."[14] Asian-American feminist theologian Rita Nakishima Brock provides another account of the power of women turning to their experiences. She states that "Feminist impulses toward inclusivity and ecumenism in the widest possible sense, while ambivalent and imperfect, are crucial for the development of depth and breadth in our visions and dreams."[15]

Brock, along with many other women of color, responds to the appeal to women's experience as a challenging hermeneutic, as *a process of reflection*, and not as a static metaphysic, a depiction of "universal female experience." The appeal to women's experience is an invitation for women to discover, analyze, and describe what those experiences have been. It is also an invitation for women to challenge, in unforeseen and unforeseeable ways, the two-gender system and to create, together, other ways of being:

> We begin to heal, in remembrance and forgiveness, by allowing anger to surface, by reconnecting to our deepest, most passionate feelings, feelings grounded in the rich complexities

13. Kwok Pui-Lan, "Mothers and Daughters, Writers and Fighters," *Inheriting Our Mothers' Gardens*, 31.

14. Ada María Isasi-Díaz, "A Hispanic Garden in a Foreign Land," *Inheriting Our Mothers' Gardens*, 97.

15. Rita Nakishima Brock, *Journeys by Heart: A Christology of Erotic Power* (New York: Crossroad, 1988), xvii.

> of our full embodied experience, and by actively reclaiming memory, memory grounded in our relationships. In consciousness-raising groups and other feminist contexts, the hearing of each person into her own speech, a process Nelle Morton describes in *The Journey Is Home*, can become a powerful tool of memory and connection. As Morton reports from her experiences, when the empathetic, receptive listening of others allows a woman to tell her own story of suffering fully from beginning to end, that woman is heard into her own liberating speech. My own experiences in such contexts and reports from friends have made me acutely aware of both the pain and healing power of honest memory. Memory that emerges from the heart of ourselves binds us to the suffering of others and provides us the routes to empowerment and self-acceptance. Such memory also makes us hungry for collective memory, for the stories of our own people, and of the truth of the life of the human species.[16]

What is this memory that makes us "hungry for collective memory, for the stories of our own people, for the truth of the life of the human species?" To interpret either the memory or the truth in essentialist terms is to miss the evocative power of articulating "the rich complexities of our full embodied experience." When we follow this hermeneutic and actually describe the texture of our lives, we elicit reflection and action in others, reflection that may, if we are successful, lead as easily, as readily to dissent as to assent.

It is my contention that the specificity of the appeal to women's experience (that white women did and do describe white middle-class experience) has invited politically transformative dissent. It is far easier to see the contrasts between one's own experiences and those of other people if the experiences are described concretely and vividly, as they are in feminist theology.

The critical power of describing our experience and having *others* see its limits can be clearly illustrated by contrasting feminist writings and those of male liberal theologians. Feminist theologians ground our theological work in the complex particularities of human life. Judith Plaskow, Mary Daly, and Carter Heyward, among others, all provide detailed accounts of women's experiences, in the past and present, of suffering, healing, joy, and endurance.

16. Ibid., 23.

The works of many male liberal theologians, while ostensibly referring to the experience of being human, elide the specificity of their claims through abstractions. Reading such abstractions, many people can fit themselves into the schemes and categories of liberal theology without seeing the fundamental difference between their experiences and those serving as the basis for theological abstractions. Paul Tillich, for example, writes of the "courage to be" in ways that seem applicable to many people in a wide range of situations. Yet, when we look carefully at what he means by courage, and by the threats that necessitate courage, a vastly different picture emerges.

Tillich's description of the power of Being as that which "eternally conquer(s) its own nonbeing" seems plausible and innocuous until we realize what he means by nonbeing. While Tillich rarely defines nonbeing, his description of one central aspect of nonbeing in *The Courage to Be* is revealing. He sees as a threat and as something to be conquered the constituent elements of human life: our belonging to history and place and our dependence on a world that is itself changing and interdependent:

> One can show the *contingency of our temporal being*, the fact that we exist in this and no other period of time, beginning in a contingent moment, ending in a contingent moment, filled with experiences which are contingent themselves with respect to quality and quantity. One can show the *contingency of our spatial being* (our finding ourselves in this and no other place, and the strangeness of this place in spite of its familiarity); the contingent character of ourselves and the place from which we look at our world; and the *contingent character of the reality at which we look, that is, our world*. . . . Contingent does not mean causally undetermined but it means that the determining causes of our existence have no ultimate necessity. They are given, and they cannot be logically derived. Contingently we are put into the whole web of causal relations. Contingently we are determined by them in every moment and thrown out by them in the last moment.[17]

Tillich interprets our interdependence as a threat. The fact that there is no necessity to our existence, that no law of nature would

17. Paul Tillich, *The Courage to Be* (New Haven, Conn.: Yale University Press, 1952), 43-44. Emphasis added.

be violated had we never been born, is seen by him as a threat to self-affirmation.

In contrast to the elusive categories of much liberal theology, feminist theologians speak concretely and vividly of experiences of suffering, healing, joy, and endurance. Our speech often, when most effective, evokes dissent. It is odd, however, that such dissent is interpreted as a sign of failure.

In 1978 Mary Daly explored, in her book *Gyn/Ecology*, the deep, often painful differences between women. Since then, even more differences have emerged. A significant difference is the challenge of women of color to white women's interpretation of the interaction of racism, sexism, and class exploitation. White women, such as Rosemary Ruether and Mary Daly, have argued that the oppression of women by men is primary, and that class exploitation and racism are derived from this primary patriarchal oppression. Many women of color disagree with this analysis and argue that racism is as much a problem for white women as for white men, and that it cannot be seen as a subset of patriarchal oppression.

This debate is far from academic, yet its political and strategic import has been missed in many white interpretations. White women have taken up, for example, Audre Lorde's critique of Mary Daly, arguing that Daly's work reflects the universalizing of white women's experience and that Daly has not listened to the voices of women of color. It is clear, however, in *Pure Lust* that Daly has listened to women of color. Writings of women of color are predominantly featured there as examples of endurance, creativity, and liveliness, and the relationship between racism and patriarchal oppression is recognized.[18] Daly continues to differ with many women of color, however, on the interpretation of the relationship of racism and sexism. This disagreement comes from taking seriously the analyses of women of color yet continuing to see things differently. The differences here are not accidental, and not at all

18. Daly responds to Audre Lorde's critique in the "New Intergalactic Introduction" to the 1990 edition of *Gyn/Ecology*. She writes that "Explosions of Diversity do not happen without conflict. . . ." Mary Daly, *Gyn/Ecology: The Metaethics of Radical Feminism* (Boston: Beacon Press, 1990), xxx–xxxi.

due to universalizing. Rather they reflect particularities of vision and of experience.

Ruether and Daly argue that the racism of white women, while real, emerges within the context of patriarchal oppression.[19] The situation for white women is akin to that of poor and working class white men. In much of the United States, racism emerges as a force pitting poor, working-class, and middle-class whites against poor, working-class, and middle-class blacks. It leads to a situation in which whites see blacks as the enemy and blame them for taking "their jobs," not seeing the structure of class exploitation that creates few jobs and jobs with low pay. In both rural and urban settings in the U.S., the phenomenon is the same. In addressing the racism of white women and of poor and working-class white men, it is essential to recognize the way racism is a subterfuge, an outlet for rage and frustration that effectively prevents women and poorer men from challenging the economic power structures that control their lives.

From the perspective of people of color, such distinctions are immaterial. Racism hurts as much, irrespective of the status of the racist doing the harm. A rock thrown by a woman hurts as much as one thrown by a man; being humiliated by white teachers (male or female) does as much damage as being denied employment by wealthy white men. These two points of view are not commensurable, yet each is essential in analyzing and working against the damage of racism.

The longing for a discourse that is complete, final, and free of conflict lingers in the interpretive strategies practiced by many Euro-American feminists. Take for example the reflections of the Euro-American feminist theorist Nancy Miller:

> When I finished (and gave) the piece "on race"—let's just say it created more problems than it solved—I began to wonder whether there was any position from which a white middle-class feminist could say anything on the subject without sounding exactly like that. . . . The rhetorical predictability of it all.

19. Rosemary Radford Ruether, *New Woman New Earth: Sexist Ideologies and Human Liberation* (New York: Seabury Press, 1975), 115–33.

> The political correctness. Just like "men in feminism." In which case it might be better not to say anything.[20]

The problem for many of us is that we are still trying to escape our skins, trying to write without sounding "white and middle-class." For those of us who are white and middle-class, the goal is to acknowledge that perspective, not evade it, and explore forthrightly the range of perspectives opened and closed by our social location. I am white and middle-strata, if not middle-class. My goal in writing is not to escape or transcend that conditioning but to understand it more thoroughly, more critically. Let me give as an example my experience in writing about African-American women's literature. In my book *A Feminist Ethic of Risk* I build a critique of much of Euro-American understandings of responsibility and power from my work with African-American women and men.[21] I describe the critique of racism that I have found in the work and writings of African-American women. In my interpretation of this literature I was constantly wary of the dangers of appropriating the work of African-American women, the dangers of speaking for African-American women, the dangers of assuming that I could interpret this literature without distorting it. I tried to make clear that my reading was partial and conditioned—that I was reading the literature of African-American women *as* a Euro-American, describing what I had learned from that literature. In spite of my efforts to avoid appropriation, the power of class and race privilege is still operative in the work. Irene Monroe, an African-American minister and womanist theologian, pointed out a glaring act of appropriation in my book. The title is *A Feminist Ethic of Risk,* and yet I find the ethic of risk in dialogue with the writings of African-American women. Monroe argues that the title is misleading. The book itself reflects political work and dialogue with womanist ethicists and activists. The title, however, names only one partner in the political-theological dialogue, feminism. A more accurate title would acknowledge in a subtitle or an alternate wording, the primacy of dialogue in the creation of feminist ethics.

20. Nancy K. Miller, "Criticizing Feminist Criticism," *Conflicts in Feminism*, 364.

21. Sharon D. Welch, *A Feminist Ethic of Risk* (Minneapolis: Fortress Press, 1990).

Do I regard the book as a failure? No. On the contrary, it was only by attempting to write about racism that I was able to learn more about how deeply it is embedded in my habits of knowing and naming. I concur, therefore, with the insights of those who argue that we need an emphasis on maintaining procedures of evaluating the conflicts of interests and interpretations that will necessarily arise as we are engaged in serious political work and theoretical discussions with people from different groups. Barbara Herrnstein Smith, in *Contingencies of Value*, highlights the imperative of eliciting and evaluating conflicting interpretations of experience:

> If, as I believe, there can be no total and final eradication of disparity, variance, opposition, and conflict, and also neither perfect knowledge or pure charity, then the general optimum might well be that set of conditions that permits and encourages . . . *evaluation*: that is, the local figuring and working out, as well as we, heterogeneously, can, of what seems to work better than worse.[22]

What we need is, quite simply, what Jane Gallop calls an ethic of criticism.[23] We need to distinguish between critiques that are based in "attending to" arguments and claims, and critiques that are simply dismissive.[24]

AN ETHIC OF CRITICISM

I believe that it is possible to find such an ethic, and that key ingredients of an ethic of criticism can be discerned from a consideration of two disparate sources—the writing of African-American women, and interpretations of the differences between American and French feminisms. I will begin with the writings of African-American women and then explore the differences between American and French feminisms.

22. Barbara Herrnstein Smith, *Contingencies of Value: Alternative Perspectives for Critical Theory* (Cambridge: Harvard University Press, 1988), 179.

23. Jane Gallop, "Criticizing Feminist Criticism," 368.

24. Ibid.

In her novel *The Salt Eaters*, Toni Cade Bambara describes an ethic of abundance, struggle, and transformation.[25] Bambara describes a black community's struggle to combine intellectual, political, and spiritual forces in work for justice. Bambara takes as one model for political work and ethical critique the soaring, healing beauty of jazz. I contend that our theoretical and strategic work can also be a soaring, healing manifestation of "sheer holy boldness." Within this ethic, power is not grounded in a guaranteed access to truth, not based in an accurate understanding of the universal human experience. Rather, power emerges from processes of listening, inventing, and responding to very particular challenges, to very particular lives and opportunities.

As we are grounded in community, our theoretical work is an exercise in "sheer holy boldness." What gives our theoretical work its power is its basis in a community of resistance and its resonance in the lives of women also struggling for liberation. Our work is *powerful* when it is itself the product of liberation and furthers and evokes liberation in others. Furthermore, our work is partial. Its trajectories are unforeseen and unforeseeable: what realities are there beyond the two-gender system, what will coalitions with women of different races and classes bring?

Bambara names the courage of creative political work that is akin to the creativity of jazz:

> She could dance right off the stool, . . . her head thrown back and singing, cheering, celebrating all those giants she had worshiped in their terrible musicalness. Giant teachers teaching through tone and courage and inventiveness but scorned, rebuked, beleaguered, trivialized, commercialized, copied, plundered, goofed on by half-upright pianos and droopy-drawers drums and horns too long in hock and spittin up rust and blood, tormented by sleazy bookers and takers, tone-deaf amateurs and saboteurs, . . . underpaid and overworked till they didn't know, didn't trust, wouldn't move on the wonderful gift given and were mute, crazy and beat-up. But standing up in their genius anyhow ready to speak the unpronounceable. On the stand with no luggage and no maps and

25. Toni Cade Bambara, *The Salt Eaters* (New York: Vintage Books, 1981).

> ready to go anywhere in the universe together on just sheer holy boldness.[26]

The theoretical and strategic differences among us are real and worthy of careful discussion and much mutually challenging and transforming work. It is somewhat ironic, but our differences are less fruitfully explored when we make too much of them, rather than too little, assuming that the discovery of the single correct foundation for ethics or the single most appropriate metaphor for the sacred would free us. Misplaced theoretical fervor arises as we forget that what defeats us is not incorrect theory per se but brute force, coercion, and social control.

The struggle against patriarchy is not an easy one. Any theory or strategy can be used against us. This could seem grim, but my conclusion is not pessimistic. I see it rather as a call for suppleness of mind, clarity of vision and purpose. We can think, organize, and act with greater focus, and given this awareness, do our theoretical work well but hold it lightly, valuing the human connections it serves more than the cerebral connections it makes. This recognition can free us for boldness in our theoretical work and strategy-planning. Realizing that there is no strategy without the risk of being outmaneuvered, no theory without the possibility of subversion, we can freely experiment with different forms of thought and action.

While there is no sure foundation in such intellectual work, it is possible to lessen our chances of defeat. Just as theory separated from community can be most easily distorted, theoretical work grounded in community offers a better chance for political success, and this for several reasons. If demonstrated faulty, incomplete, or even distorted, the base remains for engendering other theories, other theologies and thealogies. Also, the very process of creating theory, including thealogy and theology, can be empowering, a process (to use Nelle Morton's language) of hearing others to speech.

With this approach to theory we can be bold ourselves and recognize the boldness of women in the past. Even if our work is later used against us, it can be generated in such a way that the

26. Ibid., 265.

process of developing theory creates the matrix of responding to such threats. As we take our own voices seriously, as we name this world with women outside the academy, as we value the process of naming as much as the result, our theoretical work can be (to use another image from Toni Cade Bambara) a way of "sporting power" for others:

> Knock and be welcomed in and free to roam the back hall on the hunt for that particular closet with the particular hanging robe, coat, mantle, veil or whatever it was. And get into it. Sport it. Parade around the district in it so folks would remember themselves. Would hunt for their lost selves.[27]

"Power" for intellectuals does not require developing a final theory of oppression and liberation. It is found in bold attempts to understand, analyze, and name, utilizing the resources of a resisting community.

In fact the ethic of "sporting power" is difficult even to see when people are thinking instead in terms of rational citizens choosing the knowable and definable good. A clear example of such oblivion is found in *Habits of the Heart*. The concern of the authors of *Habits of the Heart* is "how to preserve or create a morally coherent life."[28] Robert Bellah, Steven Tipton, Richard Madsen, Ann Swidler, and William Sullivan interviewed white middle class Americans. The resulting text is rich and thought-provoking. The discussion of the interviews is especially well-done, detailed enough to enable alternative interpretations of the data they present.

One of the people interviewed and discussed in the book is a white middle-class man whose ethic seems similar to Toni Cade Bambara's depiction of the ethical and political strategies of sporting power. Wayne Bauer is a tenant organizer working with the Campaign for Economic Democracy. His goal in working with people who are working-class or living in poverty is "to give them a sense of power about their own lives."[29] He helps people organize in

27. Ibid., 266.

28. Robert N. Bellah, Richard Madsen, William Sullivan, Ann Swidler, and Steven M. Tipton, *Habits of the Heart: Individualism and Commitment in American Life* (New York: Harper and Row, 1985), vi.

29. Ibid., 18.

response to what they identify as the most pressing crises affecting them. The result is people feeling alive, effective, and connected. Bauer says, "I see them coming out feeling like, well hell! we affected something . . . it's very beautiful to see and very exciting to be a part of."[30]

The authors of *Habits of the Heart* ask Bauer for more: "What specific kinds of things should these newly liberated people create in society?"[31] Bauer refuses to answer for the people with whom he works. His response is interpreted as "a weak idea of justice," his vision of economic and political democracy is seen as "strangely without content," and it seems as though freedom becomes "a virtual end in itself."[32]

Accustomed to responsible people determining for others as well as for themselves how power and wealth are distributed, the authors of *Habits of the Heart* cannot imagine a system of justice in which it is essential that people decide together the forms and structures of their lives. Wayne Bauer cannot decide alone what housing policy should be, cannot determine in the abstract "what a just society would look like."[33] As we live wholeheartedly an ethic of sporting power, the definitions of a just society will be endlessly, constantly evolving and changing, changing to meet the exigencies of current social and political needs and possibilities.

It is at this point that the conversation between American and French feminists becomes most important and extremely muddled. Not only the French, but American thinkers as well reject over-inflated, misleading claims for Reason as the primary means of adjudicating different interests and combatting injustice. The recent exchange between Daryl McGowan Tress and Jane Flax in the journal *Signs* is instructive on this issue. Tress argues that the only means of combatting injustice is "the primacy of reason."[34] She believes that "it is *only reason*, at work in any person, that would

30. Ibid., 19.

31. Ibid.

32. Ibid., 24.

33. Ibid., 26.

34. Daryl McGowan Tress, "Comments on Flax's 'Postmodernism and Gender Relations in Feminist Theory,' " *Signs: Journal of Women in Culture and Society* 14 (1988), 197.

have some measure of ability to stand apart from the practices of injustices and to identify them; *reason alone is independent of contingencies* and is universal and available to everyone."[35] While Tress's fears are shared by many activists and theoreticians, her solution, a universally available and historically transcendent reason, seems increasingly suspect. Surely there are other grounds for compassion, justice, and liberation than an elusive and indeed illusory shared reason.

In her reply to Tress, Jane Flax mentions other political and social constituents of justice. She notes, "There are many ways in which such qualities [liberation, stable meaning, insight, self-understanding, the self and justice] may be attained—for example: political practice; economic, racial and gender equality; good childrearing; empathy; fantasy; feelings; imagination; and embodiment."[36] Flax advocates a proliferation of diverse practical prerequisites of justice and fluid understandings of the concrete embodiments of justice. In each case, I find it important to note the power of difference—different practices working toward at times common, at times divergent ends, "solid practices" (of respectful childrearing, of empathy) producing fluid concepts of the self, society, and justice.

I have often thought that it is at this point that American and French feminists have the most to say to each other, and I have been surprised and dismayed by debates in which the discussion of difference by French feminists is used to dismiss the work of American feminists such as Mary Daly, Susan Griffin, and Adrienne Rich. I am not alone in this concern. Ann Snitow criticizes a common interpretation of radical feminism: "the revisionist image of extreme essentialism (such as Mary Daly's in *Gyn/Ecology*) as the basic matrix of feminist thought from which a radical "nominalism" has more recently and heroically departed, calling all categories into doubt."[37] Teresa de Lauretis is also critical of analyses that reduce the radical

35. Ibid.

36. Jane Flax, "Reply to Tress," *Signs: Journal of Women in Culture and Society* 14 (1988), 202.

37. Ann Snitow, "A Gender Diary," in *Conflicts in Feminism*, 9–43, 17.

feminist theory of the self found in Daly, Griffin, and Rich to "an essential womanhood, common to all women."[38]

Why has radical feminist theory been relegated to the nether world of simplistic unified selves and French feminist thought taken as the marker of a truly liberating openness? With Ann Snitow, I find that this comforting division elides the complexity within the many variants of feminist theory.[39] The simple division between essentialist and anti-essentialist elides the fluidity of the radical feminist self and ignores the individualism and elitism of Luce Irigaray's and Hélène Cixous' celebration of difference. In the following pages I will first examine the lack of significant difference in the work of Irigaray. I will then explore the presence of constitutive difference in the work of Mary Daly. I will conclude with a discussion of the way in which Irigaray's and Cixous' descriptions of the differences within and between individuals can serve as a metaphor that aids our analyses of the dynamic interaction between culturally and politically distinct groups.

IRIGARAY, CIXOUS, AND THE PLAY OF DIFFERENCE

A common confusion marks many of the American projects that attempt to use the work of Luce Irigaray and Hélène Cixous. Many American authors fail to see that while American theorists tend to emphasize the differences between groups, these French theorists stress the play of difference that marks the individual subject. The use of French theorist Irigaray as a theoretician of the differences between groups of women is especially misleading. The difference extolled by Irigaray is the fluidity and difference of the individual self.[40] She does not discuss the differences between various groups of women, for her focus, although unacknowledged, is the fractures and ambiguities of the self of the Western elite. As the African-American critic Barbara Christian reminds us, the analysis of post-

38. Teresa de Lauretis, "Upping the Anti (*sic*) in Feminist Theory," in *Conflicts in Feminism*, 255–70, 258.

39. Ann Snitow, "A Gender Diary," in *Conflicts in Feminism*, 9–43, 17.

40. Luce Irigaray, *This Sex Which Is Not One*, trans. Catherine Porter (Ithaca, New York: Cornell University Press, 1985).

modern theorists is culture specific and not true of the dynamics constitutive of language and self-formation in all peoples.[41]

The confusion is understandable. Irigaray, for example, in her two most influential books, does refer to themes central to the politics of difference. In *Speculum of the Other Woman* she criticizes the Freudian construction of woman and her sexuality, arguing that woman "is reduced to a function and a functioning whose historic causes must be reconsidered: property systems, philosophical, mythological, or religious systems."[42] There is a complementary acknowledgment of historical specificity in *This Sex Which Is Not One*. Here Irigaray affirms the importance of the dual task of exposing "the exploitation common to all women" and finding "the struggles that are appropriate for each woman, right where she is, depending on her nationality, her job, her social class, her sexual experience, that is, upon the form of oppression that is for her the most immediately unbearable."[43]

These affirmations lead us to expect a modulation of claims by Irigaray, a recognition that the construction of Woman she so carefully criticizes is a Western, elite phenomenon, and a recognition that the subversive, fluid "self" she extols is similarly culturally specific. Unfortunately, that is not the case. In the work of Irigaray there is nothing from working-class women or women of color and precious little about the concrete political and cultural differences that shape women's lives. In sharp contrast to Irigaray's work, the political debates central for many American feminists focus on the understanding and mediation (through conflict and/or coalition) of differences between groups of women, each group asserting a fluid, complex, multilayered yet particular identity. Irigaray claims that "woman never speaks the same way. What she emits is flowing, fluctuating. *Blurring*." While undoubtedly characteristic of the speech and experience of some women, "blurring" does not describe the fierce affirmation of self and community that funds feminist political work throughout the world.[44]

41. Barbara Christian, "The Race for Theory," *Feminist Studies* 14 (Spring 1988), 75–76.

42. Luce Irigaray, *Speculum of the Other Woman*, trans. Gillian C. Gill (Ithaca, New York: Cornell University Press, 1985), 129.

43. Irigaray, *This Sex Which Is Not One*, 166–67.

44. Ibid., 112.

THE FLUIDITY OF THE RADICAL FEMINIST SELF

Mary Daly addresses these concerns in *Pure Lust*. She writes that "the title *Pure Lust* is double-sided. On one side, it Names the deadly dis-passion that prevails in patriarchy." The "end" of "pure lust" is "the braking/breaking of female being, . . . the obliteration of natural knowing and willing, . . . our innately ordained Self-direction toward Happiness."[45] This language of "natural," and "innately ordained" is frequently misread as static and essentialist. Daly is making a quite different claim. That which is "natural" is intrinsically fluid, dynamic, and *changing*. Daly claims that our "innate be-ing" is a *verb*, not a noun. She identifies as "natural" and "elemental" *a process of being in relation*, not a fixed essence or content:

> Primarily, then, *Pure Lust* Names the high humor, hope, and cosmic accord/harmony of those women who choose to escape, to follow our hearts' deepest desire and bound out of the State of Bondage, Wanderlusting and Wonderlusting with the elements, connecting with auras of animals and plants, moving in planetary communion with the farthest stars. This Lust is in its essence astral. It is pure Passion: unadulterated, absolute, simple sheer striving for abundance of be-ing. It is unlimited, unlimiting desire/fire.[46]

This process of Pure Lust, though called ontological, is quite different from the ontology of fixed essence, of a universal humankind with a knowable and specifiable universal experience. Daly states, again and again, that women belong to different "tribes," have great individual diversity, and cannot even be regarded as being members of a single species.[47] As she says:

> *It renders the old philosophical concept of "species" obsolete*, especially as a tool for conceptualizing and Naming the be-ing of biophilic creatures. Such ones cannot be confined to any static species, *for our essences are changing, metapatterning*.

45. Mary Daly, *Pure Lust: Elemental Feminist Philosophy* (Boston: Beacon Press, 1984), 2.
46. Ibid., 3.
47. Ibid., 352.

> When I write Metaphorically of the "souls" of women as our telic focusing and metapatterning principle, then, I am not restricting the term to express the classical Aristotelian idea of substantial form determining an individual as a member of a fixed species. . . . Springing off from Aristotelian structure, and from the language of modern science as well, the Spirited Searcher may speak of the soul not as that which confines an individual within a "species," but rather as a principle of uniqueness/diversity. . . .[48]

The commonality that exists among women is not a given, not a universal female essence, but *a relation that is created* as we attend, with respect and openness, to the meanings and challenges of each others' lives:

> For it is clear that Lusty women are profoundly different from each other. Not only are there ethnic, national, class and racial differences that shape our perspectives, but there are also individual and cross-cultural differences of temperament, virtue, talent, taste, and of conditions within which these can or cannot find expression. There is, then, an extremely rich, complex Diversity among women and within each individual. But there is also above, beyond, beneath all this a Cosmic Commonality, a tapestry of connectedness which women as Websters/Fates are constantly weaving. The weaving of this tapestry is the Realizing of a dream, which Adrienne Rich has Named "The Dream of a Common Language."[49]

For Daly, what is ontological is our grounding in processes of interaction, our participation in "Powers of Be-ing [that] are constantly unfolding, creating, communicating—Be-ing more."[50] Our elementally inspired memories are created, not "always there," created by connections with people and with nature:

> A woman who can evoke her childhood experiences of gazing at the moon and stars on clear nights, or lying on the grass, or listening to the sea, or watching the sunset is Elementally inspired. When she can recall early experiences of the smell of leaves on an October day, the taste of raspberries at a picnic,

48. Ibid., 352–53.
49. Ibid., 26–27.
50. Ibid., 30.

> the feel of sand warmed by the sun, she is empowered. Energized by her own unique Elemental memories, she can break through the maze of "adult categories." Her reawakened, recharged aura expands its rays, shining through the film of societally imposed schemata, rendering visible the deep connections.
>
> Enormous breakthroughs to the spheres of deep Memory can be occasioned by the accidental recurrence of a body posture. Feminists becoming aware of our bodies in new/ancient powerful ways know that this far-from-accidental process reconnects us with Metamemory. Women who study self-defense and various forms of the martial arts, for example, sometimes describe a vivid remembering of bodily integrity and coordination which they had known as young girls, before the heavy indoctrination of adolescence forced feminization upon them.[51]

Elemental memories do not exist without concrete acts, without participation in a culture that teaches us to live, openly and freely, in and through our bodies and our complex, intricate relationships of mutual interdependence. Women, working together to recover such processes, are involved in a movement of creation, not in the discovery of fixed essences. As Daly states, feminism is a verb:

> In this true and radical sense, feminism is a verb; it is female be-ing. Unlike sadopseudofeminism fabricated by the fathers, which is a thing, a reified state, feminism as Realizing is constant unfolding process. It was/is inevitable that women who conceive of feminism as a thing, a state, would come at some point to believe themselves to have moved "beyond feminism." But if one understands feminism to mean the radical, ontological process of Realizing female Elemental potency, one does not move "beyond" it. One moves with it. *Feminism* is a Name for our moving/movement into Metabeing.[52]

THE COMPLEMENTARITY OF FRENCH AND AMERICAN FEMINIST THEORY

How best to describe the claims to truth of fluid yet describable, particular identities? It is here that the insights of some French feminists and those of American feminists and womanists can be

51. Ibid., 356–57.
52. Ibid., 194.

powerfully integrated and can lead to an articulation of the logic of naming, the logic of identity-formation that, to use the language of Mary Daly, sparks and spins rather than forms, ranks, normalizes, and molds.[53] I apply to the political and collective Irigaray's description of the evocative, transformative relationship between "two" women. Irigaray claims that the experience of women's knowing and loving cannot be contained in patriarchal depictions of logic or in patriarchal descriptions of a love predicated on a clear distinction between the self and other. She writes of the challenge of speaking without utilizing a static logic: "How can we speak so as to escape from their compartments, their schemas, their distinctions and oppositions. . . . Disengage ourselves, *alive,* from their concepts? . . . You know that we are never completed, but that we only embrace ourselves whole."[54] Irigaray describes the fluidity of life, a fluidity incomprehensible if one searches for "solid ground":

> You are moving. You never stay still. You never stay. You never "are." How can I say "you," when you are always other? How can I speak to you? You remain in flux, never congealing or solidifying. What will make that current flow into words? It is multiple, devoid of causes, meanings, simple qualities. . . . These movements cannot be described as the passage from a beginning to an end. These rivers flow into no single, definitive sea. These streams are without fixed banks, this body without fixed boundaries. This unceasing mobility. This life—which will perhaps be called our restlessness, whims, pretenses, or lies. All this remains very strange to anyone claiming to stand on solid ground.[55]

53. Teresa de Lauretis makes a similar defense of radical feminist thought. "I would insist that the notion of experience in relation both to social-material practices and to the formation and processes of subjectivity is a feminist concept, not a poststructuralist one . . . and would be still unthinkable were it not for specifically feminist practices, political, critical, and textual: consciousness raising, the rereading and revision of the canon, the critique of scientific discourses, and the imaging of new social spaces and forms of community. In short, the very practices of those feminist critics Weedon allocates to the 'essentialist' camp." "Upping the Anti (*sic*) in Feminist Theory," 260.

54. Irigaray, *This Sex Which Is Not One,* 212.

55. Ibid., 214–15.

This life, with its "unceasing mobility," cannot be comprehended in categories that imagine a "one," or even the "one and the many":

> We are luminous. Neither one nor two. I've never known how to count. Up to you. In their calculations, we make two. Really, two? Doesn't that make you laugh? An odd sort of two. And yet not one. Especially not one. Let's leave *one* to them: their oneness, with its prerogatives, its domination, its solipsism. . . . And the strange way they divide up their couples, with the other as the image of the one.[56]

Irigaray writes of a love that does not require sacrifice of "one" to "another." She speaks of a love that emerges from plenitude, not from lack. "We are not lacks, voids awaiting sustenance, plenitude, fulfillment from the other."[57] The love that emerges from plenitude enlarges the world, and the joy that is achieved in such love is not static: its movement is the product of pleasure. "When you kiss me, the world grows so large that the horizon itself disappears. Are we unsatisfied? Yes, if that means we are never finished. If our pleasure consists in moving, being moved, endlessly. Always in motion: openness is never spent nor sated."[58]

Cixous also explores the economy of abundance. What she describes in individual women, womanists celebrate on the communal level. For Cixous, the gift as excess, as spending and abundance, is women's essential attribute.[59] In reading the theory and literature of African-American women, and in working with African-American women, I have learned that the gift as excess also characterizes communal life and the joyous, sustained struggle against injustice.

At the same time, I find the crux of the divergence between French feminists and womanist ethicists, novelists, and critics in the interpretation of the literary, psychological, and linguistic strategies that destroy the economy of abundance and laughter. For Cixous, the enemies are clear:

> For the German Romantics, the same bastions had to be destroyed as for us. Logocentrism and idealism, theology, all

56. Ibid., 207.
57. Ibid., 209.
58. Ibid., 210.
59. Verena Andermatt Conley, *Hélène Cixous: Writing the Feminine*, expanded edition (Lincoln: University of Nebraska Press, 1991).

> supports of society, the structure of political and of subjective economy, the pillars of property. The repressive machine has always had the same complicities, homogenizing reason, reductive, unifying which has always allied itself with the master, the unified subject [*sujet un*], stable, socializable.[60]

According to Verena Andermatt Conley, Cixous argues that the unified subject is tied to the "outmoded literary convention" of character. Cixous, like other members of the French *avant-garde,* sees "representation as politically reactionary." In order to effect social change, she "break(s) up character and unity," both "linked to a linear conception of time." The alternative is a fiction that "produces a surplus of reality."[61] Cixous is engaged in the production of "a political poetic," and criticizes literary forms that other groups embrace as the means of also producing a writing of affirmative excess, abundance.[62]

Barbara Harlow has noted the assertion of the revolutionary, liberative act of representation and character in resistance literature of people throughout the Third World.[63] Toni Cade Bambara's reflections on her work illustrate this political engagement through fiction, in which she represents "unified selves" struggling for life and dignity. Bambara's fiction explores a factor that enables and sustains moral critique and political resistance: the ability of African Americans to resist the multiple oppressions that cripple human life. Her work is carefully nuanced, acknowledging the defeats and costly victories of her people. She describes the tensions motivating her work:

> I despair at our failure to wrest power from those who have it and abuse it; our reluctance to reclaim our old powers lying dormant with neglect; our hesitancy to create new power in areas where it never before existed, and I'm euphoric because everything in our history, our spirit, our daily genius—suggest we do it.[64]

60. Ibid., 19.
61. Ibid., 24–25.
62. Ibid., 125.
63. Barbara Harlow, *Resistance Literature* (New York: Methuen, 1987).
64. Toni Cade Bambara, "Salvation Is the Issue," in Mari Evans, ed., *Black Women Writers (1950–1980): A Critical Evaluation* (Garden City, New York: Doubleday Anchor Books, 1984), 46.

Bambara names the "givens" from which she works: the recognition that African Americans "are at war"; the belief that "the natural response to oppression, ignorance, evil, and mystification is wide-awake resistance"; the belief that "the natural response to stress and crisis is not breakdown and capitulation, but transformation and renewal."[65] She says that her work is part of this natural resistance and renewal; her writing is a way of "participat[ing] in the empowerment of the community that names me."[66] Grounded in a community of resistance, Bambara writes stories of renewal and transformation:

> Stories are important. They keep us alive. In the ships, in the camps, in the quarters, fields, prisons, on the road, on the run, underground, under siege, in the throes, on the verge—the storyteller snatches us back from the edge to hear the next chapter. In which we are the subjects. We, the hero of the tales. Our lives preserved. How it was, how it be. Passing it along in the relay. That is what I work to do: to produce stories that save our lives.[67]

Contrast Bambara's writing to "save our lives" with Cixous' interpretation of her own work and the lack of a collective public for her fiction:

> When I write a fictional text, who is my interlocutor? To whom do I write? I cannot name the instance which then works on the unconscious of my language. It must be a mixture of myself, of God, of the absolute, etc.—since the public has neither a face nor a presence. There is also a part of censorship of which I am conscious. I felt over the years that I was threatened inside by effects of censorship.[68]

Cixous finds herself writing fiction without a public. This stance may be appropriate and liberating in its own context. But in other contexts, in the American struggle of feminists and womanists against racism, against patriarchal oppression and for the play of

65. Ibid., 47.
66. Ibid., 42.
67. Ibid., 41.
68. Hélène Cixous, in Conley, *Hélène Cixous: Writing the Feminine,* 166.

connection and life, we can write and work in concert with specific, identifiable publics.

In fact, it is through grounding in these communities that our work gains its political and ethical power. The problem of much American interpretation of Irigaray and Cixous is in its identifying particular linguistic strategies as the cause of cooptation: the use of characters, representation, and the unified self. Rather, the causes of cooptation are to be found in freezing the processes of engagement.

What linguistic and political strategies keep the processes of engagement open? How do we participate in a logic of identity-formation that sparks and spins rather than forms, ranks, normalizes, and molds? Feminist theorists on both sides of the "essentialist" divide try to honor the radical openness of creative thought and action. Irigaray evokes the unforeseen and unforeseeable dynamism of lives/selves open to others and open to growth:

> Something of the consummation of sexual difference has still not been articulated or transmitted. Is there not still something held in reserve within the silence of female history: an energy, morphology, growth or blossoming still to come from the female realm? Such a flowering keeps the future open. The world remains uncertain in the fact of this strange advent.[69]

Irigaray's haunting intimation of "a flowering that keeps the future open" is strikingly akin to Daly's hopes for the evocative impact of *Gyn/Ecology*:

> I have always seen *Gyn/Ecology* as part of a Movement, including my own Voyage. . . . When I set it free so it could be in the world, I did not see it as a work of perfection. For some women it could be an Awakening shock, for others a Source of information, or a springboard from which they might Leap into their own A-mazing Searches, Words, Metaphors. . . . I looked forward to the profusion of New Creation, which I believed could emerge from women of all races, cultures, classes—from women all over this planet, speaking/Be-Speaking

69. Luce Irigaray, "Sexual Difference," in *French Feminist Thought: A Reader*, ed. Toril Moi (New York: Basil Blackwell, 1987), 129.

> out of our various and vital heritages. I thought of our rich and radiant Diversity.[70]

What can best honor this rich, radiant, and conflictual Diversity? What can best serve the "energy still to come from the female realm?" My answer, for now, is an appeal to women's experiences, an evocation of more stories, more details, more conflicts, coalitions, and relationships. I affirm the words of Mary Daly, themselves inspired by Nelle Morton: "In the beginning was not the word. In the beginning is the hearing."[71]

70. Mary Daly, *Gyn/Ecology*, 1990 ed., xxx.
71. Mary Daly, *Gyn/Ecology*, 424.

8

Irigaray and the Divine

ELIZABETH GROSZ

Irigaray's recent writings on the divine have evoked shock, outrage, disappointment, and mystification in her readers. To many, she seems to have succumbed to the most naive essentialist reliance on religion to overcome or to provide solutions for women's sociopolitical and psychical oppression. In this chapter, I will defend her against these accusations by explaining how this recent interest is directly linked to her ongoing critique and displacement of the founding concepts of Western philosophy. Her analysis of discourses of the divine is not altogether different from her analysis of psychoanalytic theory. Her fascination with the divine is foreshadowed in her earlier writings; more particularly, it is the center of a cluster of loosely related interests. Among the more significant linkages are those she posits between (1) the domain of ethics (which, I would claim, is based on a reading of Levinas's notion of ethics as an encounter with alterity), (2) her notion of God and the divine (derived from her readings of Feuerbach, Levinas, and Schüssler Fiorenza, among others), (3) her notion of the elements or the elemental (based on her reading of Empedoclean ontology and the later Merleau-Ponty), and (4) her notion of sexual exchange, an exchange based on irreducibly different sexes as partners (derived from her bringing together of the structuralisms of Lévi-Strauss, Saussure, Marx, and Lacan). I hope in this essay to outline briefly the points of intersection and realignment of these concepts in her recent writings,[1] and also to indicate some of the ways in which this recent work continues yet transforms her earlier work on psychoanalysis.

Irigaray's (earlier) work on the borders of psychoanalytic theory—one ear in its ambit, the other outside, listening to what it cannot hear—provides if not a method, strictly speaking, then at least a series of questions that can with equal relevance be asked of any forms of (patriarchal) knowledge. Her question, if it can be reduced to one, is this: given that this body of knowledge or mode of representation presents the interests of only one sex, how would such knowledge look if it were able to represent adequately women's interests? This question is directed to psychoanalysis in Irigaray's writings of the 1970s: if Freud and Lacan provide conceptions of sexuality, the drive, desire, the object, the unconscious, and so forth, only from the point of view of masculinity, then how can these masculinist accounts be reread from other perspectives so that women's autonomy is a real possibility? How can psychoanalytic texts be read as both necessary, insofar as they explain the

1. Published translations of which I am aware include the following: "Divine Women" (Sydney: Local Consumption Occasional Papers 8 [1986]); "Women, the Sacred and Money," *Paragraph* 8, 1986); "The Fecundity of the Caress" in *Face-to-Face with Levinas*, ed. R. Cohen (Albany: State University of New York Press, 1986); and "Equal to Whom?" *differences* 2 (1990). Among other, more general texts relevant to understanding her position, see "Women's Exile," *Ideology and Consciousness* 1 (1977); "That Sex Which Is Not One" in *New French Feminisms*, ed. E. Marks and I. Courtivron (New York: Schocken Books 1981); "When the Goods Get Together," ibid.; "When Our Lips Speak Together," *Signs* 6, no. 1 (1980) (also in *This Sex Which Is Not One* [Ithaca, N.Y.: Cornell University Press, 1985]); "And One Doesn't Stir without the Other," *Signs* 7, no. 1, 1981 (also in *Refactory Girl* 23 [1982]); "For Centuries We've Been Living in the Mother-Son Relation," *Hecate* 9, nos. 1–2 (1983); "Any Theory of the 'Subject' Has Always Been Appropriated by the 'Masculine,' " *Trivia* (Winter, 1985). It appears as if, at long last, translations of many of her most recent texts will become available in English.

present structure and recent history of women's social subordination, and insufficient, insofar as they provide no way of questioning, let alone transforming, this social subordination? She demonstrates that the very texts and language of psychoanalysis simultaneously reveal its investments in male domination, yet allow alternative readings, readings that remain contrary to or different from its received interpretations. Like all texts, psychoanalytic texts (even the unconscious itself) are not inert objects controlled by their authors. Texts are material objects, and as matter, they are available for a very wide range of uses and potentially infinite readings.

A text's "viscosity," its materiality, its superabundance regarding an author's intentions, and its resistance to ownership is seen by Irigaray as a counterpart to the resistance or recalcitrance of the female body and sexuality in patriarchal culture. This parallelism, or, in her terms, "isomorphism," between bodies—especially women's bodies—and texts is not random. It is only insofar as female bodies are textually inscribed that they are constituted as lacking. It is only through textual incision that men are constructed as phallic. Thus a transformation in modes of writing is the condition of a transformation in modes of corporeal inscription and thus a transformation in bodies themselves.

If the broad question of sexual difference, autonomy, or specificity characterizes and informs all of Irigaray's writings, her philosophical and political goals seem to have undergone an inflection. Her broad goal in the 1970s was the interrogation of phallocentric texts through the articulation of a repressed femininity. In the 1980s, her new interests can be summed up in the title of her 1984 text, *The Ethics of Sexual Difference*. She has moved from the problematic of the independence, autonomy, and differences of the two sexes, to that of examining the conditions and possibilities of the modes of exchange between the two sexes. *Speculum* and *This Sex* were necessary starting points—necessary to make clear both how knowledges have defined woman as man's other and how conceptions of masculinity or, more commonly, humanity, are dependent on the silencing and denigration of femininity. The assertion of women's irreducible differences from men is only a preliminary stage of a transformation in social, theoretical, and representational relations. Although this assertion is a prerequisite, by itself it cannot engender new kinds of relations between the sexes. Establishing models and procedures whereby the two sexes, considered in their irreducible specificity, can be partners in a relation of exchange rather than exploitation implies the possibility of an exchange guaranteed not through the interchangeability of exchanging subjects (subjects presumed to be the same), but between subjects acknowledged as different. An entirely different mode of economy follows. Irigarary's more recent writings are an attempt to rethink models of exchange based upon difference and recognition and acceptance of the sexual otherness of the other, the interaction of a dual sexual symmetry.

I should state at the outset that I do not believe that Irigaray is advocating a return to the model of piety and devotion offered by the well-worn feminine emblem, Saint Teresa.[2] This would simply reinsert women back into the confines of men's modes of self-worship guaranteed by a God built in their image. Nor is she concerned with resurrecting or creating female goddesses from a mythic prehistory. Her concern with the notion of the divine or God is, rather, part of a project of creating an ideal self-image for women, an ideal to which women may aspire and through which they may make cultural artifacts, as men have created ethics, religions, sciences, and forms of life and love under the justification and authority of God. Irigaray is explicit in her rejection of these patriarchal traditions and representations of God and the divine:

> Man found a way to avoid this finitude in a *uniquely* masculine God. God created him in his own image. . . . He scarcely limits himself in himself, amongst his selves: he is father, son, spirit. Man did not let himself be defined by another genre: feminine. His only God was to correspond to the human type which we know is not neutral as far as the difference of sex goes.[3]

2. Saint Teresa is Lacan's emblem of a *jouissance* or pleasure that women may experience—in sexual love or in religious devotion—that is "beyond the phallus." Yet for Lacan, although women can experience this pleasure, they cannot know or say anything about it. Compare Lacan, "God and the Jouissance of the Woman," *Feminine Sexuality*, J. Rose and J. Mitchell (New York: W. W. Norton, 1985); and Irigaray's response in "Cosi Fan Tutti" in *This Sex Which Is Not One*.

3. "Divine Women," 4.

Indeed, Irigaray is scathing about what Lacan calls "good old God," for this concept has enabled men to disavow their debt to femininity and, especially, maternity. Because men can present God as the Ultimate and Divine Creator and because they can regard themselves as formed by Him in His image, they have effectively contained women outside the sphere of the Divine while relying upon women's resources. She sees the Catholic church, and, by implication, all patriarchal religions, as forms of women's oppression:

> When this minister of God only, of God the Father, pronounces the words of the Eucharist: "This is my body, this is my blood" according to the cannibalistic rite which is secularly ours, perhaps we could remind him that he would not be here if our body and our blood hadn't given him life. . . . And that it is us, women-mothers, whom he thus gives to be eaten.[4]

In place of patriarchal religion, Irigaray advocates neither a role-reversed female-dominated religion nor a more encompassing, truly "human" model. She refuses to abandon the category of the divine, as many others in the twentieth century have; instead, she attempts to tie notions of God and the divine to women's struggles for personal and social autonomy, thus politicizing them. She attempts to formulate the conditions of an entirely new way of envisaging the divine:

> Far from thinking that we should continue the process of deification on the pattern of our ancestors and their totem animals, that we should make a regression back to the siren goddesses, in particular against the men gods, it seems to me that we certainly have to incite a return to the *cosmic*, but at the same time asking ourselves why we were stopped as we were becoming *divine*.[5]

As in her relation to psychoanalytic theory, her relations to Christianity remain ambivalent; she neither accepts in wholesale terms nor does she reject outright the discourses associated with either institution. Instead, she tries to utilize their own insights

4. *Le corps-à-corps avec la mère* (Montréal, Quebec: Editions de la Pleine Lune, 1982), 37.

5. "Divine Women," 3.

against their pronouncements to highlight the limitations of each. Thus just as she uses Freud's notions of repression and the unconscious to show what of femininity psychoanalysis must repress, so too she uses what she considers are the real insights of Christianity against its manifest misogyny. For her, Christianity offers a model of "the respect for the incarnation of all bodies (men's and women's) as potentially divine: nothing more or less than each man and each woman being virtually gods."[6]

As she makes clear, however, "this message, especially as it concerns women, is most often veiled, obscured, covered over."[7] If Christianity makes explicit the fact that "spiritual becoming" and "corporeal becoming" are one and the same thing, Christianity must, in fact, be seen as a form of the cultivation and not at all as a renunciation of the sexual.[8] Christ is not only a God, but a God incarnated in human (here, male) sexual form. It is only by the purification and neuterization of Christ's corporeality that women's corporeality can be posited as the locus of sin. Moreover, while providing clues, hints as to what a divinity for women might be, Christianity must ultimately remain inadequate for women insofar as it is modeled on a Father-son genealogy, one in which women are either ignored or reduced to the status of mother. Only when the relation of mother and daughter can be conceived as divine, only insofar as woman can become divine in and of herself, and not simply as mother, wife, or lover, will a notion of divinity appropriate to women become possible. To understand Irigaray's notion of the divine, we must examine three themes in her writing that are intimately bound up with divinity: her conception of the elemental, of female autonomy, and of sexual exchange. I will look briefly at each.

THE ELEMENTAL

The metaphoric play of the elements is part of Irigaray's continuing strategy of developing a model or theoretical paradigm to enable

6. "Equal to Whom?" 64.
7. Ibid.
8. Ibid., 65.

women's subjectivity, desire, and social place to be autonomously designated. It is part of her search for a corporeal or *charnel* philosophy appropriate to the body and situation of women. If, as she has argued in *This Sex Which Is Not One*, models based on physics, chemistry, biology, or evolution are all implicated in a rampant yet rarely recognized phallocentrism, then it is necessary to depart from these paradigms—while recognizing their historical role in forming our self-understanding—in order for women to be understood on less constricting models. Her metaphor is based on her reading of the pre-Socratics, particularly Empedocles.

For Empedocles, the fundamental principle of being is endless change, infinite becoming. Matter is the arrangement of four different types of unchangeable particles; all objects are the result of their intermingling. The alliance each element makes with the others is described by Empedocles as love or attraction; conversely, material objects are destroyed through hate or strife. The unity of things is thus a consequence of the plurality and harmony of their elements. Love is the intermingling—the harmonious coming together—of differences. Empedocles's representation of the four elements provides an apposite metaphor of the meeting of different substances, a perilous and provisional union of differences that, through love, can yield unpredicted productivity—a rich metaphor for the possibilities of autonomy and interaction between sexually different subjects—a kind of heterosexuality without heterosexism.

In using the terminology of alchemy, Irigaray turns to a prehistoric or protohistorical worldview, one preceding the imposition of a "reasoned" science, in both ancient Greece and medieval Europe. She turns to a logic of interactive forces operating as combinatory particles—a logic of transmutation—and thus, like the dialectic, a logic of *becoming*. Earth, air, fire, and water, the primal elements, combine in varying degrees to create the (significatory) structure of reality, both individual and collective. The elements constitute the ingredients of a type of subjectivity and faculties within a subjectivity (for example, their particular combinations constitute what were called "the passions") as well as the relations pertaining to the social and natural world: "I wanted to go back to this natural material which makes up our bodies, in which our lives and environment are grounded: the flesh of our passions."[9]

To defend her against the anticipated and usual charges of essentialism, it needs to be said clearly that her use of the four elements represents a fable or mythic unfolding of a fantasied—an impossible—origin, to be read in the manner of Freud's *Totem and Taboo* or Nietzsche's *Thus Spake Zarathustra*, rather than as historical "archeology."[10] They have a discursive rather than a referential status. In the case of the elements, resonances with the later writings of Merleau-Ponty must also be recognized. Like Irigaray, he uses the emblem of the four elements to rethink carnality, the flesh, outside its traditional binary terms in which mind is opposed to body, self to other, and nature to culture. The flesh is the most elementary of terms, comprising the subject and the world and the subject in and as the world:

> The flesh is not matter, is not mind, is not substance. To designate it, we should need the old term "element" in the sense it was used to speak of water, air, earth and fire, that is, in the sense of a *general thing*. . . . The flesh is in this sense an "element of Being."[11]

The elemental, in sum, provides Irigaray with a language with which to represent a materiality and a corporeality outside the traditional patriarchal framework and more acceptable for representing women's corporeal-material existence. Her argument relies on an earlier account of the patriarchal debt to maternity, to women's reproductive abilities, that remains the silent support of patriarchy. Her concept of the four elements provides a corporeal foundation for the creation of an account of a transcendental or divine order, which she believes is necessary for articulating an autonomous femininity: such a transcendence is the condition, as

9. "Equal to Whom?" 1.

10. See Lacan's comments on God, in *Feminine Sexuality*; and in *The Four Fundamental Principles of Psychoanalysis*, trans. Alan Sheridan (New York: W. W. Norton, 1981) where he discusses the Cartesian concept of God from the *Meditations*.

11. Merleau-Ponty, Maurice, *The Visible and the Invisible* trans. Alphonso Lingis (Evanston, Ill.: Northwestern University Press, 1969), 139.

de Beauvoir almost recognized, of women's elevation from the category of other to the status of subject.

GOD AND THE DIVINE

In Irigaray's writings, the notion of God (or gods) functions to anchor several interrelated concepts. God is the ontological framework of our understanding of reality and the conditions of perception of this reality in each of us: God frames the genesis of space, time, and their contents (persons, nature, elementary particles) by speaking, naming, and constituting distinctive particles. In this way God divides and categorizes the particles. God is thus, as Descartes recognized, the source and justification of (Western) knowledge. Second, God provides a framework and a horizon for the constitution of the subject's identity as a subject. Third, God provides an ideal of perfection, a becoming that is particular to each sex. Irigaray does not use a concept of God as a static, frozen image, but as a "sensible transcendental,"[12] that is, as a term designating a material process of completion and integration, a movement always tending toward and becoming its own ideal. And fourth, God is an emblem of a supreme form of alterity that institutes ethics: one can love the other only if one also loves oneself and (a) God. "Gods are necessary and linked to the constitution of an identity and a community."[13]

Irigaray's God is neither naturalistic nor personal, neither forgiving nor judgmental. God is not the totality, unity, origin, or purpose of the world, but the principle of the ideal, a projection of the (sexed) subject onto a figure of perfection, an ego-ideal specific to that subject, a mode of self-completion without finality. God is the condition of men's finitude, their identities as law-abiding subjects, and their being situated in a genre. Irigaray plays on the full resonances of the term "genre": a term able to summarize men's domination of personal and familial structures (genre as "genus,"

12. Her phrase in *L'Ethique de la différence sexuelle* (Paris: Editions de Minoit, 1984).

13. "Divine Women," 12.

"family," or "humankind"); of knowledge (genre as "kind," "manner," or "sort," the imposition of categories), of cultural achievement (genre as "style," "aesthetic type") and of social relations (genre as "fashion," "taste," or "style"):

> Man can exist because God helps him to define his *genre*, to situate himself as a finite being in relation to the infinite. . . . To set up a genre, a God is needed. . . . Man did not let himself be defined by another genre: feminine. His only God was to correspond to the human type which we know is not neutral as far as the difference of sex goes.[14]

God is the term necessary for positioning one's finite being in both the context of other finitudes (sexual, social, terrestrial) and in the context of the infinite. God provides the genre, the context, the milieu and limit of the subject, and the horizon of being against which subjectivity positions itself. For this reason, Irigaray refuses to abandon the language of patriarchal religion, although she retains a distance from it. The position of God as ideal and horizon needs to be retained as a political, aesthetic, and ethical ideal:

> If women lack a God they cannot communicate, or communicate amongst themselves. The infinite is needed, they need the infinite in order to share *a little*? Otherwise the division brings about fusion-confusion, division and tearing apart in them/her, between them. If I can't relate to some sort of horizon for the realisation of my genre, I cannot share while protecting my becoming.[15]

Her use of the concept of God is thus an inversion and displacement of its theological or religious sources. God serves as an image or metaphor of being situated in space and time as a subject of a particular kind and of the capacity for an autonomous identity, insofar as the subject aspires to a perfection that is the actualization of its potentialities. In this sense, her work must also be seen as the culmination of an ethical and ontological project fundamentally initiated by Spinoza. God represents being positioned in a place: social, natural, interpersonal. God, then, is not a personage regulating, governing, or judging these positions nor one's mode of

14. "Divine Women," 4.
15. Ibid., 5.

occupying them. God is a name to describe the possibilities of awareness, and transcendence, of these positions.

If God represents, inhabits, the celestial order and men and women are fundamentally terrestrial, Irigaray is fascinated with exploring that which is between the divine and the human, the bird and the fish, man and woman: the angel. The angel is the messenger of the divine, a messenger who announces divine events: proclaiming the union of the sexes (in marriage) and the productivity of sexual exchange (particularly in birth but also in death). The angel always traverses and displaces distinct identities and categories, being a divine union of contraries:

> The angels tell of a journey between the envelope of God and the world, the micro and the macrocosm. They announce that this journey is accessible to the body of man. And especially to women's body. They represent and speak of another incarnation, another *parousia* of the body. Irreducible to philosophy, theology, morality, the angels appear as messengers of the ethics evolved by art—sculpture, painting or music—without which something other than the gesture which they represent cannot be said.[16]

Yet, although the angel signifies the possibility of a bridge between heterogeneous orders (divine-mortal, male-female), it remains traditionally disembodied, sexually neuter, intangible, a form of the unity of sexual diversity never incarnated, never material. They move between one order and another, but occupy neither. They are thus able to act as images or models of a possible occupation of a middle ground by the two sexes in their meeting. These two sexes, while seeking the status of the angelic or divine, would not become *neutral* or *neuter*, but would retain their sexes in their marriage. Her ideal union of the sexes involves the corporealization of the angelic, an attribution of a body and a sex to that always moving, shimmering being. The *embodied* that is, the sexed angel, may represent the possibility of a divine—nonencompassing—union. It thus represents the possibility of a *sexual ethics*.

> A sexual or carnal ethics would require that the angel and the body be found together. A world to construct or reconstruct

16. *L'Ethique*, 22–23.

> . . . from the smallest to the greatest, from the most intimate to the most political, a genesis of love between the sexes would be still to come. A world to create or recreate in order that man and woman can again or finally cohabit, meet and sometimes remain in the same place.[17]

Thus, for Irigaray, the divine is not simply the reward for earthly virtue, all wishes come true; it is rather the field of creativity, fertility, production, an always uncertain and unpreempted field. It is the field or domain of what is new, what has not existed before, a mode of transcendence, a projection of the past into a future that gives the present new meaning and direction. The divine is a movement, a movement of and within history, a movement of becoming without *telos*, a movement of love in its Empedoclean sense.

SEXUAL AUTONOMY AND EXCHANGE

The question of sexual difference has been displaced in Irigaray's more recent writings in favor of the postulation of an exchange between the sexes. Although she sees that women require unmediated, positive relations with other women, she also sees that it is necessary for women to be able to enter relations of exchange with men without sacrificing their positive self-conceptions. The question of the meeting of the two sexes is one that preoccupies her here. How can a meeting between the two sexes take place? If the sexes are characterized by irreducible difference—morphological, reproductive, biological, psychological, social—how can a common ground or meeting place between them be formed? What ground between them, what commonness left untouched by phallocentrism, enables them to speak, to understand, to share, to create?

This problematic of the unity in the heterogeneity of the two sexes underlies her explorations of the divine, the theological, and the philosophical. It is a concern that has occupied her work since the 1980s. In rather bald terms, she states her preoccupation with the productivity of the couple:

> I think that man and woman is the most mysterious and creative couple. That isn't to say that other couples may not also

17. Ibid., 23.

> have a lot in them, but man and woman is the most mysterious and creative.
>
> Do you understand what I am saying: people who are sexually different and who create a different relation to the world.[18]

Very often this mysterious creativity is narrowed into the creation of a child, a symbol of love between the sexes. Yet the fecundity of the exchanges between the two sexes cannot and should not be reduced to procreation; it is the fertility necessary for the production of a new world as much as for a new life.

This meeting and mingling of the two sexes is, of course, not without its perils and dangers, particularly for the woman. On the one hand, there is always a danger of a regression to stereotyped heterosexuality. Here the woman once again conforms to a logic that oppresses her, when she takes on the role of opposite, other, or counterpart to the one. On the other hand, she also risks remaining on a parallel with, yet never meeting, her "other"—each sex living in its own homosexual economy without a point of mediation between them, each talking at and not with the other. She has written about the risks involved in women opening their femininity to a relation with men's masculinity—the risks of fusion, engulfment, absorption, anger, hatred, invasion. In a very moving and personal discussion of passion, Irigaray ranges over the emotional responses effected by interpersonal commitments to heterosexual exchange:

> It was at breakfast. We separated at your work time. You gave me something to do for the day. I asked you for that. I will flee outside myself in you. Also the outside world. I cannot stay in the world. I am in it and not in it. I don't escape from you, me, us, towards some Other, no . . .
>
> You absorbed me or you come back again to me to protect yourself from [death]. When I suffer, you are hurting in me, I think that you have abandoned your mortal limits. That my risks are redoubled to carry you in me. Redoubled? Or infinite? Overwhelmed by a peril beyond my life. Nothing that can save me without you outside of me.[19]

18. In *Hecate* 9: 199.
19. "Ou et comment habiter?" *Les Cahiers du Grif* (March 1983).

Irigaray asks how to establish a time and place, subjectivities and positions, whereby the two sexes can touch each other without loss or residue: where one is not autonomous at the expense of the other; where one does not occupy the negative and the other the positive poles of a fixed opposition; where there is mutual recognition, mutual caressing, the satisfaction of the needs of both. Such a relation cannot exist if either sex has no positive identity, no relation of autoeroticism or positive evaluation of their bodies, and no positive relation to members and ideals of their own sex. These are necessary preconditions that, in the case of both sexes (though in quite different ways) have remained out of reach. Men, for example, to retain a positive identity have had to relinquish a bodily autoeroticism. In renouncing the polymorphous pleasures of the rest of the body for the singular pleasures and benefits bestowed on a phallic organ and subjectivity, men have given up the realm of the corporeal and have forced women to occupy it for them. Women, in contrast, relinquish their homosexual, particularly their maternal, connections and thus the possibilities for a positive, autonomous self-conception in remaining the guardians of the men's corporeality. They have, consequently, given up their own.

In "Divine Women," Irigaray seeks to create at least some of the conditions necessary for women to develop an autonomous self-conception. Among the necessary conditions is a concept of God and the divine, that is, a historically possible future. For it is only if women have their own concepts of the divine that a divine fecundity between the sexes may occur. The love of God, for Irigaray, is a love of the self, and this self-love is the prerequisite of love of the other. Self-love implies recognizing from whence we come (from women—mothers, all of us), where we are now (politically, philosophically), and a future in which we can become more than this (which Irigaray calls "God"). "God holds no obligations over our needs, except *to become*. No task, no obligation burdens us except that one: become divine, become perfect, don't let any parts of us be amputated that could be expansive for us."[20]

Irigaray announces the threshold of a new era of relations between the sexes, which has the potential to supersede all social,

20. "Divine Women," 10.

sexual and significatory relations in a transvaluation and transfiguration of existing religions. Her project, like that of the angel, is to announce the birth of a new epoch, a new type of exchange and coexistence. The meeting of two different beings—the open acceptance of a different subjectivity—has yet to occur. When it does, it will open up knowledge, social practices, productions, even life and death themselves, to a new set of values and meanings.

Her model of a relation between the two sexes that may accede to the divine involves the postulation of each having its own place, its own specifications, features, needs, desires, and corporeal identities. It implies that each sex has accepted its own finitude, has accepted what the other's position has to give and what it is able to receive from the other without loss to itself. The maximization of the capacities and latent or undeveloped skills, a trajectory toward actualization of potentials that may otherwise not be revealed, continuous self-completion, these are some of the transformations that may occur in a meeting of differences. An economy of the gift may occur without the presumption of an underlying identity between giver and receiver, who must reciprocate with a symbolically identical gift. This is an economy that is all circulation with no real exchange—no exchange, because there is no heterogeneity between giver and receiver, no stretching of either position so that it may touch (upon) the other. Ritual exchange always functions to ensure (temporal) sameness. An exchange that genuinely involves taking and giving implies disparate identities, disparate needs, between which different gifts may or must circulate.

Irigaray attempts to outline some of the ingredients of a model of exchange that acknowledges the two different sexes as both givers and receivers. The gifts thus exchanged can be communication or language, sexual pleasure, the satisfaction of mutual need, a child, a home (place), a position that affirms its participants in the process of producing something new. Sexual difference heralds the era in which women and men are not neutralized under a universal or androgynous humanity abstracted from the sexed body, but rather, one in which production can be seen to be the contribution of women and men, and one in which men and women, through their difference, find a commonness between them:

> How can one mark this limit of a place, of the place, except by sexual difference? But, in order for ethics to be possible, it

> is necessary to constitute a possible place to live for each sex, each body, each flesh. Which supposes a memory of the past, a hope for the future. Memory assures a bridge of the present, and disconcerts the symmetry of the mirror which annihilates the difference of identity.
>
> This needs time, space and time. And thus, perhaps we are again passing an epoch where *time should redeploy space*. New morning of the world? Recasting immanence and transcendence, especially through this *threshold* which has never been questioned as such: the feminine sex.[21]

Her exploration of God, the celestial, and the angelic as the intermediary between the mortal and the immortal are tropes, images, or representations that Irigaray reclaims in struggling for women's autonomy. They are the names of ideals that have been stolen from women and that must be stolen back. If God and the divine provide the horizon for self-idealization, a model to emulate, then reclamation of the names and attributes of patriarchal religion is a necessary condition for identities determined by sexual difference. God is the Other in relation to which each sex, each subject, is positioned. In constructing a God using the shadows of one's own image, Irigaray believes that the seeds or possibilities of a divine fecundity or creativity may blossom. This is not a religious conversion, a leap of faith; it is a political and textual strategy for the positive reinscription of women's bodies, identities, and futures in relation to and in exchange with the other sex.

21. *L'Ethique*, 24.